D1101274

3

WALTHAM FOREST LIBRARIES

024 391 613

Plant Based Nutrition and Health

Stephen Walsh, PhD

WALTHAM FOREST PUBLIC LIBRARIES	
024 391 613	
MS	19/12/03
613.2	£12.95
S	

The Vegan Society

2003

First published September 2003

Copyright © 2003 Stephen Walsh

All rights reserved. No part of this publication may
be reproduced, stored in a retrieval system, or
transmitted, in any form or by any means, electronic,
mechanical, photocopying, recording, or otherwise,
without the prior permission of the author.

Edited by Vanessa Clarke

ISBN 0-907337-26-0 (paperback)
ISBN 0-907337-27-9 (hardback)

Published by The Vegan Society
Donald Watson House, 7 Battle Road,
St Leonards-on-Sea, East Sussex TN37 7AA,
United Kingdom. www.vegansociety.com

Cover: www.clipart.com and Doughnut Design.

Printed in England by Biddles Ltd, King's Lynn,
www.biddles.co.uk

Nothing printed should be construed to be Vegan Society
policy unless otherwise stated. The Society accepts no
liability for anything in this book. The information in this
book is not intended to take the place of advice provided
by medical professionals.

To Vanessa Clarke

Author's Foreword

I am committed to a 100% plant-based (vegan) diet as a way of improving life for humans and other animals and reducing damage to the environment that we all share.

My professional background is in process systems analysis, using mathematical models to predict how biological or chemical processes will respond to changes and the actions required to achieve a desired result. I obtained my PhD from Imperial College of Science, Technology and Medicine in 1993. After lecturing full time at Imperial College for four years, I went to work in industry as a senior systems engineer, continuing to lecture part time. My current work involves tackling a wide variety of problems by analysing data, developing models and optimising decisions to improve results.

Several years ago, I decided to apply these methods to human nutrition. I felt that my skills could make a useful contribution in sifting through relevant scientific studies, consolidating the knowledge available into models which would predict the health effects of specific choices, and using these models to develop realistic recommendations for achieving optimal health.

This project involved examining thousands of published papers and refining my observations through discussions with other researchers and with fellow vegetarians and vegans. Along the way, I became Chair of the UK Vegan Society and Science Coordinator of the International Vegetarian Union. I became actively involved in these two long established organisations so that I could both help their members and learn from them. I am not interested in research for the sake of fine debating points but to help people improve their lives. My thanks to all who have responded to my talks and articles with comments and questions that have kept me searching and learning.

All the recommendations in this book are based on human studies. No use has been made of any information obtained by harming animals as I regard such procedures as both unethical and irrelevant to recommendations for humans. The key references are listed at the back of the book for those wishing to explore further.

Contents

Chapter 1

Introduction

This book is a guide to using plant foods to promote a long and healthy life while simultaneously reducing human and animal suffering and environmental damage. The dietary choices that we make can add ten extra years of healthy life and open up the prospect of a sustainable future for all. The information in this book is derived from scientific studies of diet, health and the environment, from the individual experiences of vegans and other vegetarians, and from our evolutionary heritage.

The main topics covered are:

- The roots of plant-based diets.
- Direct evidence on plant-based diets and life expectancy.
- How to achieve and maintain a healthy weight.
- Using colourful foods to promote good health.
- The lessons to be learnt from the unfolding understanding of homocysteine and health.
- The central role of calcium *balance* rather than calcium *intake* in health, and choices to optimise calcium balance.
- Making fats work *for* your health and not *against* it.
- How to compensate for lack of vitamin D due to living far from the equator and for low levels of iodine and selenium in foods grown in deficient soil.
- Meeting protein, iron, and zinc needs entirely from plant foods.
- Plant-based diets from birth to old age.
- Pros and cons of Mediterranean (Cretan), Japanese (Okinawan) and high raw food diets.
- Simple recipes to help put the guidance into practice.
- Guidelines for maximising health using plant-based diets.

The focus of this book is on how to increase healthy life expectancy. Interactions between diet and health are complex, so a dietary change which reduces the risk of, say, heart disease may at the same time increase the risk of depression, aggressive behaviour or cancer. In general, therefore, the diet that we follow should be tailored to long term good health rather than to preventing any particular disease, even one as important as heart disease.

It is hoped that the dietary guidelines in this book will help those moving towards a more plant-based diet to forge ahead with confidence and enthusiasm and allow established vegans to fine tune their diets and become even healthier.

Throughout the book, the emphasis is on support for individual choice rather than any uniform prescription. As we grow and age, our needs change. At any given stage of life, one size does not fit all. This book highlights those areas where individual variation is particularly important. As well as indicating the best choices for the average person, it explains how to recognise individual needs and adjust eating habits accordingly.

Chapters 4 to 13 each end with a page of simple guidelines. Readers not already familiar with the topics covered may find it useful to turn to the guidelines before tackling the rest of the chapter which addresses the evidence behind these guidelines. Chapter 15 brings all the guidelines together in an overall summary.

Chapter 2

The roots of plant–based diets

Human beings are members of the family of great apes (hominoids), all of whom – with the exception of relatively modern humans – follow diets which are at least 95% plant based. The staples of our great ape relatives – the chimpanzee, the bonobo, the highland and lowland gorillas and the orang-utan – are fruits and leaves, with the addition of small amounts of roots, nuts, seeds, flowers, insects and in some cases eggs and small animals. Human hunter-gatherers – a link with our more recent prehistory – get anything from 10% to 90% of their calories from plants, the proportion of animal products increasing with distance from the equator.

Our evolutionary history gives limited guidance on optimal amounts of animal foods for human health. By picking a particular place and time, one can invoke the evolutionary argument in favour of virtually any proportion of calories coming from plants – begging the question of whether our great ape heritage or our recent hunter-gatherer heritage has shaped us more.

That is not to say that our heritage gives us no guidance on healthy diets: those characteristics of our evolutionary diet which have been relatively constant provide important pointers as to what we are adapted to require. However, as evolutionary pressures centre on reproductive success, and as adaptation is imperfect, evolutionary arguments can never have the last word on optimal diets to maintain good health into advanced years.

Only in recent years have human eating patterns, at least in developed countries, become a matter of habit and choice rather than necessity. An Inuit living above the Arctic Circle before the support of modern transportation networks would have to rely in the main on killing animals for food. A tropical hunter-gatherer would have more choice, but must still be guided largely by the principle of maximum calories for minimum effort. With late Stone Age hunting tools and no agriculture, this often meant that animals formed a substantial part of hunter-gatherer diets even in relatively hospitable climates.

With the development of agriculture, economy of effort came to greatly favour plant foods – allowing a huge population expansion from about 10 million hunter-gatherers to 6,000 million modern agriculturalists. The storage of grains and other seeds for winter replaced the hunting of animals as the key to survival. Since humans do not thrive on a diet of seeds alone, however, hot on the heels of the seed-fuelled agricultural revolution came domestication of animals and the use of meat and milk from farmed animals.

The growth of the human population means that an animal-centred diet is now possible only for a minority. The higher the percentage of calories from animals, the more land, energy and water have to be devoted to meeting human food requirements, the greater the pressures on the environment and the greater the likelihood of conflict over resources. Human ingenuity continues to try to square the circle with fish farming, genetic engineering and ever more sophisticated use of chemicals and irrigation. The fact remains, however, that the lower the percentage of calories derived from animals, the easier it becomes to meet the needs of all humans while sparing some of the planet for other species and treating any remaining farmed animals with more decency.

Some agricultural societies adopted an entirely vegetarian pattern based on seeds supplemented by fruit, vegetables and milk, but for most human populations meat and fish remained a significant part of the diet. In more recent history, individuals within populations felt able to choose a diet that differed from their neighbours, and groups such as the Pythagoreans in Greece and the Essenes in the Middle East adopted a vegetarian, plant-centred diet.

With industrialisation, the element of choice in diet expanded and vegetarianism blossomed, particularly in English-speaking countries, which had been exposed most directly to the vegetarian traditions of India. Early vegetarians were motivated by a combination of admiration for the Indian philosophy of Ahimsa (active avoidance of harm to any living being and the promotion of wellbeing) and a belief that eating flesh had adverse effects on health.

The link between the consumption of saturated fat and the prevalence of heart attacks has provided a reason to move towards a plant-based diet for personal benefit. Mad Cow Disease (bovine spongiform encephalopathy) with its human counterpart Creutzfeld Jacob Disease (CJD) has highlighted the risks of disease posed by modern farming practices.

The industrialisation of animal farming, summed up by the term "factory farming", has provoked widespread revulsion at the suffering involved.

Many environmentalists have turned to vegetarianism, recognising that a plant-based diet requires far less land, energy and water.

This triad of benefits to people, animals and the environment has fuelled a spectacular growth in the number of people choosing not to eat meat, despite cultural traditions claiming that meat is vital for health. About 1 in 20 people in the UK and the USA now describe themselves as vegetarian and a rapidly growing proportion (10% to 20%) of these have adopted a 100% plant-based (vegan) diet. The variation of dietary choices between countries, and more particularly between individuals within countries, provides a rich source of information to help determine what is the best diet for humans.

Chapter 3

Healthy life expectancy

Healthy life expectancy for humans has never been longer than it now is in economically developed countries. The World Health Organisation measures and publishes Health Adjusted Life Expectancy (HALE) figures for most countries in the world. In calculating the figures, the important fact that few people would wish to live longer with severely declining health is taken into account by a built-in adjustment for years lived with impaired health. For example, dementia or *continuous* severe migraine is regarded as reducing the value of years of life by 75% so that four years lived with such a condition counts as only one health-adjusted year. HALE is currently the best available measure of population health.

The United Nations Food and Agriculture Organisation measures and publishes food supply data, including the percentage of calories from plant foods. This only approximately reflects the percentage of calories consumed from plants as it does not allow for food wasted rather than consumed, but so long as the proportion of food wasted is similar for animal products and for plant products it will provide a good measure of actual eating habits.

Figure 3.1 shows how Health Adjusted Life Expectancy varies with plant calories for the 23 countries classified by the UN as "established market economies" and for which the required information is available. This selection excludes countries where poverty restricts access to adequate calories and clean water, thus allowing the comparison to be limited to relatively similar developed countries.

The country where people enjoy the longest healthy life expectancy is Japan, where an unusually high percentage of calories comes from plants. However, the percentage of calories from plants is

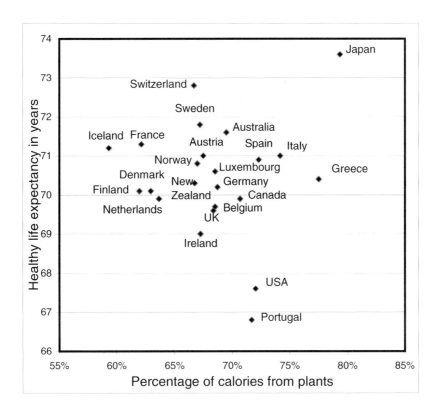

**Figure 3.1: Health Adjusted Life Expectancy and
percentage of calories from plants**

not significantly associated with healthy life expectancy among the countries in figure 3.1. This is not surprising, as diets with the same percentage of plant calories can differ greatly in quality, and non-dietary factors also have a major impact on life expectancy.

For instance, smoking is a major cause of death, and poverty can restrict access to health services and a secure environment. Portugal is the poorest member of this group of countries, which may explain its lower life expectancy. Inequalities of income within a country can mean that the benefits of a secure environment are not shared by all the population. The USA has an unusually wide gap between rich and poor and this contributes to its relatively low average healthy life expectancy.

Clearer insights can be obtained by looking at the health of individuals within countries. By measuring the characteristics of many individuals, it becomes possible to make adjustments for non-dietary influences such as smoking, exercise and number of children, and to consider many different aspects of diet at the same time. Many studies have measured the diets of a group (cohort) of individuals and monitored subsequent deaths. Five such studies have included large numbers of vegetarians.

The earliest major report from these studies was published in 1978 and compared disease mortality in vegans ("pure vegetarians") with that in other vegetarians and in meat eaters. All individuals in this study were Californian Seventh Day Adventists. The observed number of deaths in each group was compared with that predicted from death rates in the general population of California.

Among Seventh Day Adventist men, vegans showed the lowest heart disease mortality, with just 14% of the expected number of deaths compared with the general population. The vegan women, however, showed 94% of the expected number of deaths.

Among men and women combined, the number of vegans who died from heart disease was 20 compared with an expected 33 deaths (60%). There were 251 deaths from heart disease among other vegetarians compared with an expected 620 deaths (40%), and 275 deaths compared with an expected 555 deaths in non-vegetarian Seventh Day Adventists (50%).

The benefit from vegetarian and vegan diets in this early study seemed to be greatest in middle-aged men and least in elderly women. It is dangerous to draw conclusions from any one study, but subsequent studies have confirmed the vegetarian advantage on heart disease and have also confirmed that the greatest reduction in the risk of heart disease is seen in men under 65 years of age.

In 1999 the five major studies of vegetarian health combined their observations to publish the most reliable information to date on the health impact of removing meat and other animal products from the diet. The five study populations (cohorts), comprising vegetarians and meat eaters, each showed much lower death rates than the general population – living about six years longer. This advantage cannot all be ascribed to vegetarianism. About half the apparent advantage can be attributed to less smoking than in the general population. Moreover, even the non-vegetarians in the studies ate less meat and more fruit and vegetables than was typical in their countries, so both vegetarians and non-vegetarians benefited from this common move towards a more plant-based diet.

Further insight came from comparing different dietary groups within the cohorts. As part of the combined analysis of the five studies, the groups were separated into meat eaters (those who ate meat at least once a week), occasional meat eaters (less than once a week), fish eaters, vegetarians (no meat or fish) and vegans (plant foods only) for further analysis.

The meat eaters in these studies showed about 50% higher death rates from heart disease than the other groups, while the vegans showed about 30% higher death rates from causes other than cancer and heart disease. The net result was that the vegans showed the same overall death rates as the meat eaters; the other groups showed about 17% lower death rates – equivalent to living about two years longer.

This pattern was also evident in one of the five studies, which compared UK vegetarians with meat eating friends who had otherwise similar lifestyles. While heart disease mortality increased dramatically with consumption of saturated animal fat and cholesterol, mortality from all causes combined showed a more complex pattern. Meat, fish and cheese intakes were not related to overall mortality. Moderate intakes of milk and eggs were associated with the lowest overall mortality, with a 25% to 30% reduction in mortality at half a pint (300 ml) of milk per day or one to five eggs per week compared with lower intakes. However, mortality rose again as intakes of milk and eggs increased.

These results demolish the contention that humans need meat for health, but they also challenge two simplistic views: that every reduction in the use of animal products inevitably leads to a further benefit in health, and that measures reducing heart disease can be assumed to reduce overall mortality.

There were also noteworthy differences between the studies. European vegetarians (mostly from two studies in the UK, with a smaller number from a study in Germany) showed less advantage, with lower heart disease deaths being balanced by deaths from other causes to give similar overall death rates.

Vegetarians in the USA showed a notable advantage over the non-vegetarians which was particularly striking for heart disease and increased with the length of time individuals had been vegetarian. Despite the higher than usual consumption of fruit and vegetables by the non-vegetarians in the studies, and their lower than usual meat consumption, vegetarianism was associated with about two years extra life expectancy. This result was found after making adjustments for higher nut consumption by the vegetarians, which was itself associated with an additional extra two years of life in both vegetarians and non-vegetarians. In one of the UK studies, fresh fruit and wholegrain bread consumption were each associated with reduced death rates.

These observations emphasise that choices *within* plant-based diets are of critical importance to getting maximum benefit. This is borne out by the progress of attempts to prevent heart attack deaths in people who have already suffered one heart attack. Trials that simply encouraged people to eat more plant fibre or less fat had disappointing results, but recent trials offering more specific guidance as to what foods to replace have been much more successful.

In France, the Lyon Diet Heart Trial (see chapter 9) substituted rapeseed (canola) oil margarine for butter and cream and boosted consumption of fruit and vegetables to a moderate extent. The result was a 55% reduction in overall mortality over a period of four years. A trial in India, in which intake of mustard oil was increased and intake of other fats reduced, resulted in a 40% reduction in deaths after one year.

The latest guidelines for prevention of coronary heart disease adopt a similar approach, emphasising increased consumption of fruit and vegetables, nuts and whole grains. High consumption of any of these three food groups is estimated to reduce heart disease risk by 20% to 30%. Replacing about 5% of calories previously consumed as saturated fat with unsaturated fats such as those found in mustard oil and rapeseed oil is estimated to reduce heart disease risk by about 40%. All these recommended changes are consistent with moving to a plant-based diet – but not just any old plant-based diet.

In addition to direct observations on diet and mortality, further insights have come from studies of the association of biological markers with health and mortality. Among the key markers are body mass index (see chapter 4), antioxidants (chapters 5 and 10), homocysteine (chapter 6), blood pressure and calcium-balancing hormones (chapter 7), cholesterol, omega-3 fatty acids and C-reactive protein (chapters 8 and 9), thyroid function (chapter 10), and growth hormones and iron stores (chapter 11). All these measures are strongly related to health and are in turn strongly related to diet.

By fine tuning our diet to improve all these markers simultaneously we can greatly stack the odds in favour of a long and healthy life.

Recent scientific findings from human nutritional research are taking the guesswork out of making optimal dietary choices, opening up the prospect of extending healthy life expectancy by a decade compared with current averages in developed countries. Some of the desired effects come naturally with moving to a more plant-based diet while others require more specific dietary choices from among the wealth of plant foods available.

From the standpoints of non-human animals and the environment, the lower the percentage of human dietary calories derived from animals the better. Studies of long term vegetarians have already shown that meat is unnecessary for optimal human health. This book explains how to optimise the contribution of plant foods to human health and shows that, if certain simple guidelines are followed, a 100% plant-based (vegan) diet has many advantages over conventional diets and cannot be bettered for promoting human health.

Whether you are already vegan or simply considering how best to replace *some* of the animal products in your diet with health-promoting plant-based alternatives, this book will help you to make informed choices for the benefit of your own health and wellbeing, the rest of humanity, other animals and the planet that we all share.

Chapter 4

Maintaining a healthy weight

The effect of diet on weight is one of the most important ways in which eating habits influence health. World wide, the biggest issue continues to be that of lower than desirable weights due to restricted calorie intake, but excess weight is a major problem in the developed world and a rapidly growing one in the rest of the world.

Desirable weight varies with height and build. Body mass index (BMI) is used to allow recommendations to be made independently of height. BMI is calculated as weight in kilograms divided twice by height in metres. For instance, a person weighing 63 kilograms (140 pounds) who is 1.7 metres (5 foot 7 inches) tall would have a body mass index of 22 (63 divided by 1.7 and again by 1.7).

The World Health Organisation (WHO) recommends that adults maintain a BMI between 18.5 and 25 and avoid weight gain of more than 5 kg (11 lb). Overweight is defined as a BMI above 25, and obesity as a BMI above 30. These thresholds are to some extent arbitrary: there is no great difference in risk between a BMI of 29 and a BMI of 31 or between 24 and 26 – but there is a major difference between 24 and 31.

Many people find calculating BMI difficult, particularly if they are used to working with Imperial rather than metric units. Figure 4.1 provides tables to make it easy to work out BMI. The first table gives the weights in stones and pounds corresponding to a wide range of BMI values for heights ranging from 4 foot 10 inches to 6 foot 6 inches. The second table gives similar information in terms of metres and kilograms. Finally, a chart illustrates how BMI varies for heights ranging from 1.4 metres to 2 metres and weights ranging from 35 to 105 kilograms and highlights the WHO recommended range.

BMI	4ft 10in	4ft 11in	5ft 0in	5ft 1in	5ft 2in	5ft 3in	5ft 4in	5ft 5in	5ft 6in	5ft 7in	5ft 8in
17	5st 11lb	6st 0lb	6st 3lb	6st 5lb	6st 8lb	6st 11lb	7st 1lb	7st 4lb	7st 7lb	7st 10lb	7st 13lb
18.5	6st 4lb	6st 7lb	6st 10lb	6st 13lb	7st 3lb	7st 6lb	7st 9lb	7st 13lb	8st 2lb	8st 6lb	8st 9lb
20	6st 11lb	7st 1lb	7st 4lb	7st 7lb	7st 11lb	8st 0lb	8st 4lb	8st 8lb	8st 11lb	9st 1lb	9st 5lb
22.5	7st 9lb	7st 13lb	8st 3lb	8st 7lb	8st 11lb	9st 1lb	9st 5lb	9st 9lb	9st 13lb	10st 3lb	10st 7lb
25	8st 7lb	8st 11lb	9st 2lb	9st 6lb	9st 10lb	10st 1lb	10st 5lb	10st 10lb	11st 0lb	11st 5lb	11st 10lb
27.5	9st 5lb	9st 10lb	10st 0lb	10st 5lb	10st 10lb	11st 1lb	11st 6lb	11st 11lb	12st 2lb	12st 7lb	12st 12lb
30	10st 3lb	10st 8lb	10st 13lb	11st 4lb	11st 10lb	12st 1lb	12st 6lb	12st 12lb	13st 3lb	13st 9lb	14st 1lb
32.5	11st 1lb	11st 6lb	11st 12lb	12st 4lb	12st 9lb	13st 1lb	13st 7lb	13st 13lb	14st 5lb	14st 11lb	15st 3lb
35	11st 13lb	12st 5lb	12st 11lb	13st 3lb	13st 9lb	14st 1lb	14st 7lb	15st 0lb	15st 6lb	15st 13lb	16st 6lb

BMI	5ft 9in	5ft 10in	5ft 11in	6ft 0in	6ft 1in	6ft 2in	6ft 3in	6ft 4in	6ft 5in	6ft 6in
17	8st 3lb	8st 6lb	8st 9lb	8st 13lb	9st 2lb	9st 6lb	9st 10lb	9st 13lb	10st 3lb	10st 7lb
18.5	8st 13lb	9st 2lb	9st 6lb	9st 10lb	10st 0lb	10st 4lb	10st 8lb	10st 11lb	11st 2lb	11st 6lb
20	9st 9lb	9st 13lb	10st 3lb	10st 7lb	10st 11lb	11st 1lb	11st 6lb	11st 10lb	12st 0lb	12st 5lb
22.5	10st 12lb	11st 2lb	11st 7lb	11st 11lb	12st 2lb	12st 7lb	12st 12lb	13st 2lb	13st 7lb	13st 12lb
25	12st 1lb	12st 6lb	12st 11lb	13st 2lb	13st 7lb	13st 12lb	14st 4lb	14st 9lb	15st 0lb	15st 6lb
27.5	13st 4lb	13st 9lb	14st 1lb	14st 6lb	14st 12lb	15st 4lb	15st 10lb	16st 1lb	16st 7lb	16st 13lb
30	14st 7lb	14st 13lb	15st 5lb	15st 11lb	16st 3lb	16st 9lb	17st 2lb	17st 8lb	18st 1lb	18st 7lb
32.5	15st 10lb	16st 2lb	16st 9lb	17st 1lb	17st 8lb	18st 1lb	18st 8lb	19st 1lb	19st 8lb	20st 1lb
35	16st 13lb	17st 5lb	17st 12lb	18st 6lb	18st 13lb	19st 6lb	20st 0lb	20st 7lb	21st 1lb	21st 8lb

BMI table in Imperial units. Find the nearest height in feet and inches along the top row. Read down that column to find the nearest weight in stones and pounds (1 stone = 14 lb). Find the BMI in the left hand column.

BMI	1.5m	1.55m	1.6m	1.65m	1.7m	1.75m	1.8m	1.85m	1.9m	1.95m
17	38kg	40kg	43kg	46kg	49kg	52kg	55kg	58kg	61kg	64kg
18.5	41kg	44kg	47kg	50kg	53kg	56kg	59kg	63kg	66kg	70kg
20	45kg	48kg	51kg	54kg	57kg	61kg	64kg	68kg	72kg	76kg
22.5	50kg	54kg	57kg	61kg	65kg	68kg	72kg	77kg	81kg	85kg
25	56kg	60kg	64kg	68kg	72kg	76kg	81kg	85kg	90kg	95kg
27.5	61kg	66kg	70kg	74kg	79kg	84kg	89kg	94kg	99kg	104kg
30	67kg	72kg	76kg	81kg	86kg	91kg	97kg	102kg	108kg	114kg
32.5	73kg	78kg	83kg	88kg	93kg	99kg	105kg	111kg	117kg	123kg
35	78kg	84kg	89kg	95kg	101kg	107kg	113kg	119kg	126kg	133kg

BMI table in metric units:

Find the nearest height in metres along the top row. Read down that column to find the nearest weight in kilograms. Find the corresponding BMI in the left hand column.

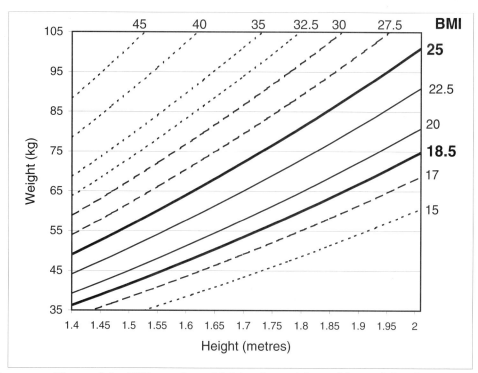

Figure 4.1: BMI graph and tables in metric and Imperial units
(The WHO recommended range is highlighted by the solid lines.)

Obesity is strongly linked with increases in blood pressure and in cholesterol and with increased risk of diabetes, cardiovascular disease and certain cancers, including breast cancer. Diabetes is particularly strongly linked with obesity. Diet and lifestyle measures to prevent excess weight gain – such as increased intake of high fibre foods and regular physical activity – also reduce the risk of diabetes at any given weight.

Weight tends to increase with age and the health risk increases with length of time at an excessive weight. Being obese from the age of 40 has been observed to reduce life expectancy by about seven years – comparable with the impact of smoking 20 cigarettes a day. Besides the damaging effects on physical health, obesity can restrict mobility and cause social and psychological problems. Despite the undoubted link between weight gain and ill health, however, the prevalence of obesity has rocketed in the developed world over the past 50 years, as has the incidence of diabetes.

During the 1990s, the percentage of obese adults in the USA rose from 23% to 31% and the percentage of obese children from 11% to 15%. Two thirds of adults in the USA are overweight. Recent figures for the UK show that 17% of men and 20% of women are obese and 45% of men and 33% of women are overweight. This trend is not driven by diet alone, but changes in diet play a key part.

An excess of just 30 calories per day in calories consumed, compared with calories required, will cause a weight gain of about 1 kg (2 lb) over a year. This difference in calorie intake between a steady weight and an increasing weight is obviously too small to be managed by calorie counting, though it could be managed by monitoring weight and cutting back on food intake or increasing physical activity to restore the balance.

Even in the absence of a conscious decision to control weight, the body has its own mechanisms for controlling weight by adjusting appetite, and these feedback mechanisms work very well in responding to minor changes in activity levels or food choices.

Some people, however, have a less effective natural feedback mechanism to reduce appetite if calorie intake is excessive, and these people are most vulnerable to becoming obese. Such individuals would have an advantage during the periodic food shortages which were common throughout much of human evolution, since fat stores built up when food is plentiful provide a useful reserve for periods of shortage. In developed countries, however, food is always easily available and many suppliers strive to make their products as appealing and as easy to consume as possible. This is not the environment to which we are adapted, so it is not surprising that more and more of us are gaining weight that we don't need and don't want.

The other key environmental change behind our expanding waistlines is the removal of the necessity for physical activity: where cars go, obesity follows. Typical hunter-gatherers walk at least 5 to 10 miles a day, accounting for an extra 500 to 1000 calories of energy expenditure. Farmers without modern machinery also have high physical activity levels. Even if our feedback mechanisms are 90% successful in compensating for this activity reduction, we are still left with a calorie excess of 50 to 100 calories a day and weight creeping up more than is ideal for health.

The key to stemming the growing levels of obesity lies in helping our inbuilt feedback mechanisms to work effectively. This is not a matter of using willpower to override hunger but of modifying our environment so that our natural levels of hunger match our needs.

One key to this is increasing physical activity. This is best built into activities that we need or want to do rather than exercise for its own sake. It is easier to sustain activities that are part of our normal lives. Walking to shops, work or social events is a great way of increasing activity. If you can avoid having a car at all or limit its use as much as possible, this will make maintaining a good level of activity easier as well as saving money and reducing pollution. Walking or running at least 20 miles (30 km) per week is enough to get most of the health benefits of increased physical activity.

Although food is constantly accessible to most people in developed countries, responding to mild hunger signals can be made less easy. Many foods are designed to subvert normal appetite control. Soft drinks are a good example: they are as easily consumed as water, but stimulate the taste buds and pack a heavy wallop of calories. Many other foods are designed to be "moreish": once you have some you want more. Biscuits, sweets, doughnuts and ice cream all come into this category: if they are in the larder most of us will eat more of them than we intend. The best way to limit consumption of such foods is by choice when out shopping rather than by willpower at home. Keep fresh fruit on display and chocolate out of sight. Eating before shopping may make it easier to exercise restraint.

A key part of appetite control is the sensation of fullness. If the foods available are calorie dense (high in fat or sugar and low in water and fibre) we can eat more before feeling full. The sensation of fullness is complex, but foods such as sweets, doughnuts and soft drinks allow us to pack in a large number of calories quickly and easily, without filling our stomachs and without giving time for the hunger signals to die down. This undermines the built-in defences against excessive eating.

Another aspect of appetite is blood sugar (glucose) regulation. If the blood glucose level starts to fall, this will trigger sensations of hunger. The carbohydrate from certain foods is rapidly released into the blood as glucose, triggering a surge in blood sugar and a compensating surge in insulin, followed by a rebound to low levels and renewed hunger. The speed of glucose release is measured by the glycaemic index, which is discussed further in chapter 9.

A further aspect of weight gain is how readily the body stores fat relative to how readily it releases fat. There is intriguing, though currently inconclusive, evidence that the balance shifts in favour of fat storage if the body is struggling to replenish calcium losses (see chapter 7).

In terms of diet, the key to avoiding unwanted weight gain is choosing foods that are low in calories and high in fibre – consistent with the characteristics of the wild plant foods that hominoids (humans and other great apes) have eaten for millions of years.

As figure 4.2 shows, unrefined plant foods provide plenty of fibre while refined grains provide only about a quarter of the fibre of their unrefined counterparts and oils and sugars provide no fibre at all. All grains, beans and root vegetables in the table are presented in terms of cooked weight. Most plant foods (boiled grains, lentils or beans, raw fruits and vegetables) provide no more than 120 calories per 100 grams and most fruits and vegetables provide much less than this. Bread provides about 250 calories per 100 grams, sugar 380, nuts about 600, and oils almost 900 calories per 100 grams.

The ease with which calories can be consumed is not entirely captured by calories per 100 grams, especially for drinks. Any easily consumed calorie source can be expected to encourage overeating and obesity. High sugar fat free soft drinks are particularly suspect. Low calorie fruits and vegetables such as oranges and broccoli, which come with plenty of water and fibre, are unlikely to promote overeating, though the contribution of fruit and vegetable *juices* is more dubious. Some high fat foods such as nuts contain plenty of fibre and need to be chewed thoroughly and are thus less likely to promote weight gain than heavy use of oils.

A diet high in fibre, low in processed sugars and low in fat is a diet on which it is difficult to gain excess weight, particularly if reasonable levels of physical activity are maintained.

	Energy (calories per 100 grams)	Fibre (grams per 100 grams)	Fibre (grams per 1000 calories)
Lentils	120	8.4	70
Beans	120	6.6	55
Oranges	50	2.5	50
Tomatoes	20	1.0	50
Cherries	60	1.9	32
Pasta, wholemeal	120	3.6	30
Avocados	160	4.8	30
Bread, wholemeal	250	7.0	28
Banana, ripe	90	2.3	26
Pumpernickel bread	250	6.5	26
Banana, underripe	90	2.3	26
Potatoes	85	1.7	20
Almonds	600	12.0	20
Hazel nuts (filberts)	630	9.5	15
Rice, brown	110	1.1	10
Bread, white	270	2.4	9
Pasta, white	130	1.0	8
Cashews	560	3.4	6
Rice, white	120	0.4	3
Sugar, brown	376	0.0	0
Sugar, white	387	0.0	0
Oil	890	0.0	0

Figure 4.2: Fibre and calorie content of common foods

Even without any fat, white bread and jam washed down with lemonade or fruit juice will pile on the weight just as effectively as white bread and margarine, but it would be extremely difficult to gain weight on extra rations of oranges, broccoli and salad.

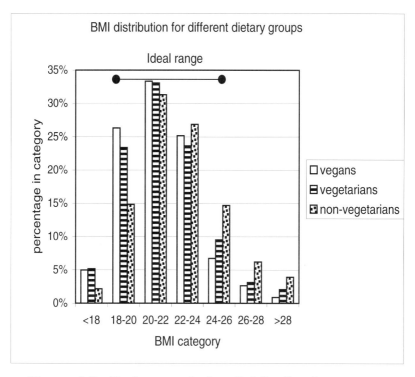

Figure 4.3: Body mass index distribution in vegans, other vegetarians and non-vegetarians

Comparisons between meat eaters, vegetarians and vegans (figure 4.3) support the expected benefit from basing one's diet on plant foods with their accompanying fibre and typically low calorie content. In developed countries, a notably different weight distribution is associated with vegetarian diets compared with omnivorous diets, and this difference increases with time on a vegetarian diet. The incidence of obesity among vegetarians is low compared with non-vegetarians with broadly similar lifestyles. Vegetarians also show an average body mass index about two units lower than non-vegetarians. BMI is slightly lower for vegans than for other vegetarians.

There is, however, considerable overlap in weight distribution between the various dietary groups – emphasising the need for diet to be tailored to the individual. The variation of BMI between individuals on similar diets, due largely to genetic factors, is much greater than the variation of average BMI between dietary groups. Some people naturally tend to be underweight, particularly on a diet high in unprocessed foods and low in fat and sugar. While this may be seen by many people as a cause for envy rather than concern, there is clear evidence from the UK study on which figure 4.3 is based, as well as from other studies, that a BMI below 18 is associated with a rapid increase in risk of death, including from heart disease. This does not seem to be explained by smoking, pre-existing disease or declining weight in old age and was observed despite a particularly favourable cholesterol profile in those with low BMI.

The optimal BMI range is probably 20 to 25, but the increase in risk from being a few units below this is much more dramatic than from being a few units above. Generally speaking, a person with a BMI of 28 has less cause for concern than one with a BMI of 17.

Figure 4.4 shows how death rate varies with BMI, based on recent studies both of vegetarians and of the general population. The death rates are expressed relative to death rates at optimal BMI. A relative death rate of 1.1 translates to a one year reduction in life expectancy. A relative death rate of two (1.1 to the power of seven) translates to a seven year reduction in life expectancy.

In younger adults, and in people who have been obese for decades, the adverse effect of obesity is somewhat higher than shown in figure 4.4, while in elderly adults the effect is somewhat lower. The adverse effect of obesity is also somewhat higher in men than in women and probably greater in whites than in blacks.

Underweight individuals should consume more calorie dense foods, make sure that food is always readily accessible when they feel hungry, and set aside enough time for eating. Physical activity should not be avoided, however, as it has many health benefits and promotes gaining weight as muscle rather than fat.

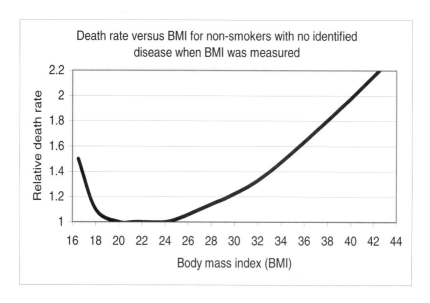

Figure 4.4: Expected death rate versus body mass index

The way fat is stored within the body may have important consequences for health which are not fully captured by measuring body mass index.   If excess fat is stored around the abdomen, creating the characteristic 'apple' shape, there is more risk of health problems than when it is stored around the buttocks and thighs – the typical 'pear' shape. Fat in the upper part of the body seems to lead to increased risk of cardiovascular disease and diabetes. Risk is greatly increased by a waist circumference of more than 88 cm (34 inches) in women and 102 cm (40 inches) in men.

An alternative way of considering shape is the waist to hip ratio (WHR).   This is calculated by dividing waist circumference by hip circumference measured at the widest point and can identify individuals who, despite being quite light or even scrawny, have a level of abdominal fat which nevertheless puts them at risk of diabetes and other problems more usually associated with high BMI. For men, a waist to hip ratio above 0.9 implies increased risk while for women a WHR above 0.8 implies increased risk.

A man with a 30 inch waist and 36 inch hips would have a waist to hip ratio of 0.83 (30 divided by 36). A woman with a 30 inch waist and 40 inch hips would have a WHR of 0.75. Both these combinations are in the healthy range.

Natural shape and build should be borne in mind in interpreting body mass index. A heavy boned or muscular person will have a lower percentage body fat for a given BMI, and a person with fat distributed evenly over their body or concentrated on their hips will have a lower risk for a similar percentage body fat than one with fat concentrated on their abdomen.

Anyone who feels healthy and looks healthy probably has little cause to worry about their weight. Although cultural influences have distorted our instinctive perceptions to some extent, they are still worth heeding. That said, the World Health Organisation's recommended BMI range of between 18.5 and 25 is a good objective reference point for the vast majority of people.

The Finnish Diabetes Prevention Study has shown that simple changes in diet and lifestyle can prevent the development of diabetes in overweight adults with high blood glucose. This study set the participants five goals: a reduction in weight of 5% or more; at least 30 minutes moderate exercise each day; total fat intake less than 30% of calories; saturated fat intake less than 10% of calories; fibre intake at least 15 grams per 1000 calories. Average weight loss was about 4 kilograms (5%) and was sustained over at least two years.

The number of people developing diabetes was 58% lower in the group encouraged to meet these targets compared with a control group who were given no special advice or encouragement. Even more strikingly, the percentage of these high risk adults who went on to develop diabetes showed a clear relationship with the number of targets met.

Number of targets met	0	1	2	3	4	5
Percentage developing diabetes	38	15	14	5	0	0

Figure 4.5: Effect of lifestyle changes on diabetes risk in overweight adults

None of the targets was dramatic or difficult to achieve, but in combination they proved highly successful in preventing diabetes. Similar results were achieved in a trial in the United States. The choices to minimise risk of obesity and diabetes are therefore clear.

Putting it into practice

Walk or run at least 20 miles a week (three miles cycling or half a mile swimming is roughly equivalent to one mile on foot).

If your body mass index is below 18.5 (see figure 4.1), increase the calorie density of your food by eating more low fibre foods high in fat and carbohydrate. Make sure that such calorie dense foods are always accessible to respond to mild hunger. Nuts, bananas and dried fruit are good snacks. Adding extra olive oil to stews or other dishes should also help.

If your body mass index is above 25 (see figure 4.1) and you are not naturally heavily built, decrease the calorie density of your food by eating more fruit and vegetables high in water and fibre. Restrict the accessibility of calorie dense foods by limiting the amount you have available. Oranges, apples and similar fruits are good snacks.

Chapter 5

The health giving rainbow

Everyone should eat a wide variety of brightly coloured fruit and vegetables. These foods are excellent sources of folate, vitamin C, carotenoids, and many other protective antioxidants, and probably of many as yet undiscovered substances that also contribute to good health. Such foods are also associated with reduced risk of cancer, cardiovascular disease, dementia and blindness and make for an attractive and stimulating diet.

Yet most people do not eat enough of these foods to maximise their chances of good health into old age: at least a pound (450 grams) a day from a variety of sources. Leafy greens, peppers, tomatoes, beetroot, oranges, carrots, cherries, plums and berries are all among the many common foods with much to commend them. Such foods are at the core of our evolutionary diet and should be returned to the heart of our modern diet to maximise potential to support health.

Unfortunately, the less colourful vegetables and fruits such as potatoes and bananas, while they are useful sources of potassium and other nutrients, are not associated with the same benefits as their more brightly coloured cousins and therefore do not count towards the intake recommended in this chapter: chips (French fries), or even baked potatoes, are no substitute for oranges and greens.

Vitamin pills and nutrient extracts are a very poor substitute for the broad cocktail of nutrients provided by brightly coloured fruit and vegetables. Certain nutrients such as vitamin C, beta-carotene, lycopene and folate act as markers for consumption of foods from the health giving rainbow, but this does not make supplements of these nutrients reliable substitutes for the foods which so plentifully and naturally provide them.

Indeed, a trial of beta-carotene supplement pills showed no significant effect and a trial of beta-carotene and retinol in combination showed an *increase* rather than a decrease in overall deaths among smokers. Similarly, trials of alpha-tocopherol (the usual form of vitamin E in supplements) found little effect on blood clotting while mixed tocopherols (typical of those provided by foods) reduced clotting. We are not adapted to megadoses of isolated antioxidants, but to the overall mixture provided by fruits and vegetables that we are naturally attracted to eating.

With this qualification in mind, it is useful to look at some of the evidence of benefits from foods high in these marker nutrients.

Lycopene is found in many bright red vegetables and is a potent antioxidant, acting in a complementary fashion to other carotenoids such as the orange-coloured beta-carotene. Increased lycopene intake, particularly from cooked tomatoes, has been found in many studies to be associated with a 50% reduction in risk of heart disease and some cancers, particularly prostate cancer. A Japanese study found high blood levels of lycopene to be associated with a 50% reduction in overall mortality.

A Dutch study found high blood levels of carotenoids to be associated with a 40% reduction in overall mortality. In the UK, increased levels of vitamin C in the blood, reflecting increased intake of fruit and vegetables, have been found to be associated with decreased overall mortality: death rates almost halved as fruit and vegetable intake increased from 150 grams per day to 300 grams per day. A study in Finland found a high intake of fruits, berries and vegetables to be associated with a 34% reduction in overall mortality.

Increased levels of vitamin C and beta-carotene are also associated with reduced risk of cognitive decline and dementia. Lutein, a carotenoid found particularly in green leafy vegetables, is found in unusually high concentrations in the eye; increased intake is associated with decreased risk of macular degeneration – the most common cause of blindness in the elderly. Increased folate intake is associated with decreased risk of bowel cancer and breast cancer and helps to reduce homocysteine levels (see chapter 6).

Fortunately, consuming a wide variety of fruits and vegetables of different colours provides an adequate guide to getting all these benefits. A high intake of fruit and vegetables also shifts the diet simultaneously towards high nutrient density and low calorie density, thus helping to maintain a healthy weight. This is especially so when such foods are eaten whole rather than taken in the form of juice, since juices provide a relatively easily consumed low fibre source of calories.

In an attempt to rank different fruits and vegetables in terms of their likely beneficial effect on health, several measures of overall antioxidant potency have been proposed which capture at least part of the combined effect of carotenoids, vitamin C and vitamin E.

The most widely publicised antioxidant measure – ORAC (Oxygen Radical Absorbance Capacity) – measures the ability of the antioxidant cocktail to quench damaging oxidation reactions driven by three different free radicals which occur naturally in the body. As the protective effect of antioxidants comes from blocking such reactions, ORAC should be particularly closely related to the effectiveness of antioxidants within the body, but it is difficult to measure and therefore not many foods have been evaluated. An alternative measure is FRAP (Ferric Reducing Ability of Plasma). FRAP is closely related to ORAC but is more easily measured – based on the reduction of ferric iron to ferrous iron – so more foods have been assessed. Figure 5.1 gives FRAP values for some common plant foods.

The pinnacle of the FRAP hierarchy is occupied by fruit. It is notable that wild berries are generally much richer in antioxidants than their cultivated cousins, but cultivated berries are still good sources.

Food	FRAP	Food	FRAP	Food	FRAP
Grains		Green pepper	1.6	Kiwi fruit	0.9
Buckwheat, whole	2.0	Brussels sprouts	1.1	Grapefruit	0.8
Buckwheat, refined	1.2	Spinach	1.0	Apricots	0.5
Barley, whole	1.1	Asparagus	0.9	Avocado	0.4
Oats	0.6	Onion	0.7	Tomato	0.3
Rye, whole	0.4	Broccoli	0.6	Apple	0.3
Wheat, whole	0.3			Banana	0.2
Rye, white	0.2	**Fruit**		Cantaloupe melon	0.2
Wheat, white	0.1	Pomegranate	11.3		
		Wild blueberry	8.2	**Nuts**	
Roots		Blackcurrant	7.4	Walnuts	21.0
Ginger	3.8	Wild strawberry	6.9	Sunflower seeds	5.4
Red beetroot	2.0	Wild blackberry	6.1	Peanuts	1.0
Swede	0.4	Sour cherry	5.5	Hazel nuts	0.5
Turnip	0.3	Cultivated blackberry	5.1	Almonds	0.2
Sweet potato	0.2	Cranberry	5.0	Cashews	0.2
Potato	0.1	Cultivated blueberry	3.6		
		Cultivated strawberry	2.2	**Beans**	
Vegetables		Yellow or red pepper	1.9	Broad beans	1.9
Chilli pepper	2.5	Grapes	1.5	Green lentils	1.0
Kale	2.3	Oranges	1.1	Soya beans	0.8
Red cabbage	1.9	Plums	1.1	Black-eyed beans	0.7
Parsley	1.7	Sweet cherry	1.0	Red lentils	0.2

Figure 5.1: Antioxidant capacity of plant foods

Melons are low in antioxidants per 100 grams, but can easily be eaten in large amounts as they are mostly water. Not surprisingly, refined grains fare very badly, but other foods such as potatoes and bananas also come close to the bottom by this measure, so the principle of favouring colourful foods stands up well.

Those nuts and seeds which are high in polyunsaturates, and thus vulnerable to oxidation, generally come with plenty of antioxidants: walnuts have a particularly high FRAP score of 21 compared with less than 0.5 for the more stable hazel nuts (filberts), almonds and cashews.

Green leafy vegetables, such as spinach, kale, spring greens (collards), broccoli, Brussels sprouts and lettuce, are the best source of bone protecting vitamin K (see chapter 7). Vitamin K requirements can be met by 100 grams per day of such foods. Vitamin K is absorbed better if green leafy vegetables are eaten with some vegetable oil.

As well as acting as antioxidants, certain carotenoids are converted in the body into vitamin A. Daily vitamin A requirements can be met by 50 grams of carrots, 100 grams of sweet potatoes or dried apricots, or 200 grams of dark green leafy vegetables such as spinach or kale. The carotenoids from carrots are absorbed better if the carrots are cooked or juiced.

Putting it into practice

Make brightly coloured fruits and vegetables – such as leafy greens, broccoli, peppers, tomatoes, beetroot, oranges, carrots, cherries, plums and berries – a major part of your diet.

Consume at least a pound (450 grams) per day from a wide variety of types and colours.

Eat at least two pounds of green leafy vegetables or broccoli and a pound of carrots each week.

Chapter 6

Homocysteine and health

The amino acid homocysteine is almost unknown among the general public but has been the subject of intense interest within the medical community since the early 1990s as evidence has accumulated that even moderately elevated levels of homocysteine go hand in hand with increased risk of birth defects, dementia, depression and death.

Independent studies in Israel, the USA, Norway and the Netherlands have reported homocysteine level to be strongly associated with mortality from all causes combined, making it potentially more important than cholesterol. Every 10% increase in homocysteine is associated with a 5% to 10% increase in overall mortality, reducing life expectancy by between six months and a year.

To understand how elevated homocysteine comes to be associated with ill effects from before birth through to death, we need to look at some vital biochemical reactions (figure 6.1). Folate is obtained from foods such as leafy vegetables and beans and is used by the body in DNA synthesis, during which folate is converted to methyltetrahydrofolate (MTHF). This is subsequently converted back to folate in a reaction which simultaneously converts homocysteine to methionine. This critical reaction relies on an adequate store of vitamin B12.

The amino acid methionine, which is also obtained from food, is the source of another vital chemical, S-adenosyl methionine (SAM). SAM provides the methyl compounds for many different methylation reactions, including DNA repair, formation of neuro-transmitters, synthesis of coenzyme Q, production of other amino acids (including carnitine and creatine), and elimination of toxins such as arsenic

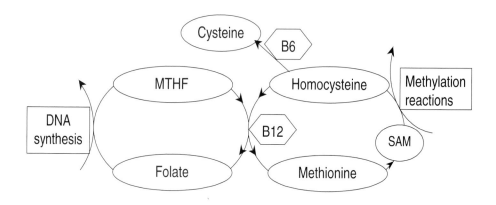

Figure 6.1: The biochemistry of homocysteine

and pyridine. Each of these methylation reactions degrades SAM back to homocysteine ready for further conversion to methionine. If homocysteine is not needed to produce methionine, it is converted with the aid of vitamin B6 to cysteine.

So folate circulates around, being consumed in the process of building DNA and regenerated with the help of vitamin B12, at the same time as homocysteine is converted into methionine to fuel methylation reactions. If there is not enough stored B12 in the body, both these vital renewing cycles are obstructed: folate gets trapped as MTHF, becoming unavailable for further DNA synthesis, while homocysteine accumulates instead of being converted into methionine to fuel the methylation reactions. As homocysteine concentration rises, the methylation reactions detect the obstruction ahead and slow down so that the pace of repair and regeneration declines. This biochemical understanding makes the many observed adverse associations of increased homocysteine levels understandable.

Kidney disease and certain rare genetic defects can cause homocysteine concentration to rise irrespective of diet. The more usual cause of elevated homocysteine, however, is low intake of any one of three B-vitamins. Vitamin B12 is required for the reaction converting homocysteine into methionine and methyltetrahydrofolate into folate, so inadequate vitamin B12 can simultaneously increase homocysteine and reduce the availability of folate. An inadequate supply of folate can slow down the provision of methyltetrahydrofolate and thus slow the conversion of homocysteine to methionine. Inadequate vitamin B6 can block the back-up disposal route converting homocysteine to cysteine.

Substantial short term increases in methionine intake fuel the methylation reactions, causing a surge in homocysteine. However, the body adapts to high methionine intake by recognising that homocysteine is not needed to replenish methionine and increasing the conversion of homocysteine to cysteine (so long as sufficient B6 is available). In the long run, typical methionine intakes have little net effect on homocysteine if intakes of B6, folate and B12 are optimal.

Unfiltered coffee, smoking and alcohol appear to increase homocysteine. Black tea has little effect. Spirits, such as whiskey and vodka, are clearly associated with increased homocysteine while other alcoholic drinks, such as beer and wine, are not. Alcohol inhibits the conversion of homocysteine to methionine, but this effect can be compensated for by good folate and B12 intakes. As with methionine, these effects are secondary: the key factor is intakes of the three B-vitamins – folate, B12 and B6.

Supplementation trials using folate, B12 and B6 to reduce homocysteine have demonstrated a reduction in symptoms of heart disease, including the rate of progression of atherosclerosis – providing further evidence of the importance of avoiding elevated homocysteine. Supplementation with 4 milligrams (mg) per day of folate reduced the incidence of neural tube defects such as spina

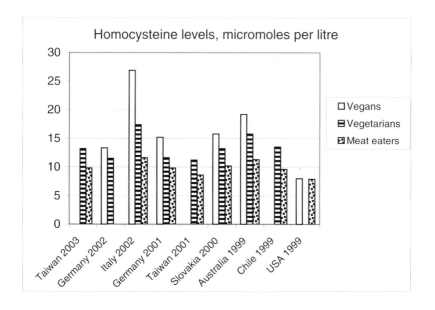

Figure 6.2: Comparisons of homocysteine levels in vegans, other vegetarians and meat eaters

bifida by about 70%. A similar trial using 0.8 mg of folic acid and 4 micrograms (µg or mcg) of B12 reduced neural tube defects by 100%.

In the early days of research on homocysteine there was considerable optimism that homocysteine levels would be lowered on a plant-based diet, due to high folate levels and moderate methionine intake. Indeed, a recent trial showed that homocysteine levels decreased within a week of switching from a typical Western diet to a vegan diet with plenty of vegetables.

However, other studies have shown that many long term vegans have blood homocysteine concentrations around 15 micromoles per litre (µmol/l) compared with desirable levels below 10. Other vegetarians also show increased levels, averaging about 12 micromoles per litre.

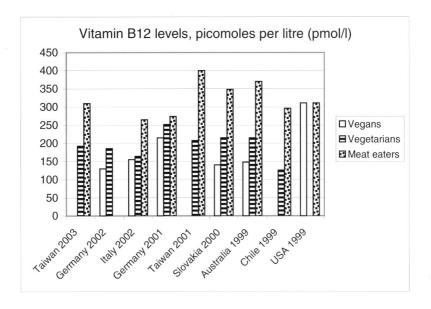

Figure 6.3: Comparisons of vitamin B12 levels in vegans, other vegetarians and meat eaters

This rise in homocysteine does not occur in those vegans ensuring an adequate B12 intake of 3 micrograms (µg) or more per day, who show the expected benefit from high folate and plentiful B6 to give homocysteine levels around 8 micromoles per litre compared with a Western average of about 10. Homocysteine levels rise with age and are slightly lower in women than in men.

Figure 6.2 shows the results of recent studies on homocysteine levels and diet.

With the exception of one study in the USA in 1999, the highest levels of homocysteine were observed in vegans, while vegetarian levels were also higher than those of meat eaters. The critical role of vitamin B12 can be seen in the comparisons of blood B12 and folate levels from the same studies (figures 6.3 and 6.4). The B12 levels of

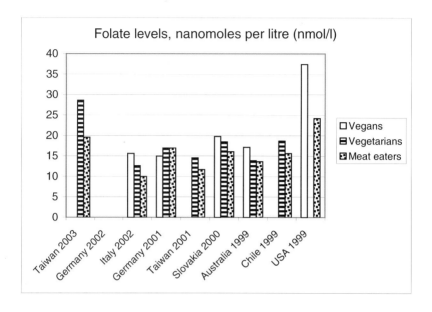

Figure 6.4: Comparisons of folate levels in vegans, other vegetarians and meat eaters

vegans were generally the lowest, while those of other vegetarians were between those of vegans and meat eaters. In contrast, vegan folate levels were generally higher than, or similar to, those of the other groups.

In the 1999 USA study, vegan B12 levels matched those of the meat eaters – due to high average B12 intakes from fortified foods and supplements – and so did homocysteine levels. To remove any shadow of doubt as to the cause of the high homocysteine levels, the Chilean study followed up by monitoring the effect of B12 supplementation. The homocysteine levels of the Chilean vegetarians dropped from about 13 micromoles per litre to 7.9 with no other dietary changes.

Average vegan homocysteine levels are about 15 micromoles per litre. Based on studies in the general population, this degree of excess homocysteine could be associated with a 40% increase in mortality from both heart disease and other causes. Low vegan cholesterol levels would be expected to reduce heart disease deaths by about 50% compared with meat eaters, so the overall result would be 30% less heart disease (0.5 times 1.4 equals 0.7), but 40% increased mortality from other causes, with little difference overall. This is almost exactly the pattern observed in the combined analysis of the five major studies of vegetarians discussed in chapter 3.

	Meat eaters	Occasional meat eaters	Fish eaters	Vegetarians	Vegans
Heart disease	1.00	0.8	0.66	0.66	0.74
Other (non-cancer) causes	1.00	0.84	0.85	0.95	1.33
All causes	1.00	0.84	0.82	0.84	1.00

Figure 6.5: Relative risk of death according to diet

The evidence suggests that getting adequate vitamin B12 could result in a 30% reduction in mortality rates for many vegans. Unfortunately, as mortality rates rise by about 10% for each year older we become, this does not translate to living 30% longer, but rather to living about four years longer (0.7 = 1.1 to the power of -4).

It should be noted that the meat eaters studied did not eat as much meat as the general population in their countries and that none of the groups included many smokers. Mortality in the general population is about 1.6 in terms of figure 6.5. **The vegans studied were therefore already living about five years longer than their typical meat-eating compatriots,** but could do even better with adequate vitamin B12.

As discussed in chapter 3, vegetarians in the USA showed more advantage over regular meat eaters than did vegetarians in the UK. The US vegetarians studied were Seventh Day Adventists, as were the vegans in the US study which found excellent vegan homocysteine levels.

Multivitamin use is more common in the USA than in Europe, and standard multivitamins in the USA include 6 micrograms of B12. This is also the US recommended dietary allowance for B12 for food labelling purposes. In contrast, the European RDA for food labelling is just 1 microgram. Fortified foods in the USA therefore often provide more B12 than their European counterparts.

Dietary practices reducing the risk of elevated homocysteine in vegetarian and vegan US Seventh Day Adventists may therefore play a significant part in the difference between the US and UK results.

Elevated homocysteine is by no means just a vegetarian problem – it is common in meat eaters due to low folate intake. Moreover, elderly meat eaters often cannot absorb vitamin B12 from meat and show a gradual decline in B12 levels, resulting - as for those vegetarians with inadequate B12 intake - in increased homocysteine levels.

All vitamin B12 is produced by bacteria, whether it is obtained from fortified foods, supplements, meat, milk or eggs. B12 for use in supplements and fortified foods is produced by fermentation (similar to beer making) using carefully selected bacteria which have not been genetically modified. This form of B12 is highly absorbable and is therefore recommended for everyone over 50 to ensure a reliable supply.

Homocysteine rises significantly a long time before B12 or folate stores drop to the level associated with classical vitamin deficiency. Folate deficiency becomes apparent as anaemia due to impaired

DNA synthesis, but may also give rise to neurological symptoms by increasing homocysteine and blocking methylation reactions.

For folate, the required blood (serum) level to minimise homocysteine is about 20 nanomoles per litre (nmol/l), corresponding to a folate intake of about 400 micrograms (µg or mcg) per day, which is easily obtained on a varied plant-based diet. This is similar to intakes now recommended for pregnant women to reduce the risk of neural tube defects. Many countries have recently adopted folate fortification of grain products to increase folate intakes.

Vitamin B12 deficiency usually becomes apparent as neurological symptoms, particularly if folate intake is high. The classic symptoms include numbness and tingling, lack of energy, blurred vision, loss of balance and limb control, poor memory, sore tongue, and personality changes such as delusions and paranoia. In infants, B12 deficiency manifests as loss of energy, appetite and alertness and can progress to coma and death. Onset is also more rapid than in adults. All symptoms are reversible *if caught early enough* but damage can be permanent, particularly in children. Breast-fed infants can become severely deficient if the mother has low B12 intake even if the mother herself has no deficiency symptoms.

Current government recommendations for vitamin B12 intake are based on reliably preventing classical deficiency and are adequate for this purpose. However, they do not consider the amounts required to minimise homocysteine. At least three micrograms per day are required to achieve this by maintaining blood B12 levels at 300 picomoles per litre (400 picograms per millilitre) or above.

If vitamin B12 is taken as a weekly supplement, then as much as 2000 micrograms may be required. The reason why the required weekly intake can vary from 20 micrograms to 2000 micrograms is that our absorption of B12 is best at very small doses, below 0.5 micrograms, from which we absorb about 70% of the available B12.

As the dose approaches 10 micrograms, the total absorbed amount flattens off at about 1.5 micrograms and only 0.5% to 2% of further increases in dose are absorbed (see figure 6.6).

The amount of B12 absorbed from 2000 micrograms may therefore be as little as 10 micrograms, which is the amount needed per week to maintain adequate B12 levels. The same weekly absorbed amount can be obtained from 3 micrograms per day spread across a couple of meals, or from a daily supplement of 10 micrograms. All B12 supplements should be chewed thoroughly to ensure good absorption.

A single weekly supplement of 2000 micrograms has the advantage that its absorption does not rely on intrinsic factor in the stomach, which is required for the efficient absorption of small amounts of B12 and is occasionally absent, particularly in the elderly. All forms of fortified foods and supplements avoid the more common B12 absorption problem in the elderly, which is inability to separate the B12 in meat from the proteins to which it is bound. This is usually due to declining stomach acidity (atrophic gastritis).

The need for B12 fortification or supplementation to keep homocysteine levels low begs the question of how plant-eating primates such as gorillas and chimps obtain adequate B12. The main answer appears to be insect consumption and bacterial contamination of soil and food. All the great apes consume significant amounts of insects as contaminants in or on their basic diet of fruits, leaves, shoots and roots. In many cases they also eat insects deliberately, as in the famous chimpanzee termite "fishing". Some primates eat faeces and large amounts of soil, which may also provide a useful source of B12.

A minority of primates have a second stomach which acts as a bacterial fermenter (similar to the rumen of grazing animals) and provides an on-board source of B12, given sufficient dietary cobalt.

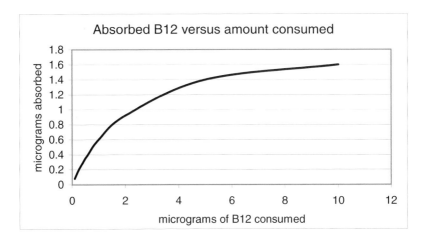

Figure 6.6: B12 absorption versus amount consumed

All other primates, like humans, require an external supply of B12 from bacteria outside their body. When primates are fed a sanitised diet, they often develop B12 deficiency.

Vegans do not deliberately eat insects, and neither soil nor faeces are particularly attractive to most modern humans. Fortunately, we now have the technology to harvest B12 directly from bacteria, thus removing the need for an intermediary and avoiding the risk of infection. Fortified foods and supplements provide a very reliable and well absorbed source of B12 with no unwanted extras.

Some vegans, particularly those following raw food diets, are nevertheless reluctant to use supplements or fortified foods. Unfortunately, none of the commonly suggested alternatives such as spirulina, nori or blue-green algae has been shown to contain sufficient true B12 to be a realistic source. Indeed, dried nori has been shown to make B12 deficiency *worse* due to the presence of large amounts of B12 analogues which interfere with the absorption and utilisation of true B12.

Analogues are compounds which are similar enough to B12 to substitute for B12 in certain bacteria but do not fulfil the vital role of vitamin B12 in humans. As the most common tests for vitamin B12 use bacteria, they can be fooled by the presence of analogues which are active for the bacteria but not for humans. For instance, the true B12 content of spirulina tablets has been shown to be just 2% of the amount normally quoted on the basis of older measurement methods which also measure B12 analogues.

The only raw plant foods that currently seem to be *possible* sources of true B12 for vegans are two types of algae: pleurochrysis carterae and chlorella. However, the quoted levels in chlorella are highly variable, availability of B12 may vary with processing and, most importantly, there has been no human study confirming that it corrects B12 deficiency. At one time, nori appeared promising as around half of its measured B12 was confirmed to be true B12, but in human feeding trials it actually *increased* symptoms of B12 deficiency rather than reducing them. In the absence of a confirmed "living food" source, and in the light of worrying evidence of poor B12 status in raw food vegans, major raw food groups such as Hallelujah Acres now recommend the use of conventional B12 supplements.

In the absence of an external source of B12, blood levels and liver stores drop gradually over time. One thousandth of current stores is lost every day in bile secretions which are only partly reabsorbed in the small intestine. As stores drop, losses in bile secretions also drop. Because small amounts of B12 are absorbed better than large amounts, the percentage of the loss that is reabsorbed increases and the rate of decline slows. For this reason, many people with minimal intake of external B12 show stable blood B12 levels, albeit usually well below the levels required to minimise homocysteine. Others continue the slide towards classical deficiency.

Individuals who choose not to include a reliable source of B12 in their diet would be well advised to get a test to see if they have adequate available B12, even if they have no classical deficiency symptoms. If probiotics or algae are being consumed, high levels of analogues in the blood may confuse the standard blood B12 test. Otherwise, the blood B12 test is adequate and a result of 300 picomoles per litre (400 picograms per millilitre) or higher indicates adequate B12. This test is readily available. A direct test of homocysteine levels is less readily available but is the best way to confirm that neither inadequate B12 nor any other factor is exposing you to unnecessary risk. The desirable level for homocysteine is less than 10 micromoles per litre and under 8 is excellent.

Vitamin B12 is also involved in another important set of reactions in the metabolism of short chain fatty acids. If this is obstructed, levels of methylmalonic acid (MMA) rise in both blood and urine. If MMA is low, this means that B12 stores are adequate. Measuring MMA therefore provides an alternative test of B12 status. This test is not confused by high blood levels of B12 analogues.

As a concluding thought on homocysteine, it should be recalled that elevated homocysteine affects health throughout life as well as reducing life expectancy, and is associated with ill effects at the start of life as well as towards the end.

Elevated homocysteine, low B12 and low folate levels are also linked with depression and with the onset and progression of dementia. S-adenosyl methionine (SAM), which fuels the methylation reactions that are blocked by elevated homocysteine, has become a well established but expensive antidepressant. Keeping homocysteine low ensures that the inbuilt mechanisms for maintaining the vital methylation reactions are not being hindered.

A study in Norway in 2000 compared the outcomes of pregnancies in the 25% of women with the highest homocysteine levels and the outcomes for the 25% of women with the lowest homocysteine.

Figure 6.7 shows the risk of various adverse outcomes in the women with high homocysteine divided by the risk for those with low homocysteine. Similar results have been found in other countries, including China where low vitamin B12 was also associated with premature birth.

Condition	Risk for women with high homocysteine	Risk for women with low homocysteine
Preeclampsia	1.32	1.0
Prematurity	1.38	1.0
Low birth weight	2.01	1.0
Neural tube defects	3.57	1.0
Club foot	2.53	1.0

Figure 6.7: Pregnancy outcomes with high or low homocysteine levels

While homocysteine levels generally rise with age, a study in Northern Ireland found that individuals in their nineties had lower homocysteine levels than individuals in their seventies and eighties – providing further confirmation of the importance of low homocysteine for healthy ageing.

From before birth to death, elevated homocysteine casts its shadow. Fortunately, the risk can be straightforwardly minimised by following the guidelines in this chapter.

Putting it into practice

Ensure a good intake of folate and vitamin B6 by eating a wide range of plant foods, particularly green vegetables, oranges and legumes (beans, peas and lentils).

Ensure a good intake of vitamin B12 by getting either

3 micrograms over the course of the day from fortified foods,

or

10 micrograms once a day from a supplement,

or

2000 micrograms once a week from a supplement.

Supplements should be chewed thoroughly to promote good absorption.

Chapter 7

Balancing calcium: a team game

Calcium is lost from the body in urine, faeces and sweat. If these losses are not balanced by calcium absorption from food, calcium will be drawn from the bones to maintain the required concentration of calcium in the blood. Calcium balance - the difference between calcium absorbed and calcium lost - is therefore critical to bone health.

If calcium loss increases, calcium balance decreases and the concentration of calcium in the blood starts to fall. This triggers the release of parathyroid hormone (PTH) and calcitriol, which in turn increase the transfer of calcium both from the digestive system and from the bones until blood concentrations are stabilised.

In children and young adults, most of the additional calcium supplied to the blood comes from the digestive system, as the bones are relatively resistant to demands for calcium to be released. Thus the overall calcium balance is only slightly degraded by increased calcium loss.

With advancing age, the bones become less resistant to demands for the release of calcium and the digestive system becomes more resistant to these demands, so the overall calcium balance is more severely reduced by increased calcium loss. Calcium balance in older adults is determined more by variations in calcium loss than by variations in calcium intake and absorption.

Even when the body is successful in maintaining calcium balance despite high losses or low intake, it does so at a price: increased levels of parathyroid hormone and calcitriol alter the calcium balance in all the cells in the body. These changes lead to increased tension in the veins and arteries, contributing to higher blood pressure, and may also alter the balance between fat breakdown and storage in fat cells, contributing to increased accumulation of body fat.

Dietary changes to increase calcium balance can therefore help to preserve bones, avoid high blood pressure with the accompanying risks of stroke and heart disease, and possibly also reduce the risk of obesity. The factors governing average calcium balance in older adults can be expressed as an equation:

Calcium balance = 5 x √calcium intake
$$+ \ 0.016 \ x \ (potassium \ intake - sodium \ intake)$$
$$- \ 1.1 \ x \ protein \ - \ 80$$

Mineral intakes are expressed in milligrams per day and protein in grams per day. The potassium is assumed to come from food and the sodium from common salt (sodium chloride). A more detailed discussion of calcium balance, including the derivation of this equation, can be found in appendix 1.

As noted, younger adults respond to a short term deficit in calcium balance primarily by boosting the calcium retention factor from the average value of 5 (in the equation) to higher values as required, while in older adults much of the deficit predicted from this equation is made up by calcium from the bones. The equation is a good approximation for people about 50 years old, while for older people average calcium absorption tends to be even lower.

The square root term on calcium intake reflects the manner in which increasing calcium intake produces diminishing returns in terms of the balance of calcium actually retained. Going from 0 to 500 milligrams (mg) of calcium per day adds 110 mg to the calcium balance whereas going from 500 to 1000 mg per day adds just 45 mg. This is a key reason why studies have found clear evidence of benefit from calcium intakes increasing from below 500 mg per day to above 500 mg per day, but have struggled to find evidence of a benefit from increasing calcium intakes beyond typical intakes in Europe, North America and Australasia of about 700 mg per day.

A further reason for the weakness of evidence for a benefit from increased dietary calcium is that not all sources are equivalent in overall effect on calcium balance as the calcium comes accompanied by differing amounts of protein, potassium and sodium.

To equate improving calcium balance with consuming more calcium is a fundamental error, as variations in balance are due more to variations in calcium loss than to variations in intake and absorption. In studies of bone loss in adults there is often a stronger protective association with potassium intake than with calcium intake, and there is a clear adverse correlation with sodium intake. This is explained by the observation that increased potassium intake reduces urinary calcium loss while increased sodium increases such loss, so with a diet low in potassium and high in sodium the body will have a constant struggle to maintain calcium balance.

In people following typical North American and European diets, calcium losses are driven with approximately equal importance by high sodium (salt) intake, high protein intake and low potassium intake. In a typical prehistoric human diet, daily potassium intake would have exceeded sodium intake by about 7,000 mg, contributing about 100 mg per day to the calcium balance. In a typical Western diet, sodium intake is similar to potassium intake, so this boost is lost. Given a protein intake of about 80 grams per day, over 1000 mg of calcium is required for balance on a typical Western diet, while with a 7,000 mg potassium excess just 200 mg of calcium is sufficient.

Absorption of calcium at a given intake varies substantially between individuals, with 10% of older women absorbing less than 3 x $\sqrt{}$Calcium intake – or 40% below average. Some individuals are more sensitive to sodium, and their calcium losses will increase more with sodium intake than indicated by the average relationship.

Even for the mythical "average person", therefore, relying on calcium intake alone to keep calcium in the bones is like fielding a football team with only strikers and no defenders. The best strategy is to reduce risk on all fronts at once by increasing potassium and calcium intake and reducing sodium intake.

Studies on blood pressure and stroke risk confirm this picture: increasing potassium and calcium and decreasing sodium provide alternative and complementary approaches to achieving the desired outcome. Some recent studies also suggest a beneficial effect of calcium on obesity. As for bone loss and blood pressure, increasing potassium and decreasing sodium can be expected to have the same impact as increasing calcium. Sodium and potassium intakes also affect blood pressure through mechanisms independent of calcium balance, but if intakes are chosen to support calcium balance these other mechanisms will also be favourably influenced.

Recent results from the Dietary Approaches to Stop Hypertension (DASH) study provide a very clear demonstration of the interaction of sodium, potassium and calcium in relation to blood pressure.

The control diet was chosen to be similar to common US diets in terms of mineral and fat intake. It was, however, unusually low in calcium.

The design of the DASH diet was inspired in part by earlier evidence that adopting a vegetarian diet reduced blood pressure, though it proved difficult to ascribe this effect to any one nutrient. The DASH diet increased vegetable and fruit consumption to boost potassium and fibre intakes, but avoided high calcium plant foods and relied on low fat dairy products to increase calcium intake.

	Potassium	Calcium	Fibre	Saturated fat	Total fat
Control diet	1700 mg	450 mg	10 g	14%	37%
DASH diet	4400 mg	1250 mg	30 g	7%	26%

Figure 7.1: Changes in nutrients in the DASH diet

The blood pressure measurements in figure 7.2 are shown as systolic (higher figure) and diastolic: the former is the pressure required to stop blood flow completely while the latter is the pressure at which blood flow becomes continuous again.

	High sodium (3.5 g)	Medium sodium (2.4 g)	Low sodium (1.3 g)
Control diet	133/83	131/82	126/79
DASH diet	127/80	126/79	124/78

Figure 7.2: Effect of reduced sodium intake and DASH diet on blood pressure

The results show that reducing sodium intake from high to medium has only a moderate effect, but reducing intake from medium to low has a much stronger effect. This is consistent with comparisons between countries in the Intersalt study, which suggested that keeping sodium intake below about two grams per day greatly reduced the prevalence of high blood pressure (hypertension).

Roughly the same benefit is obtained from either increasing calcium and potassium intakes (DASH diet) or substantially decreasing sodium intake. Combining both changes gives a modest further improvement.

Other results from the DASH study indicate that about half the benefit comes from the changes in potassium and fibre intakes and most of the rest from the changes in calcium and fat intakes.

Increasing potassium intake and decreasing salt intake is a commonly advocated strategy for reducing blood pressure. Others suggest that increasing calcium is the best strategy. The DASH results, and other direct observations of human health, show that these strategies can be productively combined for maximum effect, as would be expected from the underlying biochemistry of calcium balance.

Few would dispute the health benefits of increased dietary potassium from fruit and vegetables, but there has been controversy about the effect of sodium intake on mortality – unsurprisingly, given the prominent role of salt in processed food manufacturing.

A study of sodium excretion and mortality in treated hypertensives observed more heart attacks in those with the lowest sodium excretion. These results are cited by food manufacturers as showing the dangers of reducing salt intake, but were probably distorted by the effects of treatment and by measuring sodium excretion after participants had been instructed to avoid high salt foods.

Two later studies observed untreated adults following their normal diet. A Finnish study found a 56% increase in mortality from all causes with a 2.3 gram (100 millimole) increase in sodium excretion in overweight adults. No effect was observed in other adults. Similarly, a US study found a 39% increase in all-cause mortality in overweight adults for a 2.3 gram increase in sodium intake, but no effect in other adults.

Overall, it is clear that high salt consumption has a strong adverse effect on overall mortality in overweight adults (body mass index above 25) – as would be expected from its effect on blood pressure and from comparisons between countries.

Helping bones to retain calcium

In all developed countries with ageing populations, thinning of bones is a major public health issue. As bones thin, the risk of fracture increases. Hip fracture is a particularly devastating injury and many people die within a year. Osteoporosis and vertebral fractures result in loss of height with age and the all too familiar bent-over stance of many elderly people. Measures to promote bone health are important throughout life to assist in building bone and to reduce later bone losses.

Much of the variation in bone loss with age, sex and race is driven not by differences in calcium loss or calcium intake but by differences in the relative responsiveness of the bones and the digestive system to demands for calcium to be released into the blood to make up any calcium loss.

Calcium loss is more likely to be replenished from the digestive system in children and young adults of all races and in blacks compared with whites. This explains why older white adults, particularly postmenopausal women, have an especially high risk of negative calcium balance and bone loss.

The first line of defence is to increase calcium and potassium intakes and to decrease sodium intake, as discussed, but there are other factors which can improve calcium balance by boosting absorption of calcium above average values. Making bones more resistant to demands to release calcium into the blood forces parathyroid hormone and calcitriol concentrations to rise until increased absorption of calcium from the digestive system makes up for the smaller contribution from the bones.

Physical activity stimulates bone building, making the bones resistant to releasing calcium. Activity promotes bone growth particularly strongly during childhood, but can also promote modest growth at older ages as well as greatly reducing bone loss. The importance of physical activity for bone health cannot be overemphasised: we should no more expect diet alone to build strong bones than we would expect it to build strong muscles.

As well as reducing calcium loss, dietary potassium helps to make bones more resistant to calcium loss by making the blood more alkaline - a double benefit for calcium balance. It is therefore not surprising that potassium intake has been found to be strongly beneficial for bone health.

Protein increases calcium loss by about one milligram of calcium per gram of protein, but it also stimulates bone building. These conflicting effects mean that increased protein intake can have either a beneficial or an adverse effect on overall calcium balance, depending on background intakes of protein and other nutrients, genetic make-up and age.

If protein intake is low, the level of growth hormones such as IGF-1 will also be low, reducing the rate of repair of bone and muscle. From such a baseline, increased protein intake may actually improve calcium balance even while increasing calcium loss. If protein intake is already adequate, any further increase will make calcium balance worse. Excessive protein intake also overtaxes the kidneys and accelerates decline in kidney function with age.

Not surprisingly, epidemiological observations on protein intake, bone loss and fracture risk have been contradictory. Very low protein intake is definitely bad for bone, while at very high protein intakes the loss promoting effect outstrips the stimulus to bone building. Moderate protein intake – about one gram of protein per kilogram of body weight per day – is probably ideal.

As protein from plants is usually accompanied by much more potassium compared with protein from animals, there is good reason to meet protein needs from plant sources (see chapter 11 for more information on plant protein sources and optimal protein intake).

Vitamin K, found in green leafy vegetables and broccoli and in some fermented foods such as natto (fermented soya beans), has a profound effect on bone resistance to calcium loss, particularly in postmenopausal women. About 100 grams per day of broccoli, lettuce or other green leafy vegetables is associated with a 30% to 50% reduction in fracture risk.

Vitamin C and magnesium also help to build and strengthen bone, and omega-3 fatty acids may also have a beneficial effect. Elevated homocysteine, on the other hand, may increase the risk of fracture.

Retinol (pre-formed vitamin A) makes bone loss and fracture more likely. In Sweden, increased milk consumption appeared to increase fracture risk until the effect of retinol – added to milk as part of a food fortification programme – was taken into account. Retinol intake above 1500 micrograms per day is associated with a dramatic increase in fracture risk and should therefore be avoided.

Many multivitamin supplements contain retinol or related compounds (any ingredient beginning with "retin"), but usually provide just 700 micrograms per day. For vegans, who consume few foods containing retinol, this amount is unlikely to cause any harm. Consumption of liver can easily result in excessive retinol intake even without supplements.

Plant carotenoids - abundant in carrots, sweet potatoes and dark green leafy vegetables - allow the body to make as much vitamin A as it needs without any adverse effect on bone health. The daily vitamin A requirement can be met by 50 grams of carrots, 100 grams of sweet potatoes or dried apricots, or 200 grams of dark green leafy vegetables such as spinach or kale.

Making bones more resistant to demands to release calcium into the blood should be complemented by measures to make the digestive system more responsive to these demands.

Adequate vitamin D stores can improve absorption of calcium from food both directly and by allowing calcitriol to be generated as needed. Inadequate vitamin D can be a major factor in reducing calcium absorption in people who live far from the equator or with limited exposure to sunlight. A study of Finnish vegans indicated that low vitamin D stores were leading to elevated parathyroid hormone (PTH) levels and that vitamin D2 supplementation may improve bone health. Vitamin D is discussed further in chapter 10.

In contrast, high caffeine consumption reduces calcium absorption. Low caffeine teas, such as redbush (rooibosch) or herb teas, provide an alternative to standard tea and coffee.

Optimising bone health through diet means ensuring good intakes of potassium and calcium and moderating sodium intake so as to make it easy to compensate for calcium loss by absorption of dietary calcium. It also means ensuring an adequate but not excessive protein intake to promote growth and repair without causing excessive calcium loss or overtaxing the kidneys.

Finally, it means ensuring a good intake of vitamin K, vitamin C and magnesium, and getting ample vitamin A from plant carotenoids rather than as pre-formed vitamin A from animal foods and synthetic supplements.

This may sound a daunting task, but fortunately it translates into quite simple guidelines for food choices which meet all these requirements.

Food choices to optimise bone health and calcium balance

Fruits, vegetables and legumes are particularly rich sources of potassium relative to calories, but all whole plant foods are good sources. Potassium and magnesium intakes on a predominantly wholefood plant-based diet are generally excellent.

Consuming between 500 and 1000 milligrams (mg) of calcium per day from calcium rich foods or supplements ensures a good overall calcium intake of 700 to 1500 mg since low calcium foods will also make a contribution. More than 1500 mg of calcium per day may reduce absorption of other minerals, particularly zinc (see chapter 11).

Kale and spring greens (collards) provide about 150 mg of calcium per 100 grams raw weight. Broccoli and cabbage provide about 50 mg per 100 grams. Oranges provide about 40 mg of calcium per 100 grams and can be readily consumed in large enough quantities to make a useful contribution. Almonds, carob and molasses each provide about 250 mg of calcium per 100 grams but are unlikely to be consumed in large amounts. While spinach and rhubarb are high in calcium, the calcium is bound to oxalates and therefore poorly absorbed.

Tofu is high in calcium only if calcium chloride or calcium sulphate has been used in making it, and some tofu is highly salted. However, calcium from tofu is well absorbed, so high calcium low sodium tofu will strongly boost calcium balance.

The calcium content of tahini is also very variable and tahini may also contain a lot of added salt. The efficiency of calcium absorption from tahini has not been directly tested and may well be relatively low. When using tahini, choose brands low in sodium and do not rely on it as a principal source of calcium.

Calcium fortified foods or calcium supplements provide a convenient source of extra calcium. If phosphate intake is low (unusual for vegans), calcium phosphate may be preferable to calcium carbonate or calcium citrate. Individuals with low stomach acidity should not take calcium carbonate between meals, as absorption will be poor. For most people, however, the bioavailabilities of calcium from the phosphate, carbonate and citrate salts are similar.

The latest results from the Nurses' Health Study in the USA found no reduction in hip fracture risk with increasing dietary calcium intake, mostly from dairy sources. Use of calcium supplements, however, was associated with a 20% reduction in hip fracture risk in the group as a whole and a 60% reduction among those with dietary calcium intakes below 625 milligrams per day.

Reducing salt intake by 5 grams per day (about half the average Western intake) will reduce calcium losses by about 30 mg per day on average. If you add salt to foods, substitute one of the widely available low sodium alternatives containing at least twice as much potassium as sodium by weight. Use low sodium bread or consume bread moderately, as bread is a major source of sodium. Better still, bake your own bread with a low sodium salt - see chapter 14 for suggestions.

By assuming an average intake of calcium of about 700 mg per day it is possible to estimate the effects of different foods on calcium balance in terms of milligrams of calcium balance per 100 grams of food.

Figure 7.3 shows some representative values for older adults. Values are given both for average calcium absorption and for calcium absorption at 60% of average, as observed in about 10% of older women. At the lower absorption efficiency, calcium intake is less beneficial and the effect of each food on calcium balance is therefore less beneficial.

Food	Gain or loss in calcium balance, mg per 100 gram portion	
	Normal absorption	60% of normal absorption
Chicken	-25	-25
Fish	-20	-22
Eggs	-15	-18
Cottage cheese	-13	-16
Cheddar cheese	38	11
Cow's milk	10	5
Fortified soya milk	8	5
Spring greens (collards)	22	14
Kale	18	13
Broccoli	8	6
Wheat grain (dry weight)	-7	-8
Almonds	18	9
Soya beans (dry weight)	16	8
Potatoes	4	4
Peppers	3	3
Oranges	6	4
Bananas	6	6

**Figure 7.3: Effect of different foods on calcium balance
(mg calcium per 100 grams of food)**

Foods such as cheddar cheese – which provide large amounts of calcium but simultaneously cause increased calcium losses – show a particularly dramatic change in their effect on calcium balance as absorption efficiency declines.

The worst foods for calcium balance are those high in protein and low in calcium such as meat, fish and eggs. Every 100 gram portion of these foods reduces calcium balance by about 20 mg regardless of calcium absorption efficiency.

The ideal foods for calcium balance are those which provide plenty of absorbable calcium while reducing calcium loss by providing plenty of potassium relative to sodium and protein. Low oxalate green leafy vegetables such as kale and spring greens are good examples. In contrast, spinach and chards are high in oxalates so their calcium is poorly absorbed.

Many foods, particularly dairy products, increase calcium loss as well as providing calcium: the overall result depends on the balance between the two effects. The adverse effect on calcium balance of cottage cheese is almost as bad as that of meat, fish and eggs.

Cheddar cheese has a beneficial effect at normal absorption efficiency, but is a very inefficient source of calcium. Out of 720 mg of calcium per 100 grams, the net contribution to calcium balance ranges from 38 mg at normal absorption to a mere 11 mg at reduced absorption: at best 5% and at worst a mere 1.5% of the calcium content is retained. This contrasts with between 10% and 6% of the calcium from a calcium supplement. Cow's milk falls somewhere in the middle at between 8% and 4%.

The final category is low calcium foods which reduce calcium loss, such as peppers, bananas and oranges. These provide everyone with a boost to calcium balance regardless of absorption efficiency.

For an individual trying to improve calcium balance, fruit and vegetables are the best foods to consume as they are rich in potassium, which reduces calcium loss: 100 grams each of red peppers, bananas, oranges, kale and spring greens will boost retained calcium by about 55 mg per day.

For the same benefit, a whopping 150 grams of cheddar cheese would be required, with an unhealthy accompaniment of 32 grams of saturated fat – almost double the daily target of less than 7% of calories (see chapter 8).

In contrast, fruits and vegetables are accompanied by minimal saturated fat and plenty of protective vitamin K, vitamin C and carotenoids.

Alkaline foods (typically high in potassium relative to protein) increase blood pH, thus protecting bone by increasing its resistance to demands for more calcium to be released into the blood.

Plant sources of protein (other than grains and some nuts) are usually alkaline, while animal sources are usually acid. Cow's milk is approximately neutral, but cheese is even more acid than meat or fish. Figure 7.4 shows the effect of protein from different foods on calcium balance and on alkali balance.

The choice of protein source used to meet protein needs can make a great deal of difference to calcium balance. A person consuming meat or fish will lose more than 20 mg of calcium from their body for every 100 grams of such foods that they eat. In contrast, beans have a moderately beneficial effect on calcium balance while providing an excellent source of protein (see chapter 11).

Our prehistoric ancestors obtained about 1500 mg of calcium per day from plants, though some of this would have been unavailable due to oxalates. High intakes of vegetables, fruits, roots and flowers would also have provided abundant potassium, magnesium, vitamin K and vitamin C, all in quantities far above modern norms. Dairy products and salt were notably absent. The same conclusions apply even more strongly to primate diets, which are very rich in all the beneficial minerals and low in sodium.

Sadly, many modern cultivated foods are much less rich in calcium than the wild plants with which we evolved, but low oxalate dark green leafy vegetables, broccoli and oranges are notable exceptions and therefore of particular importance for modern humans.

Food	Change in calcium balance (mg per gram of protein)	Change in alkali balance (millimoles per gram of protein)
Chicken	-1.0	-0.5
Fish	-0.9	-0.4
Eggs	-1.3	-0.9
Cottage cheese	-1.1	-0.7
Cheddar cheese	1.5	-0.9
Cow's milk	2.9	-0.1
Fortified soya milk	2.9	-0.3
Spring greens	7.4	1.4
Kale	5.5	2.8
Broccoli	2.7	1.0
Wheat grain (dry)	-0.5	-0.6
Almonds	1.1	0.1
Soya beans (dry)	0.4	0.3
Potatoes	1.8	2.2
Peppers	3.2	3.9
Oranges	6.2	4.1
Bananas	5.9	6.7

Figure 7.4:   Effect of one gram of protein from different foods on calcium balance and alkali balance

Human use of dairy products is a recent and unnecessary development: a diet rich in vegetables, fruits and legumes and low in salt provides the best path back to good calcium balance and healthy bones.

Putting it into practice

To promote strong bones, healthy blood pressure and low risk of stroke, eat plenty of fruit, vegetables and legumes, as these are rich in potassium; reduce sodium intake; consume at least 500 milligrams of calcium per day from calcium rich foods or supplements.

Food	Milligrams of calcium per 100 grams
Kale or spring greens	150
Broccoli or cabbage	50
Oranges	40
Fortified plant milks	40 to 140 – typically 120
Tofu	Variable - check label

Get an adequate protein intake from plant foods (see chapter 11).

Maintain an adequate store of vitamin D (see chapter 10) and get a good intake of vitamin K from at least 100 grams per day of green leafy vegetables or broccoli.

Limit caffeine consumption.

Get your vitamin A from plant carotenoids in brightly coloured fruits and vegetables, not from retinol or supplements (see chapter 5).

Finally, don't forget physical activity: just as exercise helps to build and maintain muscle, it also helps to build and maintain bone.

Chapter 8

Fats for health

The proper place of fats in a healthy diet is one of the most controversial topics in public debate on nutrition, with recommended total intakes varying from less than 10% of calories to about 50% of calories and recommendations for different types of fat varying just as widely.

Advice from national and international scientific committees is, however, much more consistent. Overall fat intake in the range of 20% to 30% of total calories is recommended for most people, with saturated fats (saturates) contributing at most 10% and preferably less than 7% of calories, and polyunsaturated fats (polyunsaturates) less than 10% of calories, including 1% to 2% of calories as omega-3 polyunsaturates. Trans fatty acids should be kept below 1% of calories.

In contrast to these recommendations, a typical Western diet provides about 15% of calories as saturated fats, 2% to 3% as trans fats and a mere 0.5% as omega-3s.

This chapter outlines the rationale behind the mainstream recommendations and explains how to apply them to a plant-based diet. Chapter 9 turns the spotlight on the key controversies about fats and health to further illuminate the rationale for the recommendations in the current chapter.

The recommendation to reduce saturated fat intake is aimed at reducing blood cholesterol levels and clot formation, both of which are major risk factors for heart disease. The risk of heart disease is greatly reduced when saturated fat intake is low and the polyunsaturated to saturated fat (P/S) ratio is about 1 to 1.

This recommendation has very strong negative implications for the consumption of animal milks and red meat, as milk fat contains over 60% saturates with a P/S of about 0.06 to 1, beef fat contains 40% saturates with a P/S of about 0.10 and lamb fat contains 45% saturates with a P/S of about 0.2. Typical plant-based diets are healthfully low in saturated fat (less than 7% of calories) and have P/S values between 1 and 2.

Trans fatty acids are produced by the processing of oils through hydrogenation to increase their shelf life and to raise their melting point so that they are solid at room temperature. They are also produced by bacteria in the stomachs of ruminants such as cattle and sheep.

Trans fatty acids increase the harmful LDL (low density lipoprotein) cholesterol while decreasing the protective HDL (high density lipoprotein) cholesterol which carries cholesterol safely out of the arteries. Saturated fat increases both types of cholesterol, so its overall effect for the same percentage of calories is less harmful than the trans fats (see chapter 9 for further information on cholesterol). However, typical trans fat consumption is about 2% to 3% of calories compared with about 15% for saturated fat, so saturated fat is still the more important risk factor for most Western populations.

The main sources of trans fats are hydrogenated vegetable oils (often used in margarines, commercial deep frying, biscuits, doughnuts and many other processed foods) and also milk and beef. The trans fat content of plant-based diets is highly variable, but can easily be made desirably low by avoiding products containing hydrogenated fats or oils.

While saturated fat and trans fat intakes need to be reduced compared with typical Western intakes, omega-3 fatty acids need to be increased. The omega-3 fats are a family of polyunsaturated fatty acids, including alpha-linolenic acid (ALNA), eicosapentaenoic acid (EPA) and docosahexaenoic acid (DHA). Mammals (other than cats) can produce EPA and DHA from alpha-linolenic acid, which is predominantly found in plants. The omega-3 fats exert a protective influence against heart disease by reducing the risk of clot formation (thrombosis), inflammation and heart arrhythmias. DHA is a major constituent of the brain and retina and is important for infant growth and development.

The main trials on fish and fish oil supplementation (EPA and DHA) indicate a reduction in mortality of 15% to 30%, while trials incorporating increased ALNA intake from plant oils and replacing saturated fats with monounsaturated fats indicate reductions in mortality of 40% to 70%. All these trials were on people who had already had one heart attack, but the results are highly consistent with observations in the general population. This evidence is discussed more fully in chapter 9 when comparing the effect of fish and fish oils with that of plant oils and discussing the long running margarine versus butter debate.

Linoleic acid (LA), the most common member of the omega-6 family of polyunsaturated fatty acids (polyunsaturates), partly counteracts the effect of saturated and trans fatty acids on blood cholesterol and may reduce the risk of diabetes.

Intakes of LA above about 6% of total calories are not ideal, however, as high intakes will displace beneficial omega-3 fatty acids from the blood and may promote damaging oxidation reactions. With low saturated fat intake, the maximum benefit from LA is probably obtained at between 4% and 6% of calories.

The optimal intake of LA is an area of genuine scientific debate: in 2003 the World Health Organisation (WHO) expert consultation group suggested an optimal range of 5% to 8% of calories, while in 2000 a working group of the International Society for the Study of Fatty Acids and Lipids recommended an intake below 3%. However, both groups recommended an omega-3 intake of at least 1% of calories. The more contentious question of optimal intake of LA is discussed further in chapter 9.

Diets with a ratio of linoleic acid to alpha-linolenic acid of more than 10 to 1 and no other direct source of omega-3s lead to mild omega-3 deficiency symptoms, with low levels of omega-3s in blood, breast milk and the nervous system. An LA to ALNA ratio of about 3 to 1 gives desirable blood levels of eicosapentaenoic acid (EPA) in humans – about 1% of total fatty acids. There is some controversy over the conversion of ALNA to EPA and DHA and this is discussed in chapter 9.

The LA to ALNA ratio in wild primate diets is generally less than 2 to 1, with a total polyunsaturate intake of about 7% of calories, but typical modern human plant-based diets have a ratio of LA to ALNA close to 20 to 1 and a total LA intake around 10%. This is clearly inconsistent with our evolutionary heritage. Fortunately, it is easy to achieve a desirable ratio of LA to ALNA by selecting appropriate plant foods.

Monounsaturated fatty acids (monounsaturates) appear to have a beneficial effect on heart disease risk provided they are not consumed in amounts promoting undesirable weight gain. Evidence for a major benefit from one to two ounces (30 to 60 grams) of nuts per day is very strong. Supplementation trials have shown that nuts high in monounsaturates, such as almonds, improve cholesterol profile by increasing the levels of good (HDL) cholesterol and decreasing the levels of bad (LDL) cholesterol without increasing the susceptibility of the cholesterol to oxidation.

Many independent observational studies have found increased nut consumption, including peanut butter, to be associated with decreased risk of heart disease and diabetes. Among Seventh Day Adventists, eating about 30 grams (one ounce) of nuts five or more times per week was associated with an extra two years life expectancy – similar to the benefit associated with consuming no meat. 30 grams of most nuts provides an extra 3% to 4% of calories as monounsaturates.

As monounsaturates make up the balance of total fat intake – along with saturates and polyunsaturates, which should contribute less than 15% of calories in combination – the question of optimal monounsaturate intake is closely linked with that of optimal total fat intake.

There is growing consensus that, in general, moderate fat diets (25% to 30% of calories) are preferable to lower fat diets, though the optimum for individuals may vary over a wider range. The issue of monounsaturate intake is discussed further in chapter 9, as is the controversy over total fat intake and cancer.

An ideal fat intake therefore consists of:

- moderate to low intake of saturates (less than 7% of total calories);
- moderate intake of linoleic acid (4% to 6% of calories);
- adequate intake of alpha-linolenic acid (1% to 2% of calories);
- minimal intake of trans fats (less than 1% of calories);
- moderate to high intake of monounsaturates, particularly from nuts (7% to 20% of calories).

The limited information available on our evolutionary diets supports reducing saturates and increasing alpha-linolenic acid.

The most detailed study of wild primate fatty acid intakes looked at wild howler monkeys consuming a wide variety of fruits and leaves. These monkeys consumed 18% of calories as fat, of which 8% was saturates, 3% monounsaturates, 3% alpha-linolenic acid and 4%

linoleic acid, giving a polyunsaturate to saturate (P/S) ratio of about 0.9 to 1 and an LA to ALNA ratio of 1.3 to 1.

Late Stone Age (Palaeolithic) human diets were estimated to contain 3% of calories as LA and 4% as ALNA, with about 1% of calories as longer chain polyunsaturated fatty acids which the body can manufacture from ALNA and LA. These diets also provided about 6% of calories as saturated fat, giving a P/S ratio of about 1.3 to 1, an LA to ALNA ratio of 0.75 to 1, and about 21% total fat. Some researchers have recently taken the view that human hunter-gatherer diets were significantly higher in total and saturated fat than this estimate, but the revised estimates still indicate a P/S ratio close to 1 to 1 and an LA to ALNA ratio below 2 to 1.

The consistency of estimates of our evolutionary fat intake makes the evolutionary argument particularly strong in this context. Fat intakes in populations with low risk of heart disease also fit the suggested ideal pattern.

Japanese recommended fat intakes, similar to typical consumption by older Japanese, are 20% to 25% total fat, split between about 6% saturates, 10% monounsaturates and 6% polyunsaturates, with an omega-6 to omega-3 ratio of less than 4 to 1.

Another population with a famously low incidence of heart disease is that of Crete, where the traditional diet includes about 40% of calories as fat but only about 8% as saturates and about 4% as polyunsaturates, the principal fat source (olive oil) being dominated by monounsaturates. Tests indicated a high level of alpha-linolenic acid in the blood of Cretan men due to a relatively low omega-6 to omega-3 ratio in their diet, with blood concentrations similar to those of the Japanese.

Chapter 9 discusses recent evidence on optimal fat intakes in more detail, while the rest of the present chapter focuses on the practicalities of achieving a desirable fat intake.

Balancing fats

No diet should include more than 7% of calories as saturated fat. This implies strict limitation of animal milk fats, palm kernel oil and coconut oil, since over 60% of their fats are saturates.

The higher the overall fat content of the diet, the more restrictive this target becomes for the selection of high fat foods. An individual consuming just 20% of calories as fat could consume fat from any source with up to 35% of the fats in the form of saturates while staying within the 7% target. An individual consuming 40% of calories as fat would need to restrict saturates to less than 17% of total fat intake to meet the same target.

Healthy high fat diets must provide most of their fat from a relatively small selection of fat sources such as olive oil, avocados, hazel nuts, macadamias, cashews, rapeseed (canola) oil and almonds. These fat sources are all mainly monounsaturated without excessive amounts of either saturates or polyunsaturates (see figure 8.1).

The foods listed in figure 8.1 are ordered on the basis of the maximum percentage of calories as fat which could be consumed from that food without exceeding the recommended limits on saturates (7% of calories), linoleic acid (6% of calories) or alpha-linolenic acid (2% of calories). The fat sources most suitable for moderate to high fat diets are those at the top of the chart, while fats from the foods near the bottom of the chart should be used sparingly.

Coconut oil and palm kernel oil will find few defenders, but many people regard sunflower seeds, walnuts and soya as healthy sources of fat. Their low position in the chart, however, means that they should not be consumed in large amounts, particularly if the overall diet is high in other sources of fat. The reason is the same in each case: their fat is mostly linoleic acid which, while beneficial in moderate amounts, is likely to be harmful in excess.

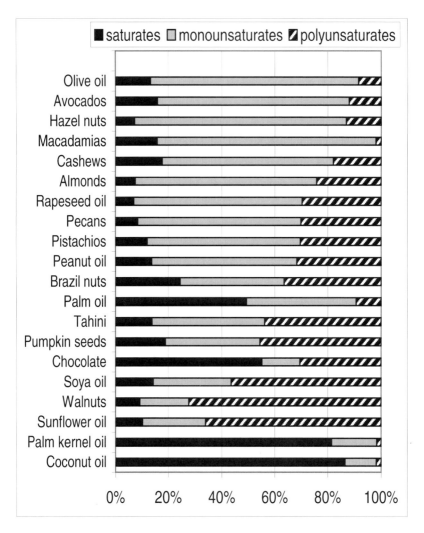

Figure 8.1: Fatty acids in common high fat plant foods

Just two tablespoons a day of soya oil would provide 6% of calories as linoleic acid, so soya oil and soya margarine should be used sparingly. Most other soya products contain protein, carbohydrate and water in addition to fat and can be used in much larger quantities: 100 grams of firm tofu or a cup of soya milk will contribute just 1% of daily calories as linoleic acid. Few people would consume more than this amount, so moderate use of tofu and soya milk will not unbalance fat intake.

Chocolate is the delight and the bane of many, and its high saturated fat content places it low on the chart. A 100 gram bar of dark chocolate would provide about 35 grams of fat, including 20 grams of saturated fat. Eaten daily, this would provide about 8% of calories as saturated fat; a 100 gram bar once a week would contribute just 1% of calories as saturated fat.

It is sometimes claimed that since much of the saturated fat in chocolate is stearic acid it is therefore not a problem. Unfortunately, while stearic acid has little effect on blood cholesterol, it is associated both with increased blood clotting and with progression of atherosclerosis. Chocolate is high in antioxidants, however, and its mood altering effects sometimes rescue a bad day. Used in moderation – 100 grams a week, say – it may actually be beneficial, but heavy use is not a good idea.

Pumpkin seeds and tahini (sesame seeds) are well known as good sources of minerals, but their place in the chart indicates a need to limit fat intake from these foods. 28 grams (one ounce) of pumpkin seeds per day would contribute 1% of calories as LA, while 28 grams of tahini would contribute about 2.5% of calories as LA. While they have a similar fatty acid profile, tahini has much more fat per gram, making pumpkin seeds the better choice as a mineral rich seed. Pumpkin seeds are sometimes promoted as an omega-3 source, but in fact they contain minimal amounts.

Palm oil is a distinctive plant fat, having a relatively high saturated fat content, though not so high as coconut oil or palm kernel oil. It can have a modest role in a healthy diet and is often found in margarines, biscuits and other processed foods, including peanut butter, due to its stability. It is sometimes hydrogenated to further increase its stability. The hydrogenated form should be avoided as far as practicable.

Brazil nuts are exceptionally high in trace minerals, notably selenium, and are best limited to about ten nuts a week to obtain the full benefit without risk of excess (see chapter 10). Ten Brazil nuts a week contribute just 0.5% of calories as linoleic acid.

Peanuts, pistachios and pecans, like Brazil nuts, can all be used in moderate amounts while meeting recommended fat intakes. 56 grams (two ounces) per day of peanuts, pecans or pistachios would contribute about 3% of calories as linoleic acid.

Almonds, cashews, macadamias, hazel nuts, avocados and olive oil can be eaten in even larger amounts if desired. Unsurprisingly, top place in figure 8.1 is held by olive oil – low in saturates and polyunsaturates, and the core of the traditional high fat diet of Crete. This group of foods can be eaten freely while maintaining a healthy fat balance.

To complete the balance, a good source of omega-3s is needed (see figure 8.2).

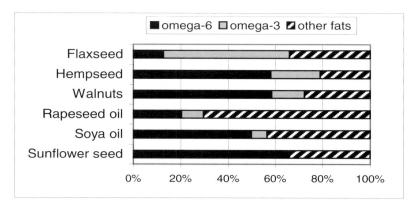

Figure 8.2: Omega-3 content of plant foods

Flaxseed (linseed) is the pre-eminent plant source of alpha-linolenic acid (ALNA), with about 80% of its polyunsaturates as ALNA. Very small amounts of flaxseed can therefore meet the need for ALNA without providing excessive polyunsaturates. A teaspoon of flaxseed oil contributes about 2.5 grams of ALNA, which translates to about

1% of calories for most people. As vegetables and fruits contribute a small but significant amount of ALNA, a teaspoon of flaxseed oil a day will take most people close to 1.5% of calories as ALNA.

As flaxseed oil is expensive and prone to oxidation, it may be preferable to buy flaxseed and grind it in a coffee grinder. Ground flaxseed can be stored in a freezer or refrigerator. A tablespoon of ground flaxseed (about 8 grams) contains about 1.7 grams of ALNA, so one and a half tablespoons are equivalent to one teaspoon of oil. Flaxseed from colder climates such as Canada is slightly richer in ALNA than flaxseed from warmer countries such as the USA.

Ground flaxseed can be eaten raw in moderate amounts, but if using much more than a tablespoon per day it is preferable to add it to sauces or bread and cook it, as this eliminates cyanogenic glycosides in the raw seed. Unground flaxseed is poorly digested and is not a good source of anything other than bulky stools.

Rapeseed provides about 30% of its polyunsaturates as omega-3s and played a key part in the Lyon Diet Heart Trial by boosting omega-3s and monounsaturates and reducing saturates. One and a half tablespoons of rapeseed oil per day would provide 1% of calories as omega-3s, 2% as omega-6s and less than 1% as saturates.

In contrast to flaxseed oil and extra virgin olive oil, which are pressed rather than chemically processed, rapeseed oil is often sold as a refined oil. However, even the refined oil has a low trans fat content and the spectacular results of the Lyon Diet Heart Trial to its credit.

Hempseed deserves special comment. It has about 25% of its polyunsaturates as omega-3s, placing it between rapeseed oil and walnuts. However, it has about 10% of its omega-3s as stearidonic acid, the first conversion product of ALNA in the body, and about 10% of its omega-6s as gamma-linolenic acid, the first conversion product of LA in the body. This makes it a stronger source of both omega-3s and omega-6s than its ALNA and LA content would suggest. One tablespoon per day of hempseed oil or five tablespoons of hempseed provide about 1% of calories as ALNA and about 3% as LA.

About 20% of the polyunsaturates in walnuts are omega-3s, so although walnuts are often listed as a high omega-3 food, getting 1% of calories as omega-3s from walnuts (28 grams or one ounce of walnuts) means getting 4% of calories as omega-6, using up most of the recommended allowance of omega-6 with just one food. That is fine if you love walnuts, but not clever if you are just after a boost to omega-3 intake.

Soya contains just 12% of polyunsaturates as omega-3s, so it is primarily an omega-6 rather than an omega-3 source. As noted, many soya foods are relatively low in total fat, so moderate use of full fat soya products such as soya milk and tofu is not problematic.

Hempseed oil and mixtures of flaxseed and sunflower oil are sometimes promoted as a "balanced" alternative to flaxseed. This confuses two issues: the balance between linoleic acid and alpha-linolenic acid in the overall diet, and the balance or otherwise in a single food. Practically any plant-based diet will provide plenty of linoleic acid, often giving an LA to ALNA ratio of more than 10 to 1, so restoring balance means *adding* omega-3s and *reducing* omega-6s.

As flaxseed has more than half its total fat as ALNA and an LA to ALNA ratio of 0.25 to 1, small amounts provide adequate ALNA without adding significant LA. Cutting down on high LA foods such as sunflower oil and sunflower seeds completes the rebalancing.

The so-called "balanced" oils are usually more expensive than flaxseed oil despite being basically just a mixture of flaxseed oil and cheaper sunflower oil: this is clearly a bad deal for everyone except the manufacturers, and a particularly bad deal for those whose diet contains more than enough LA already.

Putting it into practice

Tropical plant oils such as coconut and palm kernel oil should be avoided because – like most animal products – they are dangerously high in saturated fat.

Products containing hydrogenated or trans fats should be avoided – check the ingredients. Deep fried foods such as chips (French fries) should be limited, as the cooking oils used are often hydrogenated or highly saturated and prolonged heating creates toxic byproducts. Unhydrogenated palm oil or groundnut (peanut) oil are best for deep frying.

A mixture of almonds, macadamias, cashews, hazel nuts, avocados and olive and rapeseed (canola) oils provides an ideal basis for a moderate to high fat diet (25% to 40% of calories as fat).

Flaxseed (linseed) and rapeseed make it easy to get the desired omega-3 intake without unbalancing the diet: *either* one teaspoon of flaxseed oil a day *or* one and a half tablespoons of rapeseed oil or ground flaxseed is sufficient. One tablespoon a day of hempseed oil or five tablespoons of hempseed would also be a good source of omega-3s.

Chapter 9

Fat wars

More than almost any other topic, the impact of fats on health inspires fierce controversy. This chapter attempts to explain the arguments and to remove the uncertainty they have created. The issues addressed are:

- Margarine versus butter.
- Plant oils versus fish and fish oils.
- Low fat dairy products and health.
- Fats and cancer.
- Conversion of alpha-linolenic acid to other omega-3 fatty acids.
- Linoleic acid and health.
- Low fat diets versus high monounsaturated fat diets.

Margarine versus butter

The processing of vegetable oils by hydrogenation to make them more stable and to raise their melting point generates trans fats. Most early margarines, particularly the harder margarines, contained substantial amounts of trans fats.

The main sources of trans fats were previously dairy products and beef, but hydrogenation substantially increased the amounts of trans fats in the food supply and introduced new types of trans fats. This led to legitimate debate as to whether such margarines were better or worse than butter in terms of human health. It also led to major changes in the way margarine is made, and many margarines now proudly boast that they contain less than 1% trans fats – a very welcome improvement. Even before this change, however, soft margarines with moderate levels of trans fats had resoundingly defeated butter in terms of heart disease risk.

The Lyon Diet Heart Trial set out explicitly to mimic the Cretan diet, but adopted a pragmatic approach. The research team, led by Michel de Lorgeril and Serge Renaud, recognised that their patients – who had all suffered one heart attack already – would be reluctant to move from butter to olive oil but would accept a margarine based on rapeseed (canola) oil.

Rapeseed oil has less than 10% saturates, with about 60% monounsaturates, 20% linoleic acid and 10% alpha-linolenic acid (ALNA). The margarine used in the Lyon study included about 6% trans fatty acids as a result of hydrogenation during production.

The dietary changes also included 20% increases in fruit and bread and modest decreases in processed and red meat. The most dramatic change, however, was the almost total displacement of butter and cream by rapeseed oil margarine. This led to reduced saturated fat intake, increased monounsaturated fat and a substantial increase (from 0.3% to 0.8% of calories) in omega-3 fat intake in the form of ALNA. Saturated fat intake was reduced to about 7.5% of calories. There was no significant increase in fish intake during the trial, but blood levels of eicosapentaenoic acid rose by about 30% due to the increased intake of ALNA.

The study was originally planned to last four years, but after just over two years it had been so successful that the ethical committee overseeing the trial felt that the results should be published immediately and made available to everyone. Mortality from all causes was reduced by 70%, primarily as a result of reductions in mortality from heart disease – far exceeding the best results obtained in drug treatment trials or in large trials of fish and fish oils.

A follow-up report after a further two years found that patients had largely continued with the trial diets and a 55% reduction in mortality was observed at this stage; deaths from cancer as well as deaths from heart disease were reduced.

Margarine manufacturers have since become more successful in producing low trans fat margarines. Unfortunately, many otherwise suitable products based on rapeseed and olive oils contain whey – a byproduct of cheese manufacture – making them unsuitable for vegans and others avoiding dairy products.

The best vegan margarines are made from palm oil mixed with soya or rapeseed oil and not hydrogenated. Moderate use is consistent with the desired overall fatty acid profile. Olive oil or rapeseed oil provides an even better alternative and can be poured straight on to bread in the Mediterranean style.

Plant oils versus fish oils

The largest trials involving consumption either of oily fish or of EPA and DHA (the main omega-3 fatty acids found in fish oils) showed reductions of only 15% to 30% in overall mortality – less than half the benefit seen in the Lyon trial using rapeseed (canola) oil.

The earliest trial of vegetable oil rich in alpha-linolenic acid (ALNA) was in Norway in the mid-1960s. This trial was a head-to-head comparison of two teaspoons per day of flaxseed (linseed) oil versus two teaspoons per day of sunflower seed oil. The trial participants were healthy men aged 50 to 59 recruited via industrial physicians. The sunflower oil increased linoleic acid intake by about 2.5% of calories while the flaxseed oil increased ALNA intake by about 2%.

Overall mortality in both intervention groups was very similar and in both cases was about 40% less than that observed in the general population. These results are consistent with a substantial benefit from both oils in Norway at that time, but are also consistent with a "healthy volunteer" effect: the trial participants may simply have been healthier than the general population. The lack of advantage for alpha-linolenic acid over linoleic acid may have been due to most of this population already having a high omega-3 intake.

As discussed in the previous section, increasing omega-3 intake through increased consumption of plant oils high in alpha-linolenic acid was a key part of the spectacularly successful Lyon Diet Heart Trial. A smaller trial in India using mustard oil, which has a similar fat composition to rapeseed oil, showed a 40% decrease in mortality in patients who had already experienced one heart attack. In the Indian trial, there was no increase in fruit and vegetable intake, so the observed effect is entirely attributable to the extra mustard oil.

Studies of people without pre-existing heart disease have also found increased ALNA intake from vegetable oil sources to be associated with reduced risk of heart disease. If the dietary ALNA comes from margarines high in trans fats, however, no benefit is observed.

Similar studies of intake of omega-3 fats from fish have mostly found a benefit only in populations with high saturated fat intake, though recent results from the Nurses' Health Study have found a benefit comparable with that observed for ALNA in the same population.

In Finland, however, studies have found no benefit despite a high intake of fish along with a high saturated fat intake. The lack of benefit in Finland is generally attributed to high mercury levels in the fish. Recent studies in the USA and Europe have confirmed that the potential benefit from omega-3s in fish is greatly reduced by mercury contamination.

Fish is the main source of toxic methyl mercury: about 20% of women consuming fish three times a month or more were found to have blood mercury levels exceeding the US safety limit, while all those women not consuming fish had blood levels within the safety limit.

Two studies published in April 2003 highlight an interesting contrast between the effects of fish oil, sunflower oil and flaxseed oil on blood levels of a substance known as C-reactive protein. High levels of

C-reactive protein indicate chronic inflammation and are highly predictive of atherosclerosis and heart disease. Neither fish oil nor sunflower oil supplementation had any effect on C-reactive protein, but flaxseed oil supplementation led to a 38% decrease in C-reactive protein. While some other markers of inflammation seem to be reduced by all sources of omega-3s, these results suggest a specific role for ALNA in reducing C-reactive protein.

The best source of omega-3s for human health appears to be plant foods. Getting omega-3s from plants also avoids the environmental pitfalls of trying to increase the consumption of fish when wild fish populations have already been driven to the brink of collapse. Fish farming is no solution, and farming of carnivorous fish such as salmon actually consumes more fish than it produces.

Low fat dairy products and health

Dairy products are a more concentrated source of saturated fat than any other food apart from a few tropical oils which are rarely used in large quantities. It is thus not surprising that consumers throughout the world have voted with their wallets for low fat dairy products to try to protect themselves from the hazards of saturated fat.

Three studies in the USA have made it clear that getting calcium from full fat dairy products is a good way to destroy any benefit that the calcium might have for cardiovascular health (see chapter 7).

The Nurses' Health Study found that a high intake of full fat milk was associated with a 67% increase in heart disease while a high intake of skimmed (no fat) milk was associated with a 22% decrease.

A study of women from Iowa found that a high overall intake of calcium was associated with a 33% reduction in deaths from heart disease while high dairy consumption showed no protective association.

A study of US men found that a high intake of calcium from supplements was associated with a 40% reduction in fatal heart disease while a high intake of calcium from dairy products was associated with a 15% *increase* in fatal heart disease.

The message to get calcium from something other than high fat dairy products is therefore clear.

The idea that the hazards of dairy products can be avoided by choosing low fat versions of dairy products has been exposed as one of the most successful deceptions of recent decades. As Professor Walter Willett, one of the world's leading epidemiologists, succinctly points out:

"Once a cow is milked, the fat from that milk is in the food supply, and someone ends up eating or drinking it."

This can be readily confirmed from statistics produced by the United Nations Food and Agriculture Organisation (see figure 9.1). In over three decades there has been no reduction at all in dairy fat consumption in the USA. In the UK, there has been a reduction in milk fat consumption due to a reduction in imports of butter, but no change in the amount of fat supplied by other dairy products.

	Fat from butter	Fat from other dairy products	Protein from dairy products
USA 1964	7	19	23
USA 1999	5	22	23
UK 1964	19	21	20
UK 1999	8	21	20

Figure 9.1:   Changes in dairy fat and protein consumption (grams per day) in the UK and USA

That this information comes as a surprise to most people is a measure of how successfully the populations of milk-drinking countries have been misled.

In some cases, the fat recycled from low fat products is sold openly as cheese (especially in pizza) and ice cream; in others, it is purveyed as a hidden ingredient in pastries, biscuits and convenience foods and even in traditionally dairy free products such as guacamole.

At the population level, cutting down on dairy fat must mean cutting down on dairy production as a whole so as to reduce the amount of dairy fat introduced into the food supply.

Fats and cancer

Despite earlier suspicions – based on misleading animal experimentation – that high fat diets might promote cancer, extensive human studies indicate little or no effect of total fat intake on cancer risk after adjustment for known risk factors. In 1996, a combined analysis of breast cancer risk in over 337,000 women from seven separate studies indicated no effect of total fat, animal fat or vegetable fat. The contribution of adult diet to breast cancer risk appears limited, with alcohol and weight gain being harmful, and folate, plant carotenoids and olive oil possibly being protective.

Colorectal cancer has also been linked with fat intake, but closer examination suggests that the real link is with high intakes of processed meats, such as sausages and bacon, and low intakes of fibre and folate.

Early studies on prostate cancer and diet also suggested a link with increased fat intake from animal products, but this link fades away when other dietary components such as lycopene, fructose and calcium are considered.

There is considerable evidence that processed meats increase the risk of colorectal cancer and that dairy products increase the risk of prostate cancer. Total fat intake, however, does not appear to be an important risk factor for the most common cancers.

Two US studies in the early 1990s found an association between increased alpha-linolenic acid and prostate cancer. In both study groups, average ALNA intake was low and came primarily from meat and milk. A re-analysis in 1998 of the data on ALNA intake and prostate cancer found that when other dietary components such as dairy calcium and fructose intake were considered the association with ALNA largely disappeared.

In the Netherlands, an attempt to reproduce the US results in a population with higher average levels of ALNA intake, largely from vegetable sources, found a marginally *protective* association.

Only one study, in Uruguay, reported an association between increased intake of ALNA from vegetable oils and increased prostate cancer risk. However, the difference between low and high intakes in this study was just 0.1 grams per day – making the apparent association biologically implausible.

In contrast, prostate cancer rates are very low in Japan where about 1% of calories (2.5 grams per day) are consumed as ALNA, mostly from rapeseed (canola) oil. Interestingly, the Lyon Diet Heart Trial observed a moderately *reduced* incidence of cancer on its high ALNA diet.

The evidence, therefore, is that ALNA intake is associated with increased prostate cancer risk only when it comes from animal products.

Conversion of alpha-linolenic acid to other omega-3 fatty acids

The key members of the omega-3 and omega-6 families are summarised in figure 9.2 in the sequence they are produced in the body from alpha-linolenic acid and linoleic acid. Dietary sources are also noted.

Omega-3 fatty acids (omega-3s)	
Alpha-linolenic acid (ALNA)	Wild fruit, berries, leafy vegetables, flaxseed (linseed), rapeseed (canola), hempseed, walnuts.
Stearidonic acid (SDA)[1]	Hempseed, animal products.
Eicosapentaenoic acid (EPA)[1]	Animal products, particularly fish and brain; traces in some algae.
Docosahexaenoic acid (DHA)[1]	Animal products, particularly fish and brain; traces in some algae

[1] Produced in the body from ALNA

Omega-6 fatty acids (omega-6s)	
Linoleic acid (LA)	Most plant foods, particularly sunflower, safflower and sesame seeds, corn, soya beans and walnuts.
Gamma-linolenic acid (GLA)[2]	Borage, evening primrose, hempseed.
Arachidonic acid (AA)[2]	Animal products.

[2] Produced in the body from LA

Figure 9.2: Omega-6 and omega-3 fatty acids

High intakes of linoleic acid or other omega-6 fats such as arachidonic acid reduce the incorporation of all omega-3s into the body, and high intakes of LA inhibit the conversion of ALNA to EPA. ALNA increases blood clotting when combined with an LA intake around 10% of calories, but decreases clotting at an LA intake around 5%.

Given an overall fatty acid intake in line with the recommendations in chapter 8, which includes no more than about 6% LA, good conversion of ALNA to both EPA and DHA has been shown to occur in humans.

The MARGARIN study in the Netherlands, which lasted two years and included 103 people consuming margarine rich in ALNA, provides a good example of the conversion of ALNA to EPA. Although linoleic acid intake also increased from 7% to 9% of calories, the ratio of LA to ALNA dropped from 16 to 1 down to 4 to 1. Measured plasma EPA levels increased by 34%, compared with a predicted increase of 36% based on a model developed prior to this study using results of earlier studies, including the Lyon Diet Heart Trial.

The concentration of EPA in blood plasma can be predicted using the following equation:

$$\text{Plasma EPA \%} = 9 \times 0.3 \times [\text{ALNA} \div (\text{ALNA} + \text{LA}) + \text{Lomega-3}]$$
$$\div \{ 0.3 \times [\text{ALNA} \div (\text{ALNA} + \text{LA}) + \text{Lomega-3}]$$
$$+ [\text{LA} \div (\text{ALNA} + \text{LA}) + \text{Lomega-6}] \}$$

Lomega-3 refers to the larger omega-3 fatty acids, which are derived from ALNA, and Lomega-6 refers to the larger omega-6 fatty acids, which are derived from LA. All the dietary fatty acids are measured in grams per day, while the plasma EPA concentration is measured as a percentage of total fatty acids.

A recent UK study compared the effects of 4.5 grams per day (almost 2% of calories) of ALNA from rapeseed oil, 9.5 grams per day of ALNA from flaxseed oil, 0.8 grams per day of a mixture of EPA and

DHA from fish oil, and 1.7 grams per day of EPA and DHA from fish oil. Thirty people were assigned to each test diet.

The blood EPA percentages before the trial (the baseline) were not significantly different between groups, so the baseline values in figure 9.3 are an average for all the groups. The control group were intended to continue their baseline diet, but actually showed an increase in EPA attributable to higher intakes of EPA and DHA than the two ALNA diet groups.

	Baseline	Control	0.8 grams EPA + DHA	1.7 grams EPA + DHA	4.5 grams ALNA	9.5 grams ALNA
Observed EPA%	1.01	1.27	1.78	2.25	2.00	2.14
Predicted EPA%	1.05	1.36	1.75	2.95	1.59	2.26

Figure 9.3: Observed and predicted plasma EPA levels

The model indicates that the observed effect of 1.7 grams per day of EPA+DHA was unusually low and the effect of 4.5 grams per day of ALNA was unusually high. The experiment nevertheless confirms that ALNA is effectively converted into EPA within the blood, as predicted by the model developed on the basis of results of earlier trials.

This study also observed that fish oil increased the susceptibility of cholesterol to oxidation, potentially increasing the risk of heart disease, whereas the high ALNA diets did not.

DHA is harder to investigate than EPA as it is primarily a constituent of brain rather than blood, and brain levels cannot be readily measured. Blood DHA levels vary with ALNA intakes in a much more complex way than EPA levels: DHA concentrations remain approximately constant over a wide range of ALNA intakes, but decrease markedly if the ratio of LA to ALNA is more than about 7 to 1 and no other omega-3s are consumed (plasma EPA about 0.4%). DHA levels may take up to a year to respond fully to dietary changes.

The most direct evidence of ALNA conversion to DHA comes from trials in populations with moderate LA intake and low intakes of all omega-3s. This combination results in low initial EPA and DHA levels and avoids inhibition of omega-3 conversion by high LA intakes.

The results of trials of omega-3 supplementation in India are therefore of particular interest. These trials found that reducing the LA to ALNA ratio from 30 to 1 down to 4 to 1 increased platelet EPA levels from levels too low to measure to 0.4%, while the conversion model predicted a change from 0.06% to 0.42%. The equation for platelet EPA levels is similar in form to that for plasma levels, but predicts EPA levels about half those in plasma. Platelet DHA levels rose by about 40%, to levels similar to those observed in Finnish omnivores.

A study of UK vegans in 1981 also observed an increase in platelet DHA with increased ALNA intake. Unfortunately, this trial lasted just two weeks – too short a time to observe the full effect.

ALNA is stored in the liver and released over a period of weeks in cholesteryl esters which can be absorbed by other tissues with the capability to synthesise DHA, including the brain. Even when DHA levels in blood do not rise, most studies using radio-labelled alpha-linolenic acid have found that about 7% of the labelled fatty acids observed in the blood are in the form of DHA, indicating that significant conversion is occurring.

In short, ALNA is predictably converted to EPA and will raise DHA levels if LA intake is moderate and DHA is below its natural plateau concentration. Increased ALNA intake will ensure that the nervous system is provided with the raw material to produce the DHA it needs. Increased consumption of alpha-linolenic acid is a safe, natural, environmentally sustainable and highly effective way of getting the benefits of omega-3 fatty acids.

Linoleic acid and health

Increased linoleic acid intake reduces blood cholesterol and may improve blood sugar control. On the other hand, it also reduces the availability of omega-3 fatty acids and can increase damaging oxidation reactions.

These conflicting effects give rise to widely differing recommendations, depending on which effects are given greatest emphasis. This explains the conflicting recommendations on linoleic acid by the WHO and ISSFAL expert groups, referred to in the previous chapter, of 5% to 8% of calories and less than 3% of calories respectively.

Our evolutionary diet generally provided 3% to 5% of calories as linoleic acid, suggesting that the truth lies somewhere between these two sets of recommendations. Linoleic acid intake should be around three times alpha-linolenic acid intake to ensure a good supply of all the omega-3s. The recommended 1% to 2% of calories as alpha-linolenic acid combined with 4% to 6% of calories as linoleic acid gives a good balance between the benefits of both without leading to excessive polyunsaturate intake.

Many human trials have investigated the effect of increased linoleic acid intake on heart disease and overall mortality. Four trials raised linoleic acid intakes to between 15% and 20% of calories, giving polyunsaturate to saturate (P/S) ratios of about 2 to 1. On average, these trials observed significantly reduced heart disease mortality but no reductions in overall mortality. Two trials using more moderate LA intakes giving P/S ratios of about 1 to 1 have been much more successful, with reductions in overall mortality of about 40%.

	Medical Committee (1968)	Dayton (1969)	Leren (1970)	Hjermann (1986)	Frantz (1989)	Singh (1992)
Polyunsaturates (mostly linoleic acid)	About 20%	17%	20%	8.3%	15%	8.7%
Saturates	About 11%	10%	8.5%	8.2%	9%	7.2%
Polyunsaturate/ saturate ratio	1.8	1.7	2.4	1.0	1.6	1.2
Percentage change in overall number of deaths	+8%	-2%	-6%	-39%	+3%	-44%

Figure 9.4: Results of studies increasing the ratio of polyunsaturates to saturates

The successful trials by Hjermann and Singh both did more than just manipulate fat intake. The Hjermann study also included advice to stop smoking, and although this had little apparent impact it may have contributed in part to the good result. The Singh study included advice to increase consumption of fruit, vegetables, beans, lentils, fish and nuts. Fruit and vegetable intake went up from 200 grams per day to 600 grams per day, with accompanying large increases in antioxidants.

The Medical Committee, Leren and Singh trials involved people who had already suffered one heart attack, while the Dayton, Frantz and Hjermann trials involved people who previously consumed high levels of saturated fat. Four of the trials reduced saturate intake and increased polyunsaturate intake dramatically, using oils high in linoleic acid. The two successful trials, however, reduced saturate intake and only *moderately* increased polyunsaturate intake. All the trials reduced blood cholesterol levels by 10% or more.

More detailed analysis of the results of these trials suggests that lowering cholesterol through high polyunsaturate intake is more beneficial in middle-aged than in elderly people. This is consistent with observational studies which show the effect of elevated cholesterol on heart disease risk to be strongest in middle age. There is also some evidence from these trials that adverse effects of high polyunsaturate intake increase with length of time on the diet.

A trial adjusting fat intake of French farmers in the Moselle region in order to reduce blood clotting found that while reducing intake of saturates was the most beneficial change, results also varied with the mixture of polyunsaturates used. An LA intake of about 5% and an ALNA intake of about 1% worked very well, while an LA intake of 9% and an ALNA intake of 0.7% did not.

The lessons from this trial were later used to good effect in the highly successful Lyon Diet Heart Trial, which deliberately reduced LA intake from 5.4% to 3.6% while increasing ALNA intake from 0.3% to 0.8% and substituting monounsaturates for saturates.

Both the direct evidence and the theoretical considerations therefore support moderate (4% to 6% of calories) rather than high or low linoleic acid consumption.

Low fat diets versus high monounsaturated fat diets

A diet limiting all high fat foods, particularly animal fats and tropical oils, is inherently low in saturated fats with a moderate to high ratio of polyunsaturates to saturates. Ensuring adequate omega-3 fats is easily achieved by small amounts of flaxseed or large amounts of green leafy vegetables without significantly increasing total fat intake. Such low fat diets are therefore consistent with the overall recommendations for intake of polyunsaturates and saturates.

A diet high in mainly monounsaturated nuts and oils can also readily meet these recommendations, with a much higher total fat intake.

These two options are the extremes of a spectrum of dietary choice which can range across total fat intakes from 10% to 40% of total calories and still satisfy the recommendations on polyunsaturates.

Evidence from comparisons between countries

The Seven Countries Study, which highlighted the adverse role of saturated fats in heart disease, also shed some light on the choice between low fat and high monounsaturated fat diets.

The two regions within the Seven Countries Study with exceptionally low deaths from heart attacks in the early 1960s were Japan, with about 10% of calories as fat, and Crete with 40%. Both consumed about 4% of calories as polyunsaturates, while Japan consumed just 3% of calories as saturated fat and Crete 8%. The most dramatic difference was in monounsaturate consumption, which was ten times higher in Crete than in Japan.

Crete markedly outperformed 1960s Japan in overall mortality, largely as a result of lower stroke mortality. The higher stroke mortality in Japan was at least partly due to much higher salt intake rather than to differences in fat intake. However, other studies have indicated reduced risk of stroke with increasing total fat intake.

Since the 1960s, Japanese total fat intake has increased from 10% to 25% and Japan has moved to first place in international tables of healthy life expectancy. Whilst it is dangerous to draw conclusions from comparisons between countries since many other factors can influence the results, there is considerable evidence from studies of individuals to support a preference for higher fat diets. The Cretan and Japanese diets are discussed in more detail in chapter 13.

As discussed earlier in the present chapter, fat intake from plants has little impact on the incidence of major cancers. The debate on fats and health therefore centres on their effect on cardiovascular disease (heart disease and stroke).

Before considering the evidence from studies of individuals, it is important to provide some background explanation of risk factors for cardiovascular disease and to introduce the concept of glycaemic load as a measure of the impact of carbohydrate intake.

Cardiovascular risk factors

Most people are aware that high blood cholesterol is a risk factor for heart disease, but this is far from the end of the cholesterol story.

There are three contributors to total cholesterol in the blood: LDL cholesterol, HDL cholesterol and VLDL cholesterol. Low density lipoprotein (LDL) cholesterol and very low density lipoprotein (VLDL) cholesterol are the baddies, promoting cholesterol deposits in the arteries, while high levels of high density lipoprotein (HDL) cholesterol actually indicate that cholesterol is being carried safely back to the liver. The ideal profile is therefore high HDL with low LDL and VLDL cholesterol, giving a low ratio of total to HDL cholesterol.

Heart disease mortality decreases steadily as total cholesterol decreases and as the ratio of total to HDL cholesterol decreases. Some studies suggest that the optimal cholesterol level in terms of *overall* mortality is between 4 and 5 millimoles per litre (160 to 200 milligrams per decilitre). However, the apparent rise in overall mortality below 4 mmol/l is largely due to pre-existing cancer or liver disease reducing cholesterol levels.

As discussed in relation to optimal linoleic acid intake, reducing cholesterol by greatly increasing omega-6 polyunsaturates may have an adverse effect on blood concentrations of omega-3 fatty acids and on mortality from causes other than cardiovascular disease. So long as this potential pitfall is avoided, however, the ideal cholesterol profile for overall health is probably total cholesterol of about 4 mmol/l (160 mg/dl) and a total to HDL ratio of 3 to 1 or less.

For each unit that the ratio rises above 3 to 1, and for each unit that total cholesterol increases above 4 mmol/l, the risk of heart disease for a middle-aged adult increases by about 30%. A person with total cholesterol of 5 mmol/l and a ratio of total to HDL cholesterol of 4 to 1 would thus have a 60% higher risk of heart disease than one with total cholesterol of 4 mmol/l and a total to HDL ratio of 3 to 1.

A further aspect of cholesterol and risk of cardiovascular disease is that LDL cholesterol is most dangerous in the form of small dense particles rather than larger particles. At any given LDL cholesterol concentration, therefore, risk can differ greatly with particle size.

All aspects of cholesterol profile are strongly influenced by fat intake, placing cholesterol at the centre of the debate on optimal intake of fats. However, cholesterol profile is far from the only risk factor for cardiovascular disease, so we need to consider whether the other factors are influenced by the choice between carbohydrates and monounsaturated fats.

Homocysteine (see chapter 6) is another important risk factor, but is related to folate and vitamin B12 rather than to fat. Blood pressure (see chapter 7) is also very important, but is primarily related to mineral intakes.

The ease with which blood clots form is a key factor in cardiovascular disease and is strongly influenced by dietary fats. Low saturated fat intakes and a low ratio of omega-6 to omega-3 fats reduce the tendency for clots to form, but monounsaturated fats have relatively little influence on blood clotting.

Inflammation, which is reflected in increased blood levels of C-reactive protein, is also strongly associated with cardiovascular disease. As discussed earlier in this chapter, alpha-linolenic acid appears to reduce C-reactive protein. C-reactive protein also increases with body mass index and body fat, and with increased intake of certain types of carbohydrate.

Diabetes, with its accompanying elevated levels of glucose and insulin in the blood, increases the risk of heart disease. The risk of diabetes is significantly influenced by the types of carbohydrate and fat eaten, but excess weight and lack of exercise are the key factors. As discussed in chapter 4, lack of physical activity and the ease of overeating particular foods seem to be more important than fat content for weight control. Diets low in saturated fat and high in fibre can be expected to reduce the risk of diabetes.

The key cardiovascular risk factors to consider in comparing low fat and high monounsaturated fat diets are therefore cholesterol and C-reactive protein.

Glycaemic load

In comparing the effects of monounsaturated fat and carbohydrate, it is important to recognise that not all sources of carbohydrates are equal. Some come accompanied by fibre and high levels of beneficial minerals such as potassium and magnesium, while others have had the beneficial components stripped out by processing. Wholemeal bread and white bread differ radically in their fibre and mineral content, and the use of wholemeal rather than white bread is associated with reduced risk of diabetes and heart disease.

Carbohydrate sources also differ in the speed with which their carbohydrate is absorbed into the blood as glucose. Speed of absorption can be measured by comparing the average rise in blood glucose over two hours for a given amount of carbohydrate. This rise is then divided by the rise in glucose observed for white bread and multiplied by 100 to give the glycaemic index. White bread therefore has a glycaemic index of 100. The foods we evolved with would typically have had a glycaemic index between 40 and 80.

The overall rise in glucose depends on both the glycaemic index and the total amount of carbohydrate. The two are combined to give the glycaemic load: each unit of glycaemic load is equivalent to one gram of carbohydrate from white bread. Foods with a high glycaemic load are more demanding on the release of insulin to drive the glucose out of the blood and into storage before it can cause damage. In turn, the release of insulin has profound physiological effects, including modifying cholesterol synthesis.

Figure 9.5 provides some examples of the glycaemic load of common plant foods at a given calorie intake. Fibre and calorie density, as presented in chapter 4 (figure 4.2), are also listed.

Foods that are high in fat or protein have a low glycaemic load, but not all high carbohydrate foods are equally high in glycaemic load.

Potatoes are exceptionally high in glycaemic load. Bread is also high in glycaemic load, though wholemeal bread is associated with reduced risk of heart disease and diabetes due to other components. Pasta and dense chewy breads such as pumpernickel have a lower glycaemic load per calorie than most grain products, while lentils and beans have an even lower load. Bananas are sometimes described as a low glycaemic food, but this depends on their ripeness: ripe bananas have almost twice the glycaemic load of underripe bananas.

Low fat diets and cardiovascular risk

Increased glycaemic load decreases levels of protective HDL cholesterol, increases levels of dangerous VLDL cholesterol and changes LDL cholesterol to smaller, denser and more dangerous

	Fibre (grams per 1000 calories)	Energy (calories per 100 grams)	Glycaemic load per 1000 calories
Potatoes	20	85	276
Sugar, brown	0	376	232
Sugar, white	0	387	232
Rice, white	3	120	220
Banana, ripe	26	90	217
Rice, brown	10	110	210
Bread, wholemeal	28	250	180
Bread, white	9	270	180
Oranges	50	50	150
Pasta, wholemeal	30	120	126
Pasta, white	8	130	126
Bread, pumpernickel	26	250	114
Banana, underripe	26	90	110
Beans	55	120	95
Cherries	32	60	75
Lentils	70	120	60
Tomatoes	50	20	29
Cashews	6	560	25
Avocados	30	160	23
Almonds	20	600	15
Hazel nuts	15	630	14
Oil	0	890	0

Figure 9.5: Glycaemic load of common plant foods

particles. High glycaemic load is also associated with increased risk of diabetes and heart disease and with increased levels of C-reactive protein, indicating dangerous inflammation.

This picture is complicated by the fact that the adverse effects of high glycaemic load are greater in inactive people and in overweight people: physical activity and low body fat allow the body to absorb glucose efficiently and therefore reduce both blood glucose concentration and the amount of insulin released to control blood sugar. High body mass index, particularly if accompanied by an ample waistline, is itself associated with increased risk of diabetes, increased total cholesterol, decreased HDL cholesterol and increased C-reactive protein.

Lean and active individuals have less to fear from high glycaemic load, so if they find that a low fat diet helps to keep them that way it may have much to commend it. The type of person most at risk from high glycaemic load is one adopting a low fat diet to try to lose excess abdominal fat without at the same time increasing physical activity. If such attempts to lose weight fail, as is likely in the absence of increased physical activity, the low fat diet will probably do more harm than good.

Overweight or diabetic individuals and those following low fat diets should pay particular attention to limiting glycaemic load. This can be achieved by choosing foods with relatively low glycaemic load per calorie. In many cases this means foods that are higher in fat or protein, but appropriate choices within high carbohydrate food types can also make a major difference: pasta and pumpernickel bread rather than conventional finely milled breads, for instance, and just ripe rather than very ripe bananas.

In general, replacing animal fats with carbohydrates will dramatically reduce total cholesterol and significantly reduce the ratio of total to HDL cholesterol, due to the combined effect of reduced saturated fat and cholesterol intakes. Replacing carbohydrates with monounsaturated plant fats will have little effect on total cholesterol but will improve the ratio of total to HDL cholesterol. This important ratio can also be improved by selecting high carbohydrate foods with lower glycaemic load.

The response of cholesterol to diet varies significantly between individuals. Some individuals will show a huge increase in VLDL cholesterol (often detected by an increase in triglycerides) and a dramatic reduction in HDL cholesterol when carbohydrate intake or glycaemic load is increased. This is more likely to happen to inactive or overweight individuals, as they often require more insulin to process carbohydrate than lean and active individuals. On the other hand, some individuals are genetically more susceptible to saturated fats, showing very high LDL and total cholesterol on conventional Western diets.

If adopting a low fat diet does not increase the ratio of total to HDL cholesterol, there is little reason for concern about potential adverse effects, but if this ratio increases by more than about 0.5 – e.g. from 3 to 1 up to 3.5 to 1 – it is unlikely that the diet will be beneficial. Total and HDL cholesterol measurements are easily obtainable, so it is easy to experiment and gain confidence that the chosen diet matches individual needs. Allow at least a month on any given diet before testing the effect on cholesterol. In the event of weight loss, test cholesterol after weight has stabilised.

Direct trials of dietary changes provide further insight into the choice between carbohydrate and monounsaturated fat. A diet with just 7% of calories as fat and no animal products other than skimmed milk and egg white has been used as part of a programme to reverse atherosclerosis. This programme showed a reduction in artery blockages, angina and the need for hospital procedures, but there was no significant decrease in the number of deaths or heart attacks.

This programme also involved other changes known to improve the ratio of total to HDL cholesterol and involved individuals who showed very high initial cholesterol levels in response to a conventional diet and thus were probably in the genetic group most likely to benefit from a low fat diet. Substantial weight loss and increased exercise combined to boost HDL cholesterol, so there was a negligible drop in HDL levels along with a major reduction in LDL cholesterol and a substantial improvement in the ratio of total to HDL cholesterol. Stress management, group support and stopping smoking were also integral parts of this programme and will have made a major contribution to the results.

Another very low fat intervention programme observed a drop in total cholesterol accompanied by an undesirable increase in the ratio of total to HDL cholesterol despite increased physical activity.

On the other hand, trials incorporating increased monounsaturated fat from sources such as olive oil and almonds have consistently shown a notable reduction in the ratio of total to HDL cholesterol.

Overall, the level of monounsaturated fat should be driven by individual preference, with the ratio of total to HDL cholesterol providing a very useful check. Nuts are a particularly beneficial source of monounsaturated fat. In general, fairly high monounsaturated fat consumption, giving a total fat intake of 25% to 30% of calories, is likely to be ideal, but lower or higher fat content may be beneficial for certain individuals.

Whether following a high or a low fat diet, choose whole plant foods with plenty of accompanying fibre and minerals. On a low fat diet, choose low glycaemic load carbohydrate sources such as pasta, pumpernickel bread, cherries, beans and lentils.

Putting it into practice

Choose vegetable oils such as olive oil and rapeseed (canola) oil rather than margarines, and low trans fat margarines rather than butter.

Get your omega-3 fatty acids from plants and plant oils, such as flaxseed (linseed), rapeseed and hempseed, rather than from fish or fish oils.

Get your calcium from non-dairy sources such as green leafy vegetables, oranges and fortified plant milks (see chapter 7) to avoid the dangers of saturated fat.

The percentage of total calories from fat is a matter for individual choice and will often come down to personal preference. For most people, a moderate fat diet with 25 to 30% of calories from fat is likely to be optimal.

In general, only adopt a low fat diet (less than 25% of total calories as fat) for health reasons if it helps to maintain a healthy weight and does not increase the ratio of total to HDL cholesterol by more than 0.5, e.g. from 3 to 1 up to 3.5 to 1.

Chapter 10

Natural imperfections

Natural is often equated with ideal, but some natural environments are more healthful than others and humans have transformed the natural environment beyond recognition. It is therefore not surprising that cracks have become apparent in nature's support for human health.

As discussed in chapter 6, modern sanitised plant foods do not provide sufficient vitamin B12 for humans or other single-stomached animals to sustain optimal health. This is not the only such gap.

Our roots lie in the tropics and subtropics, but the search for more space for a growing population has led us far beyond our roots to less hospitable environments, increasing the risk of certain deficiencies, particularly vitamin D, iodine and selenium.

Vitamin D

The most direct effect of human migration to higher latitudes is that many of us now live in regions where for much of the year there is insufficient ultraviolet (UV) light to generate vitamin D from the action of sunlight on our skin.

Pale skins maximise the effect of limited UV exposure. At latitudes above about 40 degrees, however, blood vitamin D levels decline markedly during winter as we cover up to keep warm and the required ultraviolet radiation declines. The importance of adequate blood vitamin D for calcium absorption was noted in chapter 7. In addition, there is growing evidence that adequate vitamin D may reduce the risk of breast and prostate cancer, type 1 diabetes, premenstrual symptoms and polycystic ovarian syndrome.

The most striking example is research from Scandinavia which found that babies given 50 micrograms of vitamin D per day as a supplement (the standard dose in the 1960s) had about one sixth of the subsequent incidence of type 1 (juvenile) diabetes compared with those not given the supplement.

Current recommended doses are much lower due to concerns about overdose, but it is certainly prudent to get at least 10 to 20 micrograms of vitamin D per day whenever sunlight exposure is inadequate for more than a few months at a time.

Good dietary sources of vitamin D are few and far between. In the UK, the average dietary intake is just 3 micrograms per day, mostly from fortified spreads and animal products. There is some debate as to whether this intake is high enough to make any meaningful difference, but it probably does make a modest difference to the winter dip in vitamin D levels, particularly if stores built up in the autumn are low.

A vegan who uses no fortified foods would have a negligible dietary intake of vitamin D and might be more exposed to the winter dip if they have not built up good stores in the summer and autumn.

The primary defence against vitamin D deficiency is frequent short periods of exposure to sunlight of as much skin as practicable while the sun is high enough (about 40 degrees or more above the horizon). 20 minutes exposure is sufficient for maximum vitamin D generation in light skinned individuals. Up to an hour may be beneficial for people with dark skin. Longer exposures increase the risk of cancer-promoting sunburn without further benefit.

Supplements may have an important role to play in winter, especially for young children and for the elderly. Young children have a high demand for vitamin D to support rapid growth, and early infancy may be the critical period for reducing the risk of type 1 diabetes.

The use of sunbeds might appear to be an alternative to supplements. However, modern sunbeds produce little radiation in the UVB wavelengths required to generate vitamin D (about 300 to 320 nanometres), as they use longer UVA wavelengths to reduce the risk of burning and skin cancer while still producing a tan. Standard sunbeds will therefore not generate vitamin D.

The required wavelengths are also blocked by the atmosphere when the sun is low on the horizon. In the UK, breast-fed babies show a seasonal variation in vitamin D levels and babies born in the autumn are especially at risk of vitamin D deficiency. Pregnant women in Scotland sometimes experience damage to teeth due to low vitamin D stores, and levels also drop in breast-feeding mothers. Older people generate vitamin D from sunlight less efficiently and may get less exposure if mobility is restricted.

For these reasons, the UK government recommends that young children should get 7 micrograms of vitamin D per day and that adults over 65, pregnant and breast-feeding women and anyone confined indoors should get 10 micrograms per day.

There are two forms of vitamin D available for food fortification and supplements: cholecalciferol (D3) and ergocalciferol (D2). Cholecalciferol is the form generated by the action of sunlight on skin and is commercially produced by exposing wool or skins obtained from slaughterhouses to radiation, or by a more complex synthesis from cholesterol. In all cases, the raw material for vitamin D3 production is derived from animals

Vegans therefore use only vitamin D2, which is the form used to fortify fat spreads in the UK. As D2 is now considered to be only about half as active as D3, suitable supplementary doses are 10 to 25 micrograms per day. Up to 50 micrograms per day would be safe for an adult, but young children should not be given more than 25 micrograms per day.

To put the dose into perspective, 20 minutes exposure to sunlight on the upper body would provide a light skinned adult with the equivalent of 50 to 100 micrograms of D3. The same exposure on hands and face alone will generate 5 to 10 micrograms of vitamin D. Longer exposures provide no further benefit in light skinned people and may increase the risk of sunburn, which in turn increases the risk of skin cancer. Dark skinned people may benefit from exposures two to three times as long.

Iodine

Iodine is essential to thyroid hormone production, and iodine deficiency can result in abnormal functioning of the thyroid gland. This may result in either depressed or accelerated metabolic function (hypo- or hyper-thyroidism).

*Hypo*thyroidism at an early age impairs brain development and may result in cretinism if the deficiency is severe. It can also appear at any age as an enlarged thyroid gland or goitre and is associated with skin problems, weight gain and increased blood levels of cholesterol and homocysteine. *Hyper*thyroidism, on the other hand, is associated with osteoporosis.

The best protection against all these problems is an adequate but not excessive intake of iodine throughout life.

For adults and children over ten, this translates to between 150 and 500 micrograms per day; for younger children, the upper limit is 17 micrograms per kilogram of body weight.

The iodine content of plant foods depends on the iodine content of the soil, which varies greatly from one part of the world to another. Iodine in the soil is low in many areas, including most regions that were covered by ice during the last Ice Age.

It is widely believed that the problem of iodine deficiency has been solved in developed countries. The two main strategies employed to eradicate deficiency – adding iodine to salt (North America, New Zealand, and much of Africa and Asia) and adding iodine to animal feed (the UK, some other European countries and, to a lesser extent, Australia) – were largely successful in eliminating iodine deficiency as a major public health issue in developed countries by the second half of the twentieth century. However, both strategies have major limitations in relation to a healthy diet.

Tying iodine supply to salt or anything else consumed in highly variable quantities is far from ideal in view of the relatively narrow range of optimal iodine intakes. The specific choice of salt also means that health conscious people may unintentionally reduce their iodine intake by reducing their consumption of salt to avoid the adverse effects of sodium on blood pressure and bone health.

The major animal sources of iodine are dairy products and fish. In the UK, iodine concentrations in milk depend on the use of iodine fortified cattle feed concentrates. In the winter months, when use of these concentrates increases, the use of cow's milk can push infant iodine intake to undesirably high levels as the iodine content in milk rises. As with iodised salt, reliance on dairy products as a route for indirect fortification means that health conscious people may unintentionally reduce their iodine intake by reducing consumption of dairy products to avoid the adverse effects of dairy fat on cardiovascular health.

Iodine intakes were below 70 micrograms per day in about half of a sample of adult vegans in the UK, and as low as 25 micrograms per day in some cases. There has been one published case of hypothyroidism from iodine deficiency in an infant of a vegan mother in the UK; this was readily corrected by iodine supplements.

Consuming plant foods grown in many different regions of the world increases the likelihood of an adequate iodine intake from plants.

An alternative strategy, involving far fewer food miles, is to use seaweeds rich in iodine. It is easy to ensure sufficient iodine by eating plenty of many types of seaweed, but in order to avoid overly high levels of iodine, which have an adverse effect on some people, the best approach is to eat small amounts of kelp (kombu), which is consistently high in iodine content.

One gram of kelp contains about 3000 micrograms of iodine, so just 15 grams of kelp *per year* is an excellent insurance policy against iodine deficiency. As this is a very small amount, the most practical method is to use ground or powdered kelp as a condiment in cooking or to take kelp tablets. Although kelp tablets have a track record of understating their iodine content, two per week (each with a stated iodine content of 150 to 250 micrograms) should be adequate but not excessive.

Taking large amounts of kelp or iodine after an extended period with a low intake would be especially unwise as the thyroid gland sometimes adapts to low intakes by growing extra (autonomous) nodules. High intakes can then over-stimulate these nodules, resulting in hyperthyroidism. It is therefore best to consume iodine in small but frequent amounts –   at least once a week.

Selenium

As with iodine, selenium levels in the soil vary greatly, causing levels in plant foods to be highly variable. The effects of low selenium intake are less well defined than those of low iodine, so most countries have no strategy to increase selenium intake. Exceptions include Finland, where it is added to fertiliser, and regions of China where intake is so low (about 10 micrograms per day) that it is associated with a special form of childhood heart disease, Keshan disease. Low selenium levels are associated with vulnerability to infections and may increase the likelihood of mental retardation in children who are also deficient in iodine.

The most well established effect of selenium is to increase levels of antioxidant enzymes (glutathione peroxidases). This effect is maximised at intakes around 40 micrograms per day, though some selenium-dependent enzymes may require up to twice this amount for maximum activity. The UK government recommends one microgram per day per kilogram of body weight, with an upper limit of 6 micrograms per kilogram per day.

Long term selenium intake can be assessed by toenail concentrations. A study in Norfolk, where soil concentrations of selenium are relatively high by UK standards, found average toenail selenium concentrations of about 0.7 parts per million (ppm) in omnivores and about 0.5 ppm in vegans. Concentrations in a sample of US men ranged from 0.53 to 7.09 ppm, with a median value of 0.8 – soil selenium concentrations vary widely across the USA.

The Norfolk results suggest that omnivores were consuming about 100 micrograms per day of selenium while the vegans were consuming about 70 micrograms per day. Another UK study found that average selenium intake was 39 micrograms per day, with vegetarians averaging just 29 micrograms per day – putting vegetarians, and to a lesser extent omnivores, at risk of inadequate intake. Optimising selenium intake is therefore of concern to all dietary groups in regions with low soil concentrations, including much of the UK.

There is intriguing but as yet inconclusive evidence that increasing adult selenium intakes to about 200 micrograms per day has a protective effect against cancer. Selenium also helps to protect against heavy metal toxins such as mercury. However, long term intakes above 800 micrograms (about 12 micrograms per kilogram of body weight) per day may result in nails and hair becoming brittle or falling out due to selenium toxicity. As usual, there is an optimal dose and an excessive dose: more is not better.

The most concentrated plant source of selenium is Brazil nuts, which contain about 20 micrograms per gram. Ten nuts (about 35 grams) therefore provide about 700 micrograms, so ten Brazil nuts a week would be a useful insurance policy for adequate selenium intake. Brazil nuts do not need to be eaten daily to provide the desired selenium, but are best consumed in frequent small amounts – at least once a week.

Brazil nuts are sometimes criticised as containing relatively high levels of radioactive heavy metals. To put this into perspective, radiation content per gram is just five times higher than bananas, which are eaten in far larger amounts.

Other minerals

Most other trace minerals either have less well established requirements or are readily available from a diet meeting the guidelines in this book and therefore need no special consideration.

Zinc and iron are generally plentiful in plant foods and are well absorbed so long as the diet is rich in vitamin C and does not contain excessive phytates (see chapter 11).

Magnesium and potassium, which are very low in typical Western diets compared with our evolutionary diet, are particularly abundant in whole plant foods (see chapter 7).

Other trace minerals such as chromium, vanadium, manganese and copper have potential benefits and should be well supplied from a varied diet based on unrefined plant foods.

Overcoming natural imperfections

In many cases, these natural imperfections can be overcome by dietary and lifestyle choices such as winter holidays nearer the equator, small amounts of kelp and a modest quantity of Brazil nuts. However, some people will find these defensive strategies difficult or undesirable. Some may not have the time or the money for a winter holiday abroad or may wish to avoid the fossil fuel pollution that such a journey entails. Others may be concerned that Brazil nuts accumulate radioactive minerals as well as beneficial trace minerals such as selenium or may dislike their distinctive taste.

For all these reasons, it would be useful to have the option of a supplement designed to address these natural imperfections. The use of supplements is now commonplace among the general population. The Harvard Medical School advocates the use of a general multimineral and multivitamin supplement to promote health, particularly extra folate or folic acid to lower homocysteine and reduce cancer risk, and vitamin D to promote bone health. As discussed in chapter 5, supplements are no substitute for healthful foods, but used judiciously they can be a convenient way of filling gaps in the quality of available foods and compensating for non-ideal circumstances such as inadequate sunlight in winter.

There is currently no ideal supplement available for people following an entirely plant-based diet, but it is useful to consider what such a supplement should provide.

Any supplement should include adequate but not excessive amounts of iodine and selenium. For children over one year, 75 micrograms of iodine per day is an ideal dose, while twice this amount would be preferable for an adult. For selenium, the upper limit for a one-year-old would be about 50 micrograms per day; about twice this amount would be ideal for an adult.

It would therefore be useful to have a supplement with 150 micrograms of iodine and 100 micrograms of selenium which could be halved for infants, or a low cost tablet containing an appropriate amount for small children, with adults taking two a day and small children just one.

For vitamin D, the daily supplementary dose should be 10 to 20 micrograms per day of vitamin D2. This is suitable for all ages and is a very useful defence when sunlight exposure is inadequate. It does not, however, alter the desirability of frequent brief exposures of skin to sunlight from spring to autumn to build up good stores of natural vitamin D.

Supplements containing vitamin A as retinol or related compounds are not ideal, in view of evidence that more than 1500 micrograms of retinol per day increases the risk of bone fractures.   Most multimineral supplements provide about 700 micrograms of vitamin A, which is a safe amount for people on a plant-based diet but may take those consuming animal products such as liver or cod liver oil to a dangerously high level. Supplements containing beta-carotene, which is converted in the body to vitamin A, are also not ideal in the light of evidence that beta-carotene in isolation lacks the beneficial effects of foods rich in beta-carotene and may even have adverse effects. In addition, much of the beta-carotene supplied commercially uses an animal-derived gelatine carrier.   Fortunately there is no difficulty in getting enough carotenoids to meet requirements for vitamin A from easily obtainable vegetables such as carrots, sweet potatoes or dark green leafy vegetables such as spring greens (collards) and kale (see chapters 5 and 7).

Given the substantial risks from elevated homocysteine (see chapter 6), a supplement providing at least 10 micrograms of vitamin B12 is desirable for anyone on a largely plant-based diet and for everyone over the age of fifty.

Folic acid (folate) and vitamin B6, the other key vitamins in minimising homocysteine, are usually abundant in a varied plant-based diet, but there would be no harm if a supplement also included 400 micrograms of folic acid and 2 milligrams of B6. This would make the supplement well suited to anyone wishing to minimise the risk of elevated homocysteine.

An ideal supplement for adults following a plant-based diet at high latitudes would therefore contain:

- 20 micrograms vitamin D2
- 150 micrograms iodine
- 100 micrograms selenium (as selenium methionine)
- 10 micrograms vitamin B12 (cobalamin)

For small children, half these amounts would be suitable.

To complete the homocysteine reducing package, the supplement could also optionally include:

- 400 micrograms folic acid
- 2 mg vitamin B6

This combination is also very suitable to protect reproductive health, as iodine and selenium are key protective nutrients during pregnancy and elevated homocysteine is strongly associated with miscarriages and birth defects.

An ideal supplement should not contain any form of vitamin A, since retinol compounds may increase bone loss and beta-carotene supplements do not show the same benefits as foods rich in beta-carotene.

Putting it into practice

EITHER

Make a point of getting frequent short periods of sunlight exposure of as much skin as possible in the autumn while the sun is still at least 40 degrees above the horizon (your shadow should not be much longer than you are) and take a mid-winter holiday nearer the equator if this is a feasible and acceptable option (vitamin D).

Consume 15 to 30 grams (half to one ounce) of kelp (kombu) in small amounts over the year (iodine).

Eat about 10 Brazil nuts a week (selenium).

Get at least 3 micrograms a day of vitamin B12 from fortified foods or 10 micrograms a day from a supplement. All B12 supplements should be chewed.

OR

Take a daily supplement containing

20 micrograms vitamin D2

150 micrograms iodine

100 micrograms selenium (as selenium methionine)

10 micrograms vitamin B12 (cobalamin)

Chapter 11

Unnecessary fears: protein, iron and zinc

In the move towards a plant-based diet, fears are often voiced about supposedly inadequate protein, iron and zinc. The root of these fears is the observation that in typical diets in developed countries meat and fish are major sources of all three, while eggs and dairy are often significant contributors to protein intake.

Iron and zinc deficiency are major problems in those developing countries where diets are restricted by poverty or local custom. Protein intake is generally sufficient if calorie intake is sufficient, except when an exceptionally low protein staple such as cassava dominates the diet. Most Western plant-based diets have been found to provide adequate zinc, iron and protein.

Nevertheless, it is worth addressing each of these concerns in detail to dispel unnecessary fears and to ensure that protein, iron and zinc intakes support optimal health.

Protein

Concern is frequently expressed about the ability of plant-based diets to provide adequate protein, but this concern is misplaced.

Protein provides a source of nitrogen for building and repairing muscle. It also provides essential amino acids which play particular roles within the body and cannot be made from other amino acids. Protein and amino acid requirements are commonly expressed in grams per kilogram of body weight, as the requirements at a given age vary roughly in proportion to weight. The requirements identified by the World Health Organisation have been accepted by most national bodies and provide a good basis for evaluating adequacy of protein supply.

These requirements vary widely with age. Babies require the highest protein and amino acid intakes per kilogram of weight to support their rapid growth, but they also require the highest calorie intake per kilogram of body weight. Calorie requirements vary from 108 calories per kilogram of body weight for a baby to 30 calories per kilogram for an elderly adult. Protein requirements vary from about 1.73 grams per kilogram for a baby to 0.75 grams per kilogram for an adult. The requirement in terms of grams of protein per calorie of food therefore varies less dramatically than one might imagine – from 16 grams per 1000 calories for a baby to 25 grams per 1000 calories for an older adult.

Contrary to widespread belief, therefore, the older adult requires a more protein dense diet than the infant. A protein content of 25 grams per 1000 calories will meet the needs of all ages. The expression of protein needs in relation to calories makes it easier to see whether a given food is an adequate source of protein.

While there are eight groups of essential amino acids, two groups are of particular interest as they are the most likely to be low in certain plant foods.   In terms of human requirements, lysine is the least plentiful amino acid in many grains and seeds, while the sulphur amino acids methionine and cysteine are the limiting factor in legumes. Methionine and cysteine are usually considered together because if there is plenty of methionine in the diet it is converted via homocysteine into cysteine (see chapter 6).

Figure 11.1 is based on World Health Organisation estimates of protein, amino acid and calorie needs. The figures are obtained by dividing the recommended protein and amino acid intakes at each age by the average calorie requirements at each age. This introduces a safety margin of about 25% compared with average requirements, though an individual with both unusually low calorie intake and unusually high protein requirements might need somewhat more protein per calorie than this calculation indicates.

	3-4 months old	2 years old	11 years old	30 years old	60 years old
Total protein	16	11	21	21	25
Lysine	0.95	0.63	0.94	0.33	0.4
Methionine+cysteine	0.54	0.26	0.47	0.36	0.43

Figure 11.1: Protein and amino acid requirements (grams per 1000 calories)

The requirements for a baby of 3 to 4 months are based on the composition of breast milk. At all other ages, the requirements are based on controlled feeding studies. As families eat a similar mix of foods, it is desirable to identify foods capable of meeting the protein needs of all age groups from weaning to old age. Due to declining calorie intake, older adults have the highest requirement for total protein per calorie (25 grams per 1000 calories). 11-year-olds have the highest requirement for both lysine (1 gram per 1000 calories) and methionine + cysteine (0.5 grams per 1000 calories).

The adult requirement for lysine is somewhat controversial, with some evidence suggesting that it could be up to two and a half times the amounts estimated by the World Health Organisation. The highest estimate would increase the requirement of a 60-year-old to 1 gram per 1000 calories. This is essentially the same as for an 11-year-old, so the uncertainty does not affect the overall requirements derived from figure 11.1.

These requirements per 1000 calories (25 grams of protein, 1 gram of lysine and 0.5 grams of methionine + cysteine) can be compared with the contents of various foods per 1000 calories.

Figure 11.2 shows that many common plant foods would meet the needs of people of all ages, even if no other food was eaten. The exceptions are shaded.

Food	Protein	Lysine	methionine + cysteine
Fruits			
Apples	3.22	0.20	0.08
Apricots	29.17	2.02	0.19
Avocados	12.30	0.58	0.36
Bananas	11.20	0.52	0.30
Blueberries	11.96	0.21	0.32
Dates	7.16	0.22	0.24
Figs	10.14	0.41	0.24
Grapes	9.30	0.21	0.46
Orange juice	15.56	0.20	0.18
Oranges	20.00	1.00	0.64
Pears	6.61	0.24	0.15
Pineapple	7.96	0.51	0.27
Plantains	10.66	0.49	0.30
Strawberries	20.33	0.83	0.20
Tangerines	14.32	0.73	0.45
Root vegetables			
Carrots	23.95	0.93	0.35
Cassava	8.50	0.28	0.24
Potato	26.23	1.64	0.77
Sweet potato	15.71	0.77	0.51
Taro	13.39	0.60	0.46
Turnips	33.33	1.33	0.59
Yam	12.97	0.50	0.34
Vegetable-fruits			
Red peppers	32.96	1.44	1.04
Tomatoes	48.42	1.79	1.05
Other vegetables			
Asparagus	99.13	4.70	2.13
Broccoli	106.43	5.04	1.93
Cabbage	57.60	2.68	1.04
Cauliflower	79.20	4.24	2.04
Kale	66.00	3.94	1.52
Spinach	129.13	7.91	3.91
Target	*25.00*	*1.00*	*0.50*

Food	Protein	Lysine	methionine + cysteine
Grains			
Brown rice	23.24	0.89	0.80
Oats	43.42	1.80	1.85
Rye bread	32.82	0.90	1.20
Wholewheat bread	39.43	1.23	1.50
Wholewheat spaghetti	42.98	0.95	1.59
Seeds			
Pumpkin seeds	41.59	3.11	1.45
Tahini	28.57	0.92	1.52
Nuts			
Almonds	36.78	1.04	0.81
Brazil nuts	21.86	0.82	2.08
Cashews	32.19	1.64	1.33
Hazel nuts (filberts)	23.81	0.67	0.79
Macadamia nuts	11.02	0.03	0.04
Peanuts	40.48	1.45	1.02
Legumes			
Baked beans	51.51	3.54	1.33
Black-eyed beans	66.64	4.51	1.68
Chick peas	54.02	3.62	1.43
Kidney beans	77.15	5.29	2.00
Lentils	77.76	5.43	1.68
Mung beans (sprouted)	96.67	5.86	1.76
Peas	66.91	3.91	1.41
Soya milk	83.33	5.42	2.64
Tofu	106.32	7.00	2.83
Animal products			
Beef	72.67	6.05	2.67
Cheddar cheese	61.79	5.14	1.93
Chicken	86.51	7.02	3.45
Egg	81.16	5.83	4.41
Lamb	63.22	5.58	2.38
Milk, full fat	53.93	4.28	1.85
Target	*25.00*	*1.00*	*0.50*

Figure 11.2: Protein and amino acid contents of common foods (grams per 1000 calories)

The first page of figure 11.2 shows fruits followed by root vegetables and other vegetables. The second page shows grains, seeds, nuts, legumes and animal products. This grouping makes it easy to see the typical characteristics of different types of plant foods.

Most fruits fare particularly badly, falling below the requirements for total protein, lysine, and methionine + cysteine. Oranges and apricots come close to meeting the targets, but many other common fruits such as avocados, bananas, figs and dates provide only half the target amount. Fruit has a great deal to commend it, but it does not usually pull its weight as a source of protein.

Root vegetables are a mixed bunch. Cassava, a notoriously poor source of protein, provides only about a third of the target, with yam and taro also faring badly. On the other hand, that Western stalwart the potato fares very well, meeting all targets and exceeding the lysine target by more than 50%.

Vegetables other than root vegetables usually comfortably meet the targets and provide a useful source of protein. However, low calorie vegetables such as tomatoes and spinach are unlikely to contribute a major proportion of overall calories.

Grains are weakest in terms of lysine, though none is far below the target. Oats are exceptional among grains in being well above target for lysine.

Seeds vary considerably. Pumpkin seeds are a rich source of protein, comparable with many beans, while sesame seeds are borderline in total protein and lysine.

Nuts also vary markedly. Macadamias are very low in protein, and hazel nuts also miss the target, but cashews and almonds meet all the targets. Peanuts, though technically legumes, have a similar protein composition to cashews and almonds.

The legume family, including beans, peas and lentils, consistently deliver three to five times the target amounts per calorie.

While some plant foods (most fruits, some root vegetables and some nuts) are low in protein relative to requirements, most common plant foods (potatoes, grains, most nuts and seeds) meet the requirements, while others (most non-root vegetables, pumpkin seeds, beans, peas and lentils) exceed the requirements by a considerable margin. There is thus no difficulty in meeting protein requirements entirely from common plant foods if a reasonable variety is eaten.

Meat, eggs and milk provide a similar level of protein to peas and beans. Eggs, which are often held up as an ideal protein source, exceed tofu as a source of methionine and cysteine, but not as a source of protein and lysine. Moreover, methionine and cysteine requirements are easily met from plants and there is particularly good reason to avoid excessive intakes.

Methionine and cysteine account for most of the effect of protein in increasing bone loss (see appendix 1) as their sulphur content is metabolised to sulphuric acid, causing the kidneys to excrete more calcium and reducing blood and urine pH. All protein increases calcium losses, but the effect of any given protein source varies according to the proportion of sulphur-containing amino acids (methionine and cysteine) and the minerals present with the protein.

Measured by effect on calcium balance, animal protein sources come out badly compared with most plant sources for equal amounts of protein (see figure 7.4) and it is much easier to consume excessive protein if animal foods are eaten regularly. High protein intake is also associated with declining kidney function in many older adults.

Relying on plants for protein makes it easy to meet protein needs for growth and repair while avoiding excessive intakes which may damage bone and kidney health.

Iron

Iron deficiency is a common problem world wide, but is less common in developed countries regardless of levels of meat consumption. To protect the body from the oxidising effects of iron in its usual form, it is stored in the body as ferritin. Iron loss is proportional to body weight and blood loss. If losses exceed absorption, stores decline.

Once blood ferritin concentrations drop below about 15 micrograms per litre, iron stores are generally inadequate to sustain optimal production of new blood cells. The supply of iron to other tissues such as muscle is also reduced. If the synthesis of new blood cells is restricted for several months, haemoglobin levels become inadequate and anaemia results. While the main symptom of iron deficiency is anaemia, there may be milder adverse effects if the ferritin level is below 15 micrograms per litre even in the absence of anaemia. Maintaining the ferritin level at above 15 micrograms per litre is therefore an appropriate measure of iron sufficiency and is accepted as such by national and international nutritional committees.

If iron loss is particularly high, usually due to heavy menstrual periods, the UK Standing Advisory Commission on Nutrition suggests that diet may not be enough to avoid anaemia, regardless of meat content, and iron supplementation may be needed. About 5% to 10% of premenopausal women fall into this category. With this exception, however, it is easy to meet iron needs from an entirely plant-based diet without any need for supplementation.

Plant-based diets easily meet and readily exceed the recommended intakes of iron in the UK, which rise to 15 milligrams per day for premenopausal women. Many common plant foods, including potatoes, wheat, oats and most berries, contain more than 10 mg of iron per 1000 calories. Lentils, soya beans, pumpkin seeds and many beans and greens contain more than 30 mg per 1000 calories.

However, there are concerns about the efficiency of absorption of the iron from some plant foods. A significant proportion of iron from meat is in the form of haem iron (as found in blood), which is more efficiently absorbed than non-haem iron and continues to be absorbed even if iron stores are high. A diet containing large amounts of red meat is therefore associated with higher iron stores.

Non-haem iron is the only form found in plants. Absorption of non-haem iron declines markedly as iron stores rise, so very high iron stores are unusual on a plant-based diet. However, on a plant-based diet incorporating plenty of fruit and vegetables, average blood ferritin levels will generally be well above 15 micrograms per litre, indicating sufficient iron stores and thus no risk of iron deficiency anaemia.

Fruit and vegetables play a vital role in iron absorption from plant foods. Absorption of non-haem iron can be dramatically reduced by phytates and polyphenols. Phytates are found in substantial quantities in unrefined seeds as a source of phosphorus for release following germination (sprouting). Polyphenols are found in tea, coffee and many fruits and vegetables, supplying antioxidants both for the plants and for the animals eating the plants.

Unsurprisingly, given our evolutionary history, other components of plant foods neutralise the inhibiting effects of phytates and polyphenols on iron absorption. The most powerful of these is vitamin C (ascorbic acid), but other organic acids also play a role in maintaining iron in a soluble and readily absorbable form.

Soya and cow's milk proteins and eggs all inhibit plant iron absorption. Meat and fish have an enhancing effect on non-haem iron absorption if vitamin C intakes are low, but if vitamin C intake is already high there is little additional effect from meat and fish. In a varied plant-based diet with fruit and vegetables at most meals, absorption enhancers neutralise the effect of inhibitors so that good overall absorption is maintained and iron stores settle at a healthful level.

Calcium reduces both haem and non-haem iron absorption by up to 50%. Its inhibiting effect reaches a maximum at calcium contents of 200 to 300 milligrams or more per meal . In contrast to phytates and polyphenols, this effect is not neutralised by organic acids. This is not a good reason to reduce calcium intake, because the very low intake required to significantly reduce the inhibiting effect on iron absorption would be detrimental to calcium balance (see chapter 7). However, if using calcium supplements it might be advantageous to take them other than at meal times – for instance, before going to bed.

Anaemia in infants is still fairly common in the UK, largely because of inappropriate weaning foods. Breast milk ceases to be an adequate source of iron after about six months, so supplementary foods are needed. The weaning foods associated with reduced risk of infant anaemia are, as expected, fruit and vegetables and meat and fish. Use of unfortified cow's milk is a major risk factor for infant anaemia as its limited iron has very low bioavailability and inhibits absorption of iron from other sources.

While Western plant-based diets are not associated with increased anaemia, they *are* associated with lower iron stores. This might seem to be a disadvantage as lower stores mean less reserves against substantial blood loss, prolonged illness or the high iron demands of pregnancy. However, there is considerable evidence that high iron stores are associated with increased risk of diabetes, heart disease and colon cancer. The evidence is complicated by the fact that as well as reflecting iron stores, ferritin levels rise in the presence of infection or inflammation, so results to date are far from conclusive.

The strongest evidence of an adverse effect of high iron stores comes from studies which have found that while vegetarians generally show lower insulin resistance (indicating lower risk of diabetes) the insulin resistance of omnivores decreases if their iron stores are reduced from a ferritin level of about 85 to about 30 micrograms per litre by frequent blood donation.

Increased mortality from heart disease in individuals with a gene promoting moderately increased iron stores also strongly supports the hypothesis that high iron stores lead to increased heart disease.

Individuals following a plant-based diet rich in vitamin C from fruit and vegetables may have the best of both worlds in terms of adequate but not excessive iron stores.

Zinc

Zinc, like iron, is found in good amounts in many plant foods. Pumpkin seeds, okra and mung beans all have more than 20 milligrams per 1000 calories, while whole wheat, oats, peanuts, cashews, soya beans, black-eyed beans and many other plant foods have more than 10 mg per 1000 calories. This compares very favourably with UK recommended intakes of 9.5 mg per day for males and 7 mg per day for females. UK vegetarians consume an average of 8 mg of zinc per day, as do non-vegetarians.

Like iron, the key issue is absorption rather than total intake. Zinc absorption is less well understood than iron absorption. Phytates inhibit absorption, but vitamin C appears less effective in enhancing absorption of zinc than it is in enhancing absorption of iron, and the combination of a high calcium intake with high phytate foods may strongly inhibit absorption.

Boosting zinc absorption involves consuming zinc rich foods, processing high phytate foods to reduce the phytate content, and separating concentrated calcium sources such as supplements from meals.

Most whole plant foods contain a good level of zinc, but unrefined seeds – one of the richest plant sources of zinc – are also high in phytate. A key phytate reduction strategy is the baking of bread. Traditional sourdough processing is especially effective, removing almost all phytate. The combined action of water and baker's yeast normally removes only about 50% of the phytate, but including some vinegar or other organic acid in the dough can increase this to 90% or more by increasing the action of the phytase enzymes in the seeds. Long proving times for the dough also help to break down phytates.

Vinegar is widely used by master bakers, but unless you bake your own bread or discuss the subject with the baker it is difficult to be sure that this process is being used to maximum effect. However, home bread baking is enjoying a revival thanks to low cost baking machines, and chapter 14 includes a bread recipe incorporating this strategy. Even without special processing, trials suggest that wholegrain bread is preferable to white bread as the increased zinc content more than compensates for reduced absorption. Unleavened bread – made with neither yeast nor sourdough – is not a good source of zinc, but other traditionally made breads are useful sources.

Simply soaking seeds has only a modest effect on phytate levels unless the seeds have been ground. However, sprouting seeds greatly reduces phytate levels as the phytate is converted to other forms of phosphorus to make it available to the new plant for growth. Mung beans can be easily sprouted and are one of the richest sources of zinc. These are the beansprouts typical of Chinese cuisine. Lentils can also be sprouted for use in dahls or salads (see chapter 14).

A varied and predominantly wholefood plant-based diet should therefore provide abundant zinc.

Protein, zinc and IGF-1

Low intakes of zinc and protein reduce growth in children and tissue repair in adults; this is reflected in a *low* level of the growth hormone IGF-1 in the blood. On the other hand, a *high* level of IGF-1 in the blood is associated with increased risk of certain cancers, including premenopausal breast cancer, prostate cancer, bladder cancer and lung cancer. Changes in IGF-1 level may be part of the reason why certain diseases decline and others increase as countries develop and diets become more varied and richer in protein.

Some studies suggest that high IGF-1 levels are strongly associated with cow's milk. This reflects the high protein and mineral intakes associated with high milk consumption. Soya milk shows a similar association with IGF-1 levels in vegans.

Average IGF-1 levels in vegans are about 10% lower than those of meat eaters and lacto-vegetarians. UK vegans who use no soya milk show IGF-1 levels about 25% below those of vegans who consume at least one cup of soya milk a day. A 25% reduction in IGF-1 may reduce the risk of the cancers mentioned in this section by between 25% and 50%, but the overall effect on health of modest reductions in IGF-1 is currently unknown.

The effect of a given food on cancer risk cannot be deduced merely from its effect on IGF-1. Some evidence suggests that soya food consumption is associated with lower risk of breast and prostate cancer, so soya may contain other components which counter the cancer-promoting effect of IGF-1. Cow's milk, however, is strongly associated with increased risk of prostate cancer.

Until further evidence is available, the best advice must be to get adequate but not excessive amounts of protein and zinc from a varied plant-based diet, within which moderate use of soya milk and other soya foods can play a useful part.

Putting it into practice

To boost protein intake in the young and the old, choose nuts over oils, wheat over rice, and include moderate amounts of beans, peas and lentils. Eat a wide variety of plant foods.

To ensure good iron stores, eat a varied mostly wholefood diet, including fruit and vegetables rich in vitamin C with most meals: oranges, peppers, dark green leafy vegetables, broccoli and cauliflower are all good choices.

To ensure good zinc stores, eat a varied mostly wholefood diet, with unsprouted whole grains mostly consumed as breads made with yeast or sourdough, and with beans and lentils soaked thoroughly and sometimes sprouted.

Chapter 12

From birth to old age

The foundations of a healthy life are laid before conception. The demands of pregnancy and breast feeding can expose nutritional inadequacies that would otherwise remain hidden.

Iodine and selenium are important for health at any stage of life, but their most dramatic effects occur during pregnancy and in early infancy. In regions where iodine and selenium intakes are both low, the incidence of cretinism is exceptionally high. Elevated homocysteine is associated with miscarriages and birth defects. Low iron absorption can lead to anaemia during pregnancy. Demand for omega-3 fatty acids is particularly high to support the child's brain development. Good vitamin D levels during pregnancy and early infancy may help to protect against type 1 diabetes and other autoimmune diseases.

The characteristics of a healthy diet do not change in the months before or during pregnancy, but the importance of following a healthy diet increases.

From birth to six months, most infants will thrive on breast milk alone, although some will show signs of being hungry and ready for something more a little before that age. Ideally, breast feeding should continue alongside other foods until about two years of age. If breast feeding is not possible, formula feed is the only reliable alternative. Soya formulas have come under attack on suspicion of adverse effects on reproductive health in later years. However, an important study in the USA interviewed adults assigned either soya or cow's milk formula in infancy and concluded that the evidence was reassuring on the safety of soya infant formula. The controversy over soya foods in later life is discussed in chapter 13.

After six months of breast feeding, the infant's iron stores built up before birth will be heading for depletion. It is therefore important to include good sources of absorbable iron to complement breast milk. Cereals used around this time should be fortified with iron. It is generally best to start with rice as a first cereal, as this is least likely to cause allergic reactions. Oats are a good second grain and provide plenty of protein. Wheat should be introduced last, as it is the most likely to cause an allergic reaction if introduced early. Small amounts of vitamin C rich fruit and vegetables such as oranges and cauliflower should be included with other solid foods to boost iron absorption.

Infants require about three times more calories per kilogram of body weight than adults, and fat is a very efficient way of delivering calories. Breast milk is 55% fat – mostly saturates. Nut butters (cashew, almond and peanut) can be introduced at about a year, so long as there is no family history of allergies, and can provide a useful source of calories and protein.

Young children's ability to deal with fibre is more limited than that of adults, so it is important to keep the ratio of calories and protein to fibre relatively high. A tablespoon per day of plant oils added to other foods can be helpful if a child is slow to gain weight. Rice, a relatively low fibre grain, and bananas, a relatively low fibre fruit, are especially useful sources of carbohydrates.

Oils provide no amino acids, while rice and bananas are relatively modest sources, so it can be helpful to include a low fibre amino acid rich food such as soya milk as breast milk intake declines. A large cup of soya milk will provide 10 grams of lysine rich protein.

So long as the infant's diet is not overloaded with low calorie fruit and vegetables, this pattern provides a sound basis for healthy growth. The balance of the diet should be made up of the family's usual foods, introduced according to general recommendations on weaning.

Vitamin drops are available at low cost and are recommended for all children to ensure an adequate vitamin D intake. If the mother's vitamin B12 intake is good, her breast milk will meet the infant's needs for B12 at least for the first year. However, it is prudent to include B12 fortified foods or to crush a B12 supplement into other food once solids are introduced.

While relatives and friends may nod sympathetically when an adult moves to a plant-based diet, the same people often become very uneasy in relation to infants. It is therefore useful to know that both major studies of the development of vegan children observed positive results.

In the UK, an extended study of 39 vegan children carried out with the cooperation of the Vegan Society reported normal growth and development in the children studied. The researchers emphasised that good growth and development is conditional on avoiding the potential pitfalls of B12 deficiency and low calorie density.

In the USA, a study of 400 vegan children from a community known as The Farm also reported normal growth and development. In the early days of The Farm, there were some problems with anaemia in infants and low B12 levels were common. This was corrected by the introduction of locally produced soya milk fortified with vitamins A and D and high levels of B12. Thereafter, good development was observed. Sadly, there continue to be occasional cases around the world of vegan infants failing to thrive due to ignorance of these basic guidelines.

Studies of The Farm also considered health during pregnancy. Only one case of preeclampsia was observed out of 775 vegan mothers. The authors concluded: "The foregone conclusion that a vegan diet during pregnancy is or even could be harmful seems unwarranted; in fact it may be beneficial, particularly in reducing the incidence of preeclampsia".

Other studies provided some reason for concern about omega-3 fatty acid intake. Levels of omega-3 fatty acids in vegetarian and vegan women's blood and breast milk and in the blood of their infants were observed to be about half those in omnivores. This was not surprising, given a dietary omega-6 to omega-3 ratio of about 20 to 1. While there is limited direct evidence of harm to either mothers or infants from these low levels, the observations provide further evidence that vegans should shift the balance of dietary fats from omega-6 to omega-3 as discussed in chapters 7 and 8.

A recent study comparing cod liver oil supplementation with corn oil (omega-6) supplementation during pregnancy and breast feeding found that the children of mothers supplemented with cod liver oil had an average IQ about 5 points higher at four years of age. IQ was not, however, correlated with docosahexaenoic acid (DHA) levels at birth but rather was inversely correlated with other fatty acids which increase in omega-3 deficiency. This indicates that any benefit comes from avoiding omega-3 deficiency rather than from consuming high levels of DHA. Moreover, the fish oil group had a lower percentage of smokers and a slightly higher parental education level, which may have exaggerated any effect.

Consuming 1% to 2% of calories as alpha-linolenic acid and no more than 6% of calories as linoleic acid will reliably prevent omega-3 deficiency (see chapters 7 and 8).

In early adolescence, growth is again rapid It is therefore important to make sure that enough high calorie foods are available to support the demands of growth. Good intakes of calcium and protein are also important to support growth and bone development. A typical adolescent plant-based diet shows some characteristic strengths and weaknesses compared with an omnivorous diet. Saturated fat intake is 50% lower and total fat intake is slightly lower. Intakes of fibre, vitamin C and folate are approximately double those of omnivores. If the selenium content of soil is low, selenium intake can be significantly lower. Vitamin D and calcium intakes are generally lower. All the latter disadvantages are readily correctable and an adolescent vegetarian diet generally conforms more closely to health recommendations than an omnivorous diet.

In the World Health Report 2002, the World Health Organisation estimates that neuropsychiatric disorders, principally depression and dementia, account for about 20% of the burden of disease in developed countries – comparable with that of cardiovascular disease. This estimate is based not so much on the contribution to mortality as on the contribution to reduced enjoyment of life.

There is a considerable overlap between dietary factors influencing cardiovascular disease and those influencing depression and dementia. Cognitive decline, culminating in dementia, is associated with elevated homocysteine, elevated LDL cholesterol or low HDL cholesterol, low levels of antioxidants and low levels of omega-3 fatty acids. Depression is associated with elevated homocysteine and low levels of omega-3 fatty acids.

A study of depressed adults in 1998 found that lower intake of alpha-linolenic acid was strongly associated with more intense depression and with lower blood levels of docosahexaenoic acid. The recommendations in chapters 5, 6 and 8 are highly relevant to reducing the burden of neuropsychiatric illnesses throughout life as well as to reducing the risk of death.

The relative importance of risk factors for mortality, and the susceptibility to various dietary deficiencies and diseases, all change with age. Older adults often show impaired ability to synthesise vitamin D from sunlight, so vitamin D supplementation can be beneficial. People using B12 fortified foods or supplements should not be troubled by B12 malabsorption due to declining stomach acidity as this mainly affects B12 absorption from meat. However, a smaller number of adults may experience a loss of intrinsic factor so that they need to rely on the less efficient route of B12 absorption which allows only 0.5% to 2% of B12 intake to be absorbed. In the UK, this condition is often addressed by regular B12 injections, but it can usually be treated just as well by high dose oral supplements (about 2000 micrograms per week).

Risk of osteoporotic fractures increases rapidly with age, particularly in postmenopausal women. In this group, vitamin K rich foods such as green leafy vegetables and broccoli are particularly important in helping bones to retain calcium (see chapter 7). Good vitamin D stores help to keep calcium absorption levels up and may also improve coordination and reduce falls.

Mineral intakes promoting good calcium balance – high potassium and calcium and low sodium – are important for bone health, but reducing protein below the recommended intake of about one gram per kilogram of body weight per day is undoubtedly a false economy. These measures may also reduce the risk of breast and colorectal cancer. Folate and vitamin B12 may reduce cancer risk by facilitating DNA repair.

In men, the same package of measures should reduce the risk of colorectal cancer and prostate cancer, though some researchers suggest that high calcium intakes may increase prostate cancer risk. There is good evidence that milk and dairy products increase the risk of prostate cancer, but little evidence that this is the result of increased calcium intake. Meat consumption is also associated with an increased risk of prostate cancer, and both meat and milk proteins boost levels of the growth hormone IGF-1.

In minimising the risk of prostate cancer, what is included in the diet is at least as important as what is excluded: plenty of lycopene from cooked tomatoes, plenty of selenium from Brazil nuts and a moderate amount of soya milk or tofu are the most plausible recipe for prevention.

Calorie requirements decline in older adults, but requirements for protein and other nutrients do not. Use of low nutrient high calorie foods such as oils and sugars should therefore be kept to modest levels and high nutrient density foods such as beans, peas and pumpkin seeds should be boosted to compensate.

Despite declining calorie needs, some older adults experience a gradual and undesired loss of weight. This is not a good thing, particularly if body mass index falls below 18.5 (see chapter 4). In this situation, high calorie nutrient rich foods such as cashew, almond and peanut butters and pumpkin seeds may prove particularly useful. Activity levels should be maintained as far as possible so as to minimise the tendency for muscle to be replaced by fat. Preventing underweight should be a high priority in dietary choices.

Vulnerability to high cholesterol levels and high body mass index is greatest during late middle age (40 to 65) and declines thereafter. The changing impact of high cholesterol means that the reduction in the risk of heart disease due to simply avoiding meat is greatest in late middle age and less apparent beyond the age of 75.

Other risk factors remain at least as important in later years. Promoting a good calcium balance is important to avoid blood pressure creeping up with age. Antioxidants play specific protective roles against blindness and dementia, which are significant threats to the elderly. Homocysteine levels tend to increase with age, partly as a consequence of declining kidney function, so optimal vitamin B12 and folate intakes are very important.

Putting it into practice

Nutrient quality is especially important shortly before conception and during pregnancy and breast feeding, with vitamin B12, folate, vitamin D, iodine, selenium and omega-3 fatty acids being of particular concern (see chapters 6, 8, 9 and 10).

Young children need more calorie dense foods and less fibre than adults. A tablespoon a day of olive oil or rapeseed (canola) oil mixed with other foods, plus a cup of soya milk, will boost calories and protein without boosting fibre. Cashew nut butter is a very good choice for children over one year with no family history of allergies.

Vitamin D is particularly important for infants and elderly people.

Postmenopausal women get special benefit from green leafy vegetables and broccoli.

Good folate and antioxidant intakes from fruit and vegetables and good vitamin B12 intake from fortified foods or supplements are especially important for elderly people.

Older adults need to focus on quality of food intake to make up for declining quantity. They should also try to avoid undesired loss (or gain) of weight.

Chapter 13

Variations on a theme

The dietary guidelines presented in this book leave plenty of room for individual choice. Healthy diets can take many different forms. Two regions stand out as possible models: Japan and Crete. Japan now tops international tables for Health Adjusted Life Expectancy (see chapter 3) while Crete has the lowest male mortality of any European region and the highest life expectancy of the study groups (cohorts) in the Seven Countries Study.

The Seven Countries Study looked at the diet and health of about 13,000 men in 16 cohorts selected from seven countries. The study cohorts were established between 1958 and 1964 and the results from 25 years of follow up have been published. Results from this study include a mixture of comparisons between cohorts and comparisons within cohorts and have made a major contribution to modern understanding of diet and mortality.

In comparisons between cohorts, increased saturated fat intake and smoking were associated with increased mortality from all causes combined, while increased vitamin C intake was associated with decreased all-cause mortality. Increased fibre intake and physical activity were associated with less body fat. In comparisons of individuals within the cohorts, increased smoking, blood cholesterol and systolic blood pressure were all associated with increased all-cause mortality. These findings have been confirmed by many other studies, but information from the Seven Countries Study continues to illuminate the relationship between diet and disease.

Three very different models are discussed in this chapter: low to moderate fat (Japanese), moderate to high fat (Mediterranean) and high raw. Finally, combining them in a "fusion" style is discussed.

Eastern promise

In the Seven Countries Study, the Japanese cohorts had unusually low mortality from heart disease (similar to Crete) but unexceptional overall mortality. However, Japan has shown rapid improvements in mortality since the 1960s and now tops international tables for Health Adjusted Life Expectancy (HALE). Recent studies have highlighted the southern Japanese island of Okinawa as especially successful in achieving healthy ageing.

The Okinawan diet has many similarities to the mainland Japanese diet: plenty of soya foods, vegetables and rice; a high intake of omega-3 fatty acids from plant oils and fish; moderate total fat and animal product intakes. The older Okinawans, who follow a more traditional diet than the younger generation, eat more soya foods than the Japanese average and, perhaps most importantly, much less salt. Buckwheat and wholewheat noodles and sweet potatoes along with rice (usually white) are the main sources of starch. Rapeseed (canola) oil is the main cooking oil. Average homocysteine and cholesterol levels are low, and obesity is rare.

In the 1960s, the fat intake of Japanese men in the Seven Countries Study was just 9% of calories. Fish consumption averaged 150 grams per day. Small amounts of meat and eggs and very little milk made up the balance of animal products. Consumption of sugar, oils and pastries was very low and average alcohol intake was just over two units a day. Legume use averaged 100 grams per day, mostly as soya products. Little bread or potato was consumed, but about a pound (dry weight) of rice was eaten daily. Use of vegetables was about average for the seven countries at 200 grams per day, but only about 30 grams per day of fruit was eaten.

Mortality from heart disease was very low, but stroke mortality was high – causing overall mortality to lag significantly behind Crete, which had similarly low heart disease mortality.

Since the 1960s, Japanese life expectancy has improved considerably. In the intervening decades, average fat intake increased from about 10% of calories to about 25% of calories, animal product consumption rose to about 20% of calories, and salt consumption fell. Despite the increased fat and animal product consumption, both saturated fat and polyunsaturated fat intakes remained relatively low (about 7% of calories each) and the ratio of omega-6 to omega-3 fatty acids remained more or less constant at about 4 to 1.

Drawing on the experience of dietary changes over recent decades, Japanese scientific committees take the view that the current diet is about right. They do not wish fat intake to increase further, but see no benefit in going back to 10% fat as in the 1960s. They are happy with the current omega-6 to omega-3 ratio of 4 to 1, though they suggest that individuals at high risk of heart disease may benefit from reducing this ratio to 2 to 1.

Cow's milk is being promoted in schools to boost children's calcium intake. This risks boosting saturated fat consumption unnecessarily. The use of calcium fortified soya milks would be a wiser strategy as well as being more in keeping with Japanese traditions.

Most other Asian countries show far lower life expectancy than Japan, but much of this is attributable to relative poverty. This makes it difficult to confirm directly the capacity of their diets to support healthy ageing. The Indians make excessive use of dairy and hydrogenated fats for cooking, and these are associated with increased risk of heart disease within India. Some other regions of Asia use coconut oil or palm kernel oil as the main cooking fats. Unlike most plant fats, these are highly saturated.

Nevertheless, many of the foods from other parts of Asia either fit in with the overall recommendations summarised in chapter 14 or can be easily adapted to do so, often simply by changing the traditional cooking fat to a high monounsaturated oil such as rapeseed (canola) or olive oil.

In traditional Japanese recipes, the most important adaptation required is to reduce the salt content. The Japanese make limited use of fruit, so the addition of extra fruit would also be beneficial. The combination of these changes would increase the ratio of potassium to sodium, thus reducing bone loss and reducing the risk of high blood pressure and stroke (see chapter 7).

Seaweed is widely used in Japanese cooking. Nori, with moderate iodine content, is the most popular and is widely used in sushi. Iodine rich seaweeds such as wakame, kombu (kelp), hijiki and arame are also eaten and in some coastal regions iodine consumption is several thousand micrograms per day, resulting in increased incidence of thyroid problems compared with regions where iodine intake is more moderate but still adequate. As noted in chapter 11, just 15 grams per year of kelp (kombu) is enough to provide the recommended iodine intake.

Soya foods have become controversial in recent years. The American Heart Association endorses 30 grams per day of soya protein as helping to lower cholesterol. There are persistent suggestions that soya might reduce risk of prostate and breast cancer, with some books recommending 50 grams or more of soya protein per day to reduce cancer risk. Soya is also promoted as reducing osteoporosis and menopausal flushes. On the other hand, it has been claimed that it causes cancer, dementia, fertility problems, painful periods and birth defects.

Soya protein does reduce cholesterol levels, but only in individuals with high initial cholesterol levels and at a much larger intake than the typical 10 grams per day in Japan. Low cholesterol levels in Japan are attributable to low intake of saturated fats and cholesterol, not to high soya consumption.

The other claims for and against soya are largely speculative, with little firm evidence of notable effects at moderate intakes. A common sense approach is to take traditional Japanese use of soya as a safe reference point. This means an average of no more than 20 grams of soya protein per day, mostly in traditional forms such as soya milk, tofu and roasted soya beans. A cup (250 ml) of soya milk provides about 8 grams of protein while 100 grams of tofu provides about 10 grams of protein.

One qualification to this is that the Japanese consume soya from an early age and the effects of starting soya consumption at a later age may be different. There is some evidence of an adverse effect on oestrogen-positive breast cancer, so women with this form of cancer are advised not to consume large amounts of soya.

Asian cooking has contributed much to modern vegetarian diets: tofu, soya milk, stir fries, curries, dahls, and many spices and flavourings. A few simple recipes are included in chapter 14 to illustrate the possibilities and a wealth of cookery books and websites are available. The Asian model is compatible with a low to moderate fat diet.

Cruising on the Mediterranean

In the 1960s Seven Countries Study, death rates in the Cretan men were about a third lower than those of the Japanese men. In more recent years, Crete has held prime position among European regions in terms of age-adjusted mortality for men. The Cretan diet has many similarities to other traditional Mediterranean diets: plenty of olive oil and bread; abundant fruit and vegetables; a moderate amount of wine; a small amount of animal products.

In the 1960s, the average daily diet of Cretan men in the Seven Countries Study included 35 grams of meat, 18 grams of fish, 25 grams of egg (two to three eggs per week), 13 grams of cheese and 235 grams (about a cup) of milk. Vegetable consumption was similar to Japan at about 200 grams per day, but fruit consumption was the highest in the Seven Countries Study at almost 500 grams per day. The staple energy foods were 400 grams per day of bread, almost 100 grams of olive oil and 200 grams of potatoes. Alcohol consumption averaged just under two units per day.

The Seven Countries Study also included Corfu, another region of Greece. Corfu was similar in most respects to Crete, but its olive oil consumption was about 25% lower, alcohol consumption was double that of Crete and fish consumption was three times higher. Death rates in Corfu were about a third higher than in Crete. This calls into question the common perception that Mediterranean diets derive their healthfulness from high intakes of alcohol and fish.

An extensive European study of the impact of fish on heart disease (see chapter 9) considered the impacts of both high blood omega-3 levels and high levels of mercury, and found that high levels of mercury from fish largely cancelled out the omega-3 benefit.

Alcohol is rated by the World Health Organisation as the third biggest contributor to *reducing* healthy life expectancy in developed countries (below tobacco and elevated blood pressure and just above elevated cholesterol and overweight).

Alcohol intake has been consistently associated with reduced deaths from heart disease and stroke, but also with increased deaths from liver disease, accidents, violence and various cancers, including breast cancer.

Studies of biomarkers of disease risk show that increased alcohol consumption increases protective HDL cholesterol while reducing both fibrinogen (blood clotting) and C-reactive protein (inflammation). These biomarker changes predict the observed reduction in cardiovascular disease.

The cancer promoting effects of alcohol can be partially countered by high folate intake. The risk of stroke can be reduced by improved calcium balance (see chapter 7) and heart disease risk can be reduced by modifying fat intake (chapters 8 and 9) and by increased fruit and vegetable consumption (chapter 5). If risk of both stroke and heart disease are reduced by these other means, the optimal intake of alcohol might drop from that currently observed

Detailed epidemiological studies ranging from Japan to Scotland consistently observed that in terms of overall mortality one unit per day for women and one to two units for men – in regular amounts, without binge drinking – is the optimum. More is harmful.

If individuals can manage their drinking within the limits associated with an overall benefit, alcohol may be a boon to health. If these limits are regularly exceeded, it would be better to stop drinking alcohol altogether. In populations without a tradition of alcohol use, its introduction could not be commended on health grounds.

When blood samples from 92 elderly Cretan men were compared with those of men from the Netherlands, the most striking differences in fatty acid composition were three times higher levels of alpha-linolenic acid, 50% higher levels of monounsaturated fats and 20% lower levels of linoleic acid in the Cretans. This reflects a dietary fat intake of almost 30% of calories as monounsaturates, 3% to 4% as polyunsaturates (as in 1960s Japan), and 8% as saturates. Wild salad vegetables such as purslane provided significant amounts of alpha-linolenic acid. Although the total amount of omega-3s consumed was not large, the modest omega-6 consumption meant that the omega-3s were well represented in body tissues.

As discussed in chapter 4, high intakes of vitamin C and lycopene from fruit and vegetables are associated with a clear reduction in heart disease and overall mortality, and high consumption of fruit and vegetables was certainly characteristic of the Cretan diet.

The amount of animal products consumed (about 12% of calories) provided about 2.5 micrograms per day of vitamin B12 and 300 milligrams of calcium, while adding about 3% of calories as saturated fat and about 150 milligrams per day of cholesterol. It would, of course, be even better to get the desired B12 and calcium without the accompaniments – as can now be readily achieved.

Despite the high percentage of fat in their diet, average body mass index (BMI) of the Cretan men was just one unit above the Japanese men in the Seven Countries Study and average skin fold thickness – a more direct measure of body fat – was slightly lower.

In all the Seven Countries Study cohorts, physical activity and dietary fibre were inversely associated with body fat, while dietary fat had a direct but less important association. All cohorts with a fibre intake above 40 grams per day, or with most of the population engaged in heavy manual work such as farming, showed low levels of body fat. The Cretans had both these characteristics, so their low body fat was not surprising.

As discussed in chapter 8, the Cretan diet provided a key inspiration for the spectacularly successful Lyon Diet Heart Trial, which reduced mortality in heart attack survivors by 55% over four years. This trial aimed at about 30% rather than 40% of total calories as fat and used rapeseed oil rather than olive oil: 40% of calories as fat is arguably too high an average intake for sedentary populations and makes it difficult to meet the recommendations on saturated and polyunsaturated fat intakes without greatly restricting food choices.

Mediterranean cooking has contributed much to the modern plant-based diet: pasta, rich tomato sauces, substantial salads, and bread with olive oil and garlic. Again, a few simple recipes are provided in chapter 14 to illustrate the possibilities and there are plenty of Mediterranean cookery books available. The Mediterranean model suits a moderate to high fat diet.

Life in the raw

A raw food diet usually entails at least 80% of food by weight being raw plant foods, with some people eating 100% raw. Many people report feeling healthier and more energetic on adopting such a diet, while others report the opposite.

In contrast with the Mediterranean and Japanese diets, there are too few long term raw food vegans for direct evaluation of raw vegan diets by comparison with other diets. We can, however, evaluate such diets against known human nutritional requirements to gain a better understanding of the ways in which appropriate raw plant-based diets could benefit health.

Raw diets include three key food groups: sweet fruit (including peppers and tomatoes), high fat plant foods, and green leafy vegetables. Raw food authorities differ in the proportions recommended: some suggest that 2% of calories from green leafy vegetables (equivalent to about 300 grams of lettuce per day) is sufficient, while others recommend that about 30% of calories should come from green vegetables. Similarly, recommendations on high fat foods such as avocados, olives, nuts, seeds and cold-pressed oils range from a few percent to about 40% of calories. The Hallelujah diet developed by George Malkmus puts special emphasis on carrot juice and barley grass, which contribute about 15% of calories.

Getting 30% of calories from green leafy vegetables is unrealistic for most people, even with the use of blended salads and juices. For instance, 900 grams of lettuce plus 450 grams of kale provides just 300 calories or about 15% of calories. Fortunately, however, such high intakes are unnecessary for nutritional adequacy and other green vegetables can also play a useful role.

Broccoli, peas and most green leafy vegetables contain higher levels of zinc, calcium and protein than most fruits and are therefore an important part of any raw diet, but about 500 grams per day of green vegetables, including a mixture of peas, broccoli, lettuce and darker leaves such as kale and spinach, is sufficient to bring mineral and protein intakes into line with general recommendations. These vegetables also provide vitamin K, which promotes healthy bones.

The best balance between sweet fruit and high fat plant foods is probably a matter of individual constitution. Some people also experience dental problems with a very high fruit intake, especially citrus fruit and dried fruit. This can be a major problem for young children. Many people will struggle to maintain weight if they do not include significant amounts of high fat foods and dried fruit.

Olives, avocados, almonds, hazel nuts and macadamias are all dominated by monounsaturated fats, which are the safest fats to consume in large quantities. Obtaining up to 40% of calories from these foods according to individual calorie needs should be perfectly healthful. It is also important to include a good source of omega-3 fats such as crushed flaxseed or its oil. Selenium can be low if food is grown in selenium deficient soil, so ten Brazil nuts a week would be a useful insurance policy (see chapter 10).

In selecting fruits, there is no need to rely on unusual or expensive items. Bananas are a good energy food, being relatively low in fibre and high in potassium. Oranges are rich in calcium, folate, potassium and vitamin C. The high potassium and low sodium content of raw vegan diets reduces the need for calcium by reducing calcium losses and can be expected also to reduce blood pressure and risk of stroke.

The various raw food dietary schools differ in their approach to vitamin B12. Some recommend that supplements should not be taken unless clear deficiency symptoms occur. David Wolfe (Nature's First Law) has suggested seven different claimed B12 sources, including unwashed or wild plants, nori, spirulina, fermented foods or a probiotic, with a B12 supplement as an alternative if these are not available. George Malkmus has recommended regular use of a B12 supplement since a study of Hallelujah dieters showed signs of inadequate B12 in most of them and further showed that a B12 supplement or *fortified* nutritional yeast (check ingredients, as many nutritional yeasts are not fortified) corrected this reliably while probiotics did not.

The confusion in this area arises from a conceptual error. Many raw food or natural hygiene advocates believe that our evolutionary diet and that of our great ape relatives did not include an external source of B12 and go on to conclude that humans should not need such a source either. In fact, all the other great apes – even the gorillas – consume insects and soil incidentally along with their normal diet of fruits, shoots, leaves and nuts. Chimpanzees show particular enthusiasm for collecting and eating termites. The blood B12 levels of most primates drop rapidly when they are fed on a hygienically grown and prepared plant-based diet. It is therefore not surprising that humans also need an external source of B12.

Many of the B12 sources suggested by David Wolfe have been directly tested and shown to be inadequate. Nori and spirulina failed to correct deficiency in macrobiotic children and did not maintain adequate blood B12 levels in a Finnish raw food community. Probiotics did not consistently correct low B12 availability in Hallelujah dieters. A UK raw food vegan went B12 deficient while growing his own food and eating it unwashed: based on measured B12 levels in soil, this is not at all surprising. Other suggested sources have not been tested so directly, but the only two published studies of B12 levels in raw food vegans both showed inadequate B12 levels.

As discussed in chapter 6, chlorella might be a *possible* source of B12, but until its effectiveness for humans has been tested directly it should not be relied upon.

The main argument for special desirability of high raw diets derives from comparison with our evolutionary diet and the diets of our great ape relatives. All the great apes eat diets centred on raw fruit (chimps, bonobos, orang-utans, lowland gorillas) or raw leaves (highland gorillas) and comprising a mixture of fruit (including large amounts of seeds), leaves, shoots, insects and often nuts. Use of cooked foods and large amounts of grain is unique to humans.

It is further suggested that a return to a diet more like that of our great ape relatives would bring great benefits to health as it is the diet to which evolution has adapted us. This is a plausible argument, and the nutrient content of such a diet matches modern nutritional knowledge in many ways: high folate, vitamin C, vitamin K, potassium and magnesium together with low saturated fat, cholesterol and sodium. However, there are important limitations to using the plant content of great ape diets as a model for modern humans.

First, insects are not plants and are a key source of B12 in most primate diets. As all B12 comes from bacteria, the absence of insect contamination of foods is readily compensated for by B12 produced by bacteria in commercial fermenters and used in supplements.

Secondly, human exposure to sunlight at high latitudes and when spending most of the day indoors is greatly reduced compared with our evolutionary exposure. During the UK winter, vitamin D from foods fortified with the vegan form (D2) can help to compensate for limited exposure to sunlight. A trip to sunnier climes during the winter would allow the vitamin D to be topped up more naturally. Infants are particularly vulnerable to vitamin D deficiency because of their high rate of bone building and should always receive a vitamin D supplement in winter. Breast milk is not an adequate source: we are designed to live nearer the equator.

Thirdly, the human gut is smaller overall than that of the other great apes and the human colon takes up just 20% of the digestive system compared with 50% in the other great apes. This results in a dramatically reduced ability to deal with fibre, indicating that humans are adapted to a lower fibre diet than the other great apes, who consume several hundred grams of fibre per day. Our Palaeolithic ancestors consumed around one hundred grams of fibre per day – equivalent to 5 kg (11 lb) of cherries or 10 kg (22 lb) of tomatoes. Simply copying the other great apes is therefore not an option.

There are various candidate explanations for this reduced capacity to deal with fibre, such as increased reliance on some combination of soft fruit, root vegetables and meat, or increased food processing.

The use of soft fruit is unlikely to have been the main factor as it would represent a restriction of the great ape diet rather than a diversification. Root vegetables are widely available and are lower in fibre than most wild fruits. Increased meat consumption probably started with homo erectus about 2 million years ago, but may only have become a major factor about 20,000 years ago with the development of more sophisticated hunting techniques.

All the great apes show some use of food processing. Chimps often use stones to crack nuts and will chew fibrous foods to remove the juice before discarding the fibre. The use of stone tools by our ancestors became common about two million years ago. Most forms of food processing would leave little trace, however, so it is difficult to verify how big a role such processing played. Nevertheless, it is plausible that food processing – including cooking – played a major part in the changes in the human digestive system compared with other great apes.

The smaller human gut reduces the calorie requirements of humans by about 10%, balancing the higher energy demands of our larger brain, which in turn makes sophisticated food processing possible. Humans may indeed have evolved in such a way as to rely on food processing.

Food processing destroys some nutrients and introduces some new compounds, but it can also inactivate toxins and increase the availability of other nutrients. Conservative cooking such as steaming or boiling causes only modest loss of some nutrients, such as folate, while enhancing the bioavailability of others, such as carotenoids. Lycopene, which appears to have profound protective effects on health, is better absorbed from cooked than from raw tomatoes. Liquidising or juicing also increases carotenoid availability from carrots, and lycopene from water melon is probably as well absorbed as lycopene from tomato juice. Cooking increases the calories available from starchy foods such as potatoes and grains and inactivates certain food toxins, thereby increasing the range of foods available to us.

Boiling or steaming does not generate significant amounts of suspect compounds, such as acrylamide and advanced glycation end products (AGEs), but cooking foods in the absence of water until they begin to brown or burn generates far more of these substances. The suggested adverse effects of such compounds from food are speculative rather than established, but cooking by boiling, steaming or short duration stir frying avoids the potential risk.

As noted earlier, the Okinawans in Japan make extensive use of cooked grains, sweet potatoes, vegetables and soya products and use little raw fruit, while the Cretans eat large amounts of bread and cook with olive oil, but there is no large group of long term raw food vegans to provide a direct comparison.

There is good direct evidence that large amounts of refined grains are associated with increased risk of heart disease and diabetes in Western populations. However, higher consumption of whole grains is associated with reduced risk of heart disease and diabetes, so the evidence suggests that grain should be consumed in unrefined (whole) form rather than eliminated altogether, at least for most people.

A few individuals have life-threatening adverse reactions to gluten (present in many grains, but notably absent from rice). The established effects of gluten range from allergic reactions and coeliac disease to varying degrees of digestive discomfort.

In addition, some individuals appear to metabolise gluten poorly, with high levels of opioid protein fragments appearing in their urine. This pattern, which also occurs with casein from animal milks, has been found in some studies to be more common in autistic and schizophrenic individuals, and symptoms sometimes improve on elimination of gluten and casein.

As a raw food diet is often a gluten free diet, it is possible that some of the people finding such diets particularly beneficial may be gluten intolerant in varying degrees.

Raw food has particular environmental advantages in that it often comes from trees (avoiding soil loss from tilling) and requires little packaging and no cooking. These characteristics benefit the health of the planet and all who share it. On the other hand, raw food often requires long distance transportation, and commercial banana production is an environmental disaster with high pesticide use affecting plantation workers and local rivers.

The trade-off is not clear cut. It is likely that local sourcing of cooked foods (e.g. Scottish oats) has the environmental edge over Jamaican bananas or airlifted strawberries, but seasonally available local fruits and nuts would have the edge over both.

One universally recognised effect of a high raw diet is weight loss, and many leading exponents of raw diets report being overweight on a conventional diet but achieving a desirable weight on switching to a raw vegan diet. This effect is no mystery, as raw plant foods are generally low calorie high fibre foods – ideal for weight loss, as was confirmed by a six-month trial in South Africa.

A common reason for abandoning raw food diets, however, is excessive weight loss, and a study of raw food eaters in Germany found underweight to be common, particularly with 100% raw diets. Including sufficient tropical fruits such as bananas and avocados, or nuts and seeds and cold-pressed oils, may be necessary to maintain a healthy weight once any desired weight loss has been achieved.

Immoderate use of carrot juice may lead to excessive absorption of carotenoids, which may lead to cessation of menstruation and ovulation in some premenopausal women as well as a disconcerting yellow-orange skin pigmentation, particularly in areas of hard skin.

The German survey of raw food eaters found that half the premenopausal women on 100% raw food diets had stopped menstruating, though this was strongly related to being underweight. Some raw food advocates suggest that the cessation of menstruation is a desirable consequence of a raw food diet, but overt menstruation is observed in chimpanzees and many old world monkeys as well as in humans.

Raw food diets which do not include sufficient green vegetables or other foods relatively high in sodium, such as celery, may lead to sodium deficiency. While increased carotenoid intake and reduced sodium intake are both recommended, either can be taken too far.

Increasing the consumption of raw fruits, nuts and salad vegetables considerably beyond current average intakes can be expected to benefit individual health and also the environment if locally produced. However, evidence to date does not justify a general recommendation of raw food diets in the sense of more than 80% of food being consumed raw – particularly for children, who need a relatively high calorie density.

Fusion

There is, of course, no necessity to adopt any of these specific models, all of which can meet the overall recommendations of this book: a mix and match approach has much to commend it.

The traditional Japanese diet is low in fruit and high in sodium. Adding a breakfast of raw fruit to a Japanese style diet could enhance both quality and variety.

The Cretan diet is arguably too dependent on olive oil due to local circumstances, and the wild salad vegetables which may have boosted their omega-3 intake are not widely available. Flaxseed (linseed), nuts and rapeseed oil could enrich the range of fat sources in the Cretan diet while providing more accessible sources of omega-3 fatty acids.

Mixing Japanese and Mediterranean styles leads one naturally to a moderate overall fat intake, while emphasising raw fruit and vegetables enhances nutrient intake and variety.

So long as the diet conforms with the overall recommendations in chapter 15, it will support good health. Within those overall recommendations, there are an infinite number of variants to match individual needs and preferences. Chapter 14 provides a few example recipes to illustrate this.

Putting it into practice

Moderate use of alcohol – one unit per day for women and one to two units per day for men – is likely to benefit health. If you can't stick to moderate use, however, it is best avoided altogether.

Raw food diets have the potential to support good health, if carefully constructed and a reliable B12 supplement included. Care is needed to ensure adequate protein and sodium and sufficient calorie density, especially for the very old and the very young.

Traditional Cretan and modern Japanese diets have a proven track record in supporting good health.

The Japanese diet would benefit from less salt and more fruit.

The Cretan diet would benefit from a greater variety of fats, such as nuts, flaxseed (linseed) and rapeseed (canola) in addition to the healthy staple olive oil. For more sedentary individuals, fat should be about 25% to 30% of total calories rather than the 40% typical of highly active Cretan farmers.

Chapter 14

Foods and recipes

The foods and recipes suggested in this chapter are easily prepared simple fare, suitable for home cooking. There are many recipe books available (see www.vegansociety.com/shop) and the International Vegetarian Union provides thousands of plant-based recipes from around the world at www.ivu.org/recipes.

Asian

Soya milk, tofu, roasted soya beans and natto

These are the main forms of traditional soya bean use in Japan. Natto, formed by fermenting soya beans, is a particularly rich source of vitamin K, but it is not widely available outside Japan and requires a special starter culture. The other foods are much more commonly available and can also be made quite easily from soya beans. Roasted soya beans, sometimes referred to as soya bean nuts, are a common snack in Japan but are not yet common in other countries.

Soya can also be fermented to make condiments such as miso and soy sauce. These are not easy to make at home but are widely available commercially. Some brands are high in salt, so read the labels carefully and do not use large quantities on a regular basis.

Nori rolls

Nori is a widely used seaweed in Japan. Its iodine content is variable, but not high, so excess iodine consumption is not a concern even at an ounce (28 grams) a week. However, it should not be relied upon as a source of iodine. It is usually sold in thin rectangular sheets.

Some people eat nori by itself as a snack, often toasting the sheet lightly first. More commonly, the sheet is used as a wrapper for a roll with short grain sticky rice and raw or stir-fried vegetables. Vinegar, sugar, soy sauce, miso or ginger can all be added to the rice as flavourings just after cooking.

Lay a sheet of nori on a plate or cutting board. Cover evenly with a cup of rice, pressing the rice firmly on to the nori, but leave the edge of the sheet furthest from you uncovered. Add the vegetables to the centre of the roll and carefully roll the nori sheet starting from the end nearest you. Wetting the far end can help seal the roll. The roll is then cut into slices to serve as a starter or as a main course.

Nori has been claimed to be a source of vitamin B12, but large amounts of dried nori (40 grams per day) have been shown to induce signs of B12 *deficiency* in healthy human volunteers. In normal culinary amounts it should cause no problems.

Lentil dahl

Dahls are a staple of many Indian diets and vary in consistency from a thin soup to a thick paste. They are usually made with small legumes such as lentils, mung beans or chick peas.

Dahls are infinitely variable in spices and accompanying vegetables, but the following example illustrates the basic approach:

    300 grams (12 ounces) Puy or other lentils
    2 to 4 tablespoons olive or rapeseed (canola) oil
    300 grams (12 ounces) carrots
    200 grams (8 ounces) onions
    2 to 4 teaspoons garam masala
    2 to 4 teaspoons dried coriander

Chop the onions and carrots and fry them gently in the oil for a few minutes with the garam masala. Add the lentils, coriander and boiling water. Bring to the boil and simmer until the lentils are soft.

If the lentils are soaked for a few hours, cooking time is reduced from about an hour to about 30 minutes. Adding the water in stages whenever the mixture looks too dry allows more precise control of the final consistency if a thicker dahl is preferred.

To improve zinc availability, soak the lentils for at least six hours and then drain them. Place them in a covered container away from direct sunshine and leave them for twelve hours to start to sprout.

If full sprouting is desired, the lentils should be rinsed once or twice a day and allowed to grow for two to three days. Green lentils and mung beans are exceptionally easy to sprout. Overnight (eight hour) soaking is suitable for most seeds, though larger seeds such as chick peas should be soaked for longer.

Mango chutney, vegan naan bread (most naan includes milk or yoghurt, so check the label carefully) and rice are good complements to the dahl. Soya yoghurt is also a good accompaniment and can be prepared as a raita by mixing with grated cucumber and cumin or mint. A side salad including some vegetables rich in vitamin C such as sweet peppers also goes well with this dish.

Mediterranean

Wholemeal bread

The basic ingredients for a large wholemeal loaf are 450 grams (one pound) of wholemeal bread flour, 300 millilitres (half a pint) of water, a teaspoon of salt, one to three teaspoons of dried yeast, one to two tablespoons of oil, and one to two tablespoons of sugar. The nutritional quality of the bread can be greatly enhanced by some simple variations.

About 10% (45 grams) of the flour can be replaced with ground flaxseed (linseed). This makes the bread a good source of well absorbed omega-3 fatty acids. The baking does not significantly damage the omega-3s but does break down cyanogenic glycosides in the flaxseed, which can be harmful in very large doses. Flaxseed adds a pleasant flavour to the bread.

Ordinary salt (sodium chloride) can be replaced by a low sodium salt in which about two thirds of the sodium chloride is replaced by potassium chloride. Though no substitute for potassium from foods, it is a beneficial alternative to sodium chloride. Using ordinary salt in this recipe would give about 0.3 grams of sodium per 100 grams of bread – compared with 0.5 to 0.6 grams per 100 grams in typical commercial breads. Using low sodium salt (a mixture of sodium chloride and potassium chloride) would give about 0.12 grams of sodium per 100 grams. The ideal daily intake of sodium is probably between 1 and 1.5 grams, while typical intakes are over 3 grams. Reducing the sodium content of bread goes a long way towards closing the gap between typical and ideal sodium consumption.

Kelp (kombu), a useful source of iodine, can also be added to the bread mix in very small amounts. A pinch of ground kelp (about a tenth of a teaspoon) *per week* is all that is needed to meet iodine needs. If preferred, the kelp can be ground and mixed with low sodium salt to make it easier to add the appropriate small amounts. A teaspoon of ground kelp (3 grams) mixed with 10 teaspoons of salt would give 0.3 grams of kelp (about 1000 micrograms of iodine) per loaf, so a loaf or two per week would comfortably meet iodine needs without risk of excess.

A tablespoon of any variety of vinegar mixed with the water helps the loaf to rise and also breaks down phytates, thus improving absorption of zinc and iron from the wheat. If baking instructions allow for a slow or a fast baking method, the slow method should be preferred so as to enhance breakdown of phytates.

Garlic bread

Garlic bread is traditionally made with olive oil, though restaurants in English-speaking countries often use butter – so take care when eating out.

For best effect, the garlic should be finely chopped or crushed through a garlic press. It can then be left to soak in the olive oil overnight to develop the flavour. Alternatively, gentle frying will rapidly develop the flavour.

If baking rather than frying the garlic bread, place the slices on a baking tray and add a liberal amount of the garlic oil. Ten minutes at a moderate heat (gas mark 2 or 150 degrees centigrade) is enough to warm the bread thoroughly and allow the oil to soak through.

Mixed salad

Salads have an endless variety. Aim for a mixture of colours and textures with at least one leafy vegetable and one other brightly coloured vegetable. Many vegetables which are more usually cooked, such as beetroot, broccoli, cauliflower and carrots, can be grated and included in salads. Spring onions (scallions) and herbs such as coriander enhance the flavour. Chopped nuts such as walnuts, almonds and cashews can be added. Fresh and dried fruit such as raisins and grated apple can also be included.

Salad dressings are as varied as the salads themselves, but the basic "French" dressing is a good starting point for experimentation. Mix three parts of olive or rapeseed (canola) oil with one part of wine or cider vinegar, add ground black pepper and mustard to taste and shake vigorously. This dressing keeps very well. Alternatively, a squeeze of fresh lemon juice takes a lot of beating.

Raw

Avocado salad

Avocado is a good base for a salad, providing an alternative to an oil based dressing. Avocados are best stored at room temperature until just slightly soft to the touch. If the avocado is perfectly ripe, the stone will be easy to remove and the flesh will be green or yellow with no brown or black patches.

The avocado should be chopped coarsely and mixed with other raw fruits and vegetables. Lemon juice makes a good dressing and also prevents discoloration. Avocados mix well with light crunchy vegetables such as peppers, tomatoes, carrots and sprouted seeds.

Banana smoothie

Not everyone enjoys plain fruit as a snack or dessert, but most people enjoy "smoothies". Combine bananas and other soft fruits such as berries with fruit juice and liquidise in a blender. Frozen bananas give a pleasant texture. Mangos are a good alternative to bananas when in season.

Fruit salad

Fruit salad makes an excellent start to the day. The gentle softness of bananas combines well with the crunchiness of apples and the sharp sweetness of oranges. Seasonal berries and cherries further enhance the mix.

Muesli

Fruit salad also goes well with home made raw muesli. Commercial rolled oats are not raw, due to the heat used in the processing, but home rolled oat groats or sprouted grains can be used instead. Chopped nuts, dried fruit and crushed seeds, such as flaxseed (linseed), hempseed and pumpkin seed, are all good ingredients.

Fusion

One of the advantages of modern society is the opportunity to sample many different styles of food and pick and mix according to personal preference. The two dishes that follow illustrate the potential of this approach.

Tomato and tofu sauce with pasta

Rich tomato sauces are a classic Mediterranean dish while tofu is typically Asian. The two combine to give a delicious and nourishing sauce to eat with pasta and salad and, if you wish, a glass of red wine. The following recipe serves three to four people.

> One large jar (700 grams or 24 ounces) of
> sugocasa (sweet chopped tomatoes)
> Two tablespoons dried basil
> Two to four tablespoons olive oil or rapeseed (canola) oil
> 200 to 300 grams (8 to 12 ounces) firm tofu
> About four tablespoons nutritional yeast (e.g. Engevita)

Heat the oil until very hot but not smoking and immediately add the sugocasa and basil. Allow to bubble fairly rapidly for three or four minutes. Mash the tofu with a fork and add it to the tomato base along with the nutritional yeast. Simmer gently for a couple of minutes and serve with salad and pasta.

Freshly ground black pepper is the perfect seasoning for this dish. The sauce freezes well.

Note that most nutritional yeasts available in the UK, such as Engevita, do not contain vitamin B12 as it is not added to this yeast culture. If relying on nutritional yeast or yeast extracts for vitamin B12, always check for cobalamin as an ingredient.

Gram flour "Spanish omelette"

Thick egg omelettes filled with chopped potatoes, onions, peppers and other vegetables are a classic Spanish dish. Gram flour (chick pea) pancakes are a common dish in parts of India. This recipe combines the two ideas to give a novel variation. The quantities given serve two as a main dish with salad. A wide variety of vegetables including tomatoes, cabbage, leeks and spinach can also be used.

> 200 grams (8 ounces) gram flour
> 300 millilitres (half a pint) water
> 100 grams (4 ounces) chopped peppers
> 100 grams (4 ounces) finely chopped potatoes
> 100 grams (4 ounces) onions
> Two to four tablespoons olive or rapeseed oil

Lightly fry the vegetables in the oil.

Slowly add the water to the gram flour and mix with a fork or whisk. It is best to form a thick paste first and then dilute this with extra water to get a smooth consistency.

Add the gram flour paste to the vegetables and cook over a low heat shaking the pan occasionally to avoid sticking. Turning the mixture over can be a bit tricky – you may need to turn it on to a plate or use a spatula and turn it in sections. Alternatively, an omelette cooker can be used, avoiding the need for turning.

For a lighter, fluffier texture, mix the gram flour paste with mashed potato. Cooked spinach gives a particularly light texture.

Thai sweet chilli sauce goes very well with this dish and helps to avoid any need for added salt. A raw salad with a variety of flavours and textures is a healthy and colourful accompaniment.

Happy eating!

Chapter 15

Summary of recommendations

The number of different aspects of diet affecting health may seem intimidating, but the key recommendations converge into a fairly simple and unrestrictive set of guiding principles.

Physical activity

First, it is important to emphasise the benefits of combining healthy eating with adequate physical activity. The removal of the need for physical activity by modern technology is a mixed blessing: it can lead to so little activity that feedback mechanisms which would normally help avoid obesity and limit bone loss cease to work reliably. Physical activity helps to maintain a healthy weight, reduces the adverse effects of excess weight, improves cholesterol profile and blood sugar control and strengthens bones. It also increases nutrient intakes by allowing more food to be eaten without unwanted weight gain.

Unless physical activity is an integral part of ordinary daily life, a deliberate effort should be made to walk or run at least 20 miles a week or achieve an equivalent level of activity. Three miles cycling or half a mile swimming is roughly equivalent to one mile on foot.

Healthy weight

While physical activity is vital to maintaining a healthy weight, diet also has a major impact. Body mass index (BMI) measures weight relative to height. It is calculated as weight in kilograms divided twice by height in metres. For instance, a person weighing 63 kilograms (140 pounds or 10 stone) who is 1.7 metres (5 foot 7 inches) tall would have a BMI of 22 (63 divided by 1.7 and again by 1.7). A BMI between 18.5 and 25 is desirable for most people – death rates increase both below and above this range. See chapter 4 for tables of body mass index in relation to height and weight.

If your body mass index is below 18.5 (e.g. weight less than 119 lb – 8 st 7 lb – or 54 kilograms for a person 5 foot 7 inches or 1.7 metres tall), increase the calorie density of your food by eating more low fibre foods that are high in fat and carbohydrate. Make sure that nutritious calorie dense foods are always accessible to respond to mild hunger. Nuts, dried fruit and bananas are good snacks. Adding extra olive oil to stews or other dishes should also help.

If your body mass index is above 25 (e.g. weight greater than 161 lb – 11 stone 7 lb – or 73 kilograms for a person 5 foot 7 inches or 1.7 metres tall) and you are not naturally heavily built, decrease the calorie density of your food by eating more fruit and vegetables high in water and fibre. Restrict the accessibility of calorie dense foods by limiting the amount you have easily available. Oranges, apples and similar fruits are good snacks.

Brightly coloured fruit and vegetables

Increasing consumption of brightly coloured fruits and vegetables, including some green leafy vegetables or broccoli, brings a wide range of health benefits only partly explained by their antioxidants, folate, vitamin K, vitamin C, fibre and potassium and by their low calorie density.

There is no need to live exclusively on such foods: a pound (450 grams) a day is sufficient to deliver the known benefits. Spinach, broccoli, carrots, peppers, tomatoes, beetroot and oranges are excellent representatives of this food group and are generally available at reasonable cost. **Eat at least two pounds of green leafy vegetables or broccoli and a pound of carrots each week.**

Vitamin B12

Vegetables, legumes and other whole plant foods provide plenty of folate, which is the first key to avoiding elevated homocysteine – a major risk factor for ill health, including heart disease. If folate is plentiful, vitamin B12 becomes the weakest link in the homocysteine chain. A reliable source of B12 is vital, with B12 from fortified foods and chewed supplements being particularly well absorbed.

All animals get their B12 from bacteria. Most grazing animals have multiple stomachs which contain bacteria that produce B12. Animals with a single stomach, including humans and all the great apes, obtain B12 from external sources including dirt and insect contamination of their food. These sources are neither practical nor desirable in our modern sanitised world. Fortunately, B12 is now conveniently harvested from bacteria through fermentation reactions and collected for use in fortified foods and supplements.

Aim for at least three micrograms of B12 per day from fortified foods or get at least ten micrograms per day from a supplement (see chapter 6). Chewing the supplement is important to ensure good absorption. Higher dose supplements may be useful for those with absorption problems due to low levels of intrinsic factor and for those who take supplements infrequently: about 2000 micrograms per week is appropriate in these circumstances.

Calcium balance

The balance between loss of calcium from the body and absorption of calcium from food is central to reducing the risk of bone thinning, high blood pressure and stroke, and may also reduce the risk of obesity. The ideal mineral intakes to improve calcium balance are plenty of potassium, calcium and magnesium and limited sodium.

Unrefined plant foods are rich in potassium and magnesium, in contrast to refined foods such as white bread and sugar. Unless refined foods are a major part of the diet, potassium and magnesium intakes will be good; if plenty of fruit, vegetables and legumes are eaten, potassium intake will be excellent.

Relying on calcium alone to protect bone health is like fielding a football team with only strikers and no defenders. Nevertheless, calcium remains an important part of the team. Intake of absorbable calcium from a plant-based diet can be very high if large amounts of dark green leafy vegetables such as spring greens (collards) and kale are eaten or if calcium fortified foods are used. It can also be undesirably low, however, if the diet is centred on grains or modern cultivated fruits (oranges are an exception and a useful source of calcium). If a further boost to calcium is desired, supplements are preferable to dairy products as they come without the unhealthy saturated fat that inevitably accompanies dairy production and will find its way into the food supply one way or another.

Sodium intake is driven mainly by the use of processed foods with salt already included and to a lesser extent by the addition of salt at the table. Replacing home use of salt with a low sodium alternative and using low sodium bread (see recipe in chapter 14) is usually enough to bring average sodium intake down to a desirable level – 1 to 1.5 grams per day.

Fats

Balancing fat intake is vital for health. Moving to a more plant-based diet cuts down on the main sources of saturated fats: milk fat contains more than 60% saturates and meat fats contain between 30% and 45% saturates. Low saturated fat intake is a key advantage of a plant-based diet, so long as it does not include large amounts of tropical oils or chocolate.

Trans fats produced by hydrogenation are even more dangerous than saturated fats, but are usually consumed in much smaller amounts. Products containing hydrogenated or trans fats should be avoided. Deep fried foods such as chips (French fries) should be limited, as the cooking oils used are often hydrogenated or highly saturated and prolonged heating creates toxic byproducts. Unhydrogenated palm oil or groundnut (peanut) oil is best for deep frying.

To get the full health benefits from fats, it is important to consume adequate amounts of both omega-6 and omega-3 polyunsaturates. While it is difficult not to get enough omega-6 on a plant-based diet, it is easy to get too much omega-6 (linoleic acid) relative to omega-3 (alpha-linolenic acid). Replacing high omega-6 oils such as sunflower, soya, safflower and corn oil with oils rich in monounsaturates such as olive oil and rapeseed (canola) oil is the most important step to avoiding excessive omega-6 consumption. Moving from sunflower and sesame seeds to almonds, cashews and pumpkin seeds further reduces omega-6 intake. A teaspoon of flaxseed (linseed) oil (or one and a half tablespoons of ground flaxseed) per day or a tablespoon of hempseed oil (or five tablespoons of hempseed), or one and a half tablespoons of rapeseed oil, completes the picture by boosting omega-3s. Better still, freshly ground seeds can be added to muesli or home baked bread. Blended oils with added sunflower or other cheap oils provide less omega-3s for the same or greater cost.

Regular moderate amounts of nuts – about an ounce (28 grams) a day – are recommended for health. About 25% to 30% of calories from fat is probably ideal for most people, though the optimum for individuals may vary over a wider range. On a lower fat diet, it is important to check that the ratio of total cholesterol to HDL cholesterol has not been significantly increased due to the decrease in fat and to make sure that weight does not drift to undesirably low levels. In general, only adopt a low fat diet (less than 25% of total calories) for health reasons if it helps to maintain a healthy weight and does not increase the ratio of total to HDL cholesterol by more than 0.5.

Those who prefer a higher fat diet but find their weight creeping up should increase physical activity, reduce calorie intake and increase fibre intake. This will not necessarily require a reduction in fat intake: eating more fruits and vegetables reduces overall calorie density in a healthy way, and replacing oils with nuts, pumpkin seeds, olives and avocados boosts intake of fibre and many useful nutrients.

A mixture of almonds, cashews, macadamias, hazel nuts (filberts), avocados and olive and rapeseed oil provides an ideal base for a moderate to high fat diet as all are rich in monounsaturated fats.

Vitamin D, iodine and selenium

Many people live too far from the equator to maintain ideal vitamin D stores in winter, and many live on land lacking in iodine or selenium. Along with the absence of vitamin B12 in hygienically processed plant foods, this means that we cannot assume that simply eating a wide variety of foods will meet our needs for all these nutrients.

To ensure that these needs are met, therefore, *either:*

Make a point of getting frequent *short* periods of sunlight exposure of as much skin as possible in the autumn while the sun is still at least 40 degrees above the horizon (your shadow should not be much longer than you are) and take a mid-winter holiday nearer the equator if this is a feasible and acceptable option (vitamin D).

Consume 15 to 30 grams (half to one ounce) of kelp (kombu) in small amounts over a year (iodine).

Eat about 10 Brazil nuts a week (selenium).

Get at least 3 micrograms a day of vitamin B12 from fortified foods or 10 micrograms from a supplement. All B12 supplements should be chewed.

Alternatively, take a daily supplement including :

- 20 micrograms vitamin D2
- 150 micrograms iodine
- 100 micrograms selenium (as selenium methionine)
- 10 micrograms vitamin B12 (cobalamin)

Avoid supplements containing more than 700 micrograms of retinol (vitamin A).

Protein, iron and zinc

It is easy to meet protein, iron and zinc needs entirely from plant foods, but it is worth following some simple guidelines to ensure that these requirements are comfortably met.

To boost protein intake in the young and the old, choose nuts over oils, wheat over rice, and include moderate amounts of legumes (beans, peas and lentils). Eat a wide variety of plant foods.

To ensure good iron stores, follow a varied mostly wholefood diet and include fruit and vegetables rich in vitamin C with most meals: oranges, peppers, dark green leafy vegetables, broccoli and cauliflower are all good choices.

To ensure good zinc stores, follow a varied mostly wholefood diet with unsprouted whole grains mostly consumed as breads made with yeast or sourdough, and with beans and lentils soaked thoroughly and sometimes sprouted (see chapter 14).

From birth to old age

Contrary to popular belief, nutritional needs do not vary dramatically from weaning to old age. There are, however, important differences in emphasis:

- Young children need more calorie dense foods and less fibre than adults. A tablespoon a day of olive oil or rapeseed (canola) oil mixed with other foods, plus a cup of soya milk, will boost calories and protein without unduly increasing fibre.

- Nutrient quality is especially important shortly before conception and during pregnancy and breast feeding, when vitamin B12, folate, vitamin D, iodine, selenium and omega-3 fatty acids are particularly vital.

- Older adults need to focus on quality of food intake to make up for declining quantity. They should also try to avoid undesired loss (or gain) of weight.

Alcohol

Moderate alcohol use – 1 unit per day for women and 1 to 2 units per day for men – is likely to benefit health. If you can't stick to moderate use, however, it is best avoided altogether.

The way ahead

These guidelines are easy to put into practice and leave plenty of room for choice to suit every individual. There is no need to go to extremes to get the benefits of a healthy diet. If your day to day diet follows the principles outlined in this chapter, there is no need to worry about occasional indulgences or deviations. Moderation has much to commend it and moderate improvements to your diet addressing the range of issues covered in this book will more reliably improve your health than taking any measure to the extreme.

Enjoy a varied and delicious plant-based diet to the benefit of your own health, other people, animals and the environment, and enjoy all that life has to offer.

Appendix 1: A model for calcium balance

Each extra millimole (mmol) of sodium in the urine is associated with 0.01 extra mmol of calcium in the urine (Massey, 1996). About 95% of dietary sodium is excreted in the urine. Short term metabolic loading studies in which sodium intake is deliberately manipulated show a slightly weaker effect, and cross-sectional studies of free-living populations tend to show a slightly stronger effect. A large cross-sectional study (Ho, 2001) found a coefficient of 0.014 rather than 0.01. Overall, a reasonable approximation is given by

$$\Delta UCa \text{ (mmol)} = 0.01 \times \Delta NaCl \text{ (mmol)} \qquad 1$$

where ΔUCa is the change in urinary calcium and ΔNa is the change in dietary sodium chloride.

The effect of protein intake on urinary calcium loss is also well established (Barzel, 1998; Heaney, 1998; Weaver, 1999). The effect is proportional to the sulphur content of cysteine and methionine in the diet (though not to the sulphur content of taurine, which is often excreted intact) and is equivalent to about 0.1 mmol of urinary calcium loss for each mmol of sulphur (S) consumed in the diet in the form of methionine or cysteine. That is

$$\Delta UCa \text{ (mmol)} = 0.1 \times \Delta S \text{ (mmol)} \qquad 2$$
$$S \text{ (mmol)} = \text{cysteine (g)} \times 8.3 + \text{methionine (g)} \times 6.7 \qquad 3$$

Heaney (1998) confirms that this effect is seen in observations of the general population. As each gram of protein in a typical diet contributes about 0.275 mmol of sulphur, the predicted effect of one gram of protein would be a calcium loss of 0.0275 mmol (1.1 mg). While the effect of protein on urinary calcium loss varies with the average sulphur content of the protein, a useful approximation is

$$\Delta UCa \text{ (mg)} = 1.1 \times \Delta \text{protein (grams)} \qquad 4$$

That is, each additional gram of protein leads to an extra milligram of calcium being lost in the urine.

Some authors consider the effect of sulphur to be due to the acid created when sulphur-containing amino acids are metabolised (2 mmol of acid for each mmol of sulphate). This is made more plausible by the observation that adding potassium bicarbonate (KHCO3) to the diet decreases the urinary calcium excretion. However, the extent of the decrease should be 0.05 mmol of calcium per mmol of bicarbonate if both effects are operating through the mechanism of net acid excretion. Lemann (1993) provides a very pertinent summary of short term metabolic loading tests:

$$\Delta UCa \ (mmol) = -0.015 \times \Delta KHCO3 \ (mmol) \qquad\qquad 5$$
$$\Delta UCa \ (mmol) = \ 0.0 \times \Delta NaHCO3 \ (mmol) \qquad\qquad 6$$
$$\Delta UCa \ (mmol) = -0.005 \times \Delta KCl \ (mmol) \qquad\qquad 7$$

The effect of bicarbonate salts is much less than would be expected if the influence of protein is due entirely to the acid it produces, and the effect of bicarbonate varies markedly depending on whether it is accompanied by sodium or potassium. The effects of sulphate from protein and the effects of bicarbonate salts therefore need to be modelled separately. The effect of other alkaline salts such as citrate is the same as bicarbonate salts.

In typical modern diets, sodium usually comes in the form of sodium chloride and potassium usually comes in the form of potassium bicarbonate or an equivalent alkali salt such as potassium citrate. Calcium loss increases by 0.01 mmol per mmol of sodium chloride, i.e. by 17 mg of calcium per gram of sodium. Calcium loss increases by 0.015 mmol per mmol of potassium bicarbonate, i.e. by 15 mg of calcium per gram of potassium. The effects are similar enough to justify combining them as a single effect based on the difference between sodium and potassium intake in grams:

$$\Delta UCa \ (mg) = 0.016 \times \Delta(Na \ (mg) - K \ (mg) \ ) \qquad\qquad 8$$

Sodium, potassium, bicarbonate and protein have not been found to affect either gut losses of calcium or losses in sweat, so the effect on urinary loss appears to be the net effect on calcium losses from the body. This is in contrast to phosphorus, which decreases urinary losses while increasing gut losses with no overall effect on calcium loss (Heaney, 1994).

To complete the model, the relationship between calcium absorption and dietary calcium intake needs to be quantified. Heaney (2000) notes that the average fractional absorption is given by:

Calcium fraction absorbed =

$$0.22 \times (\text{daily calcium in grams})^{(-0.44)} \qquad\qquad 10$$

Gonnelli (2001) presents a similar relationship, but with slightly lower absorption at all intakes and a more rapid decline in absorption as intake increases – about $0.18 \times (\text{daily calcium in grams})^{(-0.6)}$ for men and $0.155 \times (\text{daily calcium in grams})^{(-0.66)}$ for women. Agnusdei (1998) indicates a fractional absorption of $0.19 \times (\text{daily calcium in grams})^{(-0.54)}$.

The relationship:

Calcium fraction absorbed =

$$0.22 \times (\text{daily calcium in grams})^{(-0.5)} =$$

$$7 \times (\text{daily calcium in milligrams})^{(-0.5)} \qquad\qquad 11$$

or equivalently:

Calcium absorbed (milligrams) =

$$7 \times (\text{daily calcium in milligrams})^{(0.5)} =$$

$$7 \times \sqrt{(\text{Calcium intake})} \qquad\qquad 12$$

can be expected to be a good approximation. However, as calcium intake increases so do urinary losses of calcium and endogenous faecal losses (loss of calcium from the gut without reabsorption). This means that the *net* absorption of calcium is less than the gross absorption indicated in equation 12.

Recker (1977) examined the effect of calcium carbonate supplementation on calcium balance in women with an average age of 57. As calcium intake rose from 530 mg to 1480 mg per day, calcium balance rose by 72 mg and calcium absorption by 108 mg. The predicted calcium absorption for the change in intake is 7 x ($\sqrt{1480}$ - $\sqrt{530}$) or 108 mg – an excellent match. However, about a third of the absorbed calcium disappears as increased losses reduce *net* absorption by one third compared with gross absorption.

The following equation will therefore be used to define the typical net absorption of calcium, while the increased losses associated with absorbed calcium will be ignored in calculating the calcium losses.

$$\text{\textit{Net} calcium absorbed} =$$
$$5 \times \sqrt{\text{calcium intake}} \qquad\qquad 14$$

The final element for computing the calcium balance is an estimate of calcium losses when all the dietary drivers (calcium, sodium, potassium and protein) are zero. Trial and error comparison with known variations in total calcium losses indicates 2.0 mmol (80 mg) per day to be appropriate.

The overall expression for the calcium balance is therefore

$$\text{Calcium balance (mg)} = 5 \times \sqrt{\text{calcium intake (mg)}}$$
$$+ \ 0.016 \times (\text{potassium intake (mg) - sodium intake (mg))}$$
$$- \ 1.1 \times \text{protein (g)} - 80 \qquad\qquad 15$$

When data on cysteine or methionine content are available, the effect of protein should be calculated more precisely, using equations 2 and 3 rather than the protein term in the equation 15.

The effect of individual foods on calcium balance can be evaluated by assuming an appropriate net fractional absorption for the range of calcium intakes being considered and evaluating the change in calcium balance due to the mineral and amino acid content of the food. For calcium intakes around 700 milligrams, the expected net fractional absorption is 5 / 2/ $\sqrt{700}$ – i.e. 0.095.

In calculating calcium balances for the food tables provided in chapter 7, food composition data were taken from the US Department of Agriculture nutritional database (USDA, 2002).

Calcium bioavailability in plants was adjusted where good data were available. The available calcium in high oxalate plants (spinach, rhubarb, Swiss chard) was reduced by 80% compared with their nominal content (Weaver, 1997). Kale, broccoli and Chinese cabbage had available calcium increased by 10% (Weaver, 1997; Benway 1993; Weaver, 1999). Soya beans and soya milk had their calcium bioavailability reduced by 25%, while other beans had their bioavailability reduced by 50% (Weaver, 1993). The bioavailability of calcium from other foods, including tofu, was not adjusted.

Application of the model to dairy products

One of the most thorough studies of the effect of milk supplementation is Recker (1985). This study examined the effect on calcium balance of adding 24 ounces (670 grams) of milk to the diet of 13 postmenopausal women. Calcium balance was measured one year after supplementation commenced and compared with control subjects who did not receive extra milk. The one year interval is vital, as it allows the bone remodelling transient to decay and the body's adaptation mechanisms to operate, so the measured balance should reflect the long term effect (Heaney, 2001).

Calcium intake increased from 680 mg per day to 1470 mg per day. The observed effect on calcium balance relative to a control group was an improvement of 45 mg per day. Using equation 15, the predicted effect on calcium balance of an extra 670 grams of cow's milk, starting from an initial intake of 680 mg per day, is 51 mg per day – a good match. If the change in calcium intake had been accomplished using calcium carbonate, the predicted change in balance would have been 62 mg. The difference reflects the losses associated with the milk and confirms the validity of the model for predicting the effect of dairy products on calcium balance.

It is also noteworthy that after allowance for calcium losses in sweat (about 50 mg per day), which were not considered in this study, the extra milk changed the overall calcium balance from a loss of 110 mg per day to a loss of 65 mg per day. Increased calcium consumption from dairy products up to the highest recommended intake therefore failed to prevent a net loss of calcium in these postmenopausal women. Nonetheless, the 40% reduction in loss observed is a significant improvement. No significant difference in bone density between the high dairy group and the control group was noted – possibly reflecting less accurate measurements at the time of the study than are now available.

Heaney (1998) argues that increased losses are of limited importance when calcium intakes are high, as the body will successfully increase calcium absorption from the gut to compensate for increased losses. There is some truth in this, in as much as the body can balance increased losses either by absorbing more calcium from the gut or by absorbing more calcium from bone. The success of the model in equation 15 in predicting the results of Recker (1985) indicates that the ability to compensate for increased losses by increased absorption of calcium from the gut is limited in postmenopausal women and that increased losses due to components of milk other than calcium are still reflected directly in reduced balance after a year of adaptation. Recker (1985) observes that "examination of the correlation between protein intake and calcium balance with calcium intake held constant showed a reasonably strong negative correlation". Increased protein intake was also associated with increased bone resorption after adjustment for calcium intake.

At least for postmenopausal women, therefore, the degree of adaptation appears to be limited, even at high calcium intakes, and the model predictions of the net effect of foods on calcium balance appear to be valid.

List of figures

7. Balancing calcium

8. Fats for health

9. Fat wars

11. Unnecessary fears

References

3. Healthy life expectancy

World Health Organisation reports

WHO (2003a): The World Health Report 2002, World Health Organisation, www.who.int/whr/2002/en.

WHO (2003b): Diet, nutrition and the prevention of chronic disease, 2003, WHO Technical Report Series 916 www.who.int/hpr/NPH/docs/who_fao_expert_report.pdf.

Food supply data

apps.fao.org/page/collections?subset=nutrition

Mortality and inequality

Sen (1999): Amartya Sen, *Development as Freedom,* 1999, Oxford University Press.

Plant-based diets and environmental issues

Beckett and Oltjen (1993): J L Beckett and J W Oltjen, *Journal of Animal Science*, 1993; 71: 818-826, Estimation of the water requirements for beef production in the United States.

Gerbens-Leenes (2002): P W Gerbens-Leenes et al., *Agriculture, Ecosystems & Environment,* 2002; 90: 47-58, A method to determine land requirements relating to food consumption patterns.

Comparisons of vegetarian and non-vegetarian mortality

Appleby (2002): Paul N Appleby et al., *Public Health Nutrition*, 2002; 5: 29-36, Mortality in British vegetarians.

Fraser (1999): Gary E Fraser, *American Journal of Clinical Nutrition*, 1999; 70: 532S-538S, Associations between diet and cancer, ischemic heart disease, and all-cause mortality in non-Hispanic white Seventh-day Adventists.

Fraser (2001): Gary E Fraser, *Archives of Internal Medicine,* 2001; 161: 1645-1652, Ten years of life: Is it a matter of choice?

Frentzel-Beyme (1994): Rainer Frentzel-Beyme and Jenny Chang-Claude, *American Journal of Clinical Nutrition*, 1994; 59: 1143S-1152S, Vegetarian diets and colon cancer: the German experience.

Key (1996): Timothy J Key et al., *British Medical Journal*, 1996; 313: 775-779, Dietary habits and mortality in 11 000 vegetarians and health conscious people: results of a 17 year follow up.

Key (1999): Timothy J Key et al., *American Journal of Clinical Nutrition*, 1999; 70: 516S-524S, Mortality in vegetarians and nonvegetarians: detailed findings from a collaborative analysis of 5 prospective studies.

Mann (1997): Jim I Mann et al., *Heart,* 1997; 78: 450-455, Dietary determinants of ischaemic heart disease in health conscious individuals.

Phillips (1978): Roland L Philips et al., 1978; 31: S191-S198, Coronary heart disease mortality among Seventh Day Adventists with differing dietary habits: a preliminary report.

Recent recommendations on heart disease

Hu (2001): Frank B Hu et al., *Journal of the American College of Nutrition,* 2001; 20: 5-19, Types of dietary fat and risk of coronary heart disease: a critical review.

Hu and Willett (2002): Frank B Hu and Walter C Willett, *Journal of the American Medical Association*, 2002; 288: 2569-2578, Optimal diets for prevention of coronary heart disease.

Kromhout (2002): Daan Kromhout et al., *Circulation*, 2002; 105: 893-898, Prevention of coronary heart disease by diet and lifestyle.

Trials using plant oils rich in ALNA to reduce heart disease
See references for chapters 8 and 9

4. Maintaining a healthy weight

Body mass index and mortality

Allison (1999): David B Allison et al., *Journal of the American Medical Association,* 1999; 282: 1530-1538, Annual deaths attributable to obesity in the United States.

Calle (1999): Eugenia E Calle et al., *New England Journal of Medicine,* 1999; 341: 1097-1105, Body-mass index and mortality in a prospective cohort of U.S. adults.

Peeters (2003): Anna Peeters et al., *Annals of Internal Medicine,* 2003; 138: 24-32, Obesity in adulthood and its consequences for life expectancy: a life-table analysis.

Stevens (2000): June Stevens, *Nutrition Reviews,* 2000; 58: 129-137, Impact of age on associations between weight and mortality.

Thorogood (2003): M Thorogood et al., *Journal of Epidemiology and Community Health,* 2003; 57: 130-133, Relation between body mass index and mortality in an unusually slim cohort.

Visscher (2000): T L S Visscher et al., *American Journal of Epidemiology,* 2000; 151: 660-666, Underweight and overweight in relation to mortality among men aged 40-59 and 50-69 years: The Seven Countries Study.

Willett (2001): Walter Willett, *Cancer Epidemiology, Biomarkers and Prevention,* 2001; 10: 3-8, Diet and cancer: one view at the start of the millennium.

Body mass index and diet

Astrup (2002): Arne Astrup, *Obesity Reviews,* 2002; 3: 57-58, Dietary fat is a major player in obesity – but not the only one.

Bray (1998): George A Bray and Barry M Popkin, *American Journal of Clinical Nutrition,* 1998; 68: 1157-1173, Dietary fat intake does affect obesity!

This paper presents an analysis of weight loss trials, suggesting that a reduction in fat intake of 10% of total calories leads to a weight loss of 16 grams per day. However, this is largely due to the inclusion of trials as short as 28 days in which changes in water retention strongly influence the results. In one case (ref 79 in this paper) weight loss was recorded at 6 months, 12 months and 18 months (-25, -6 and +1 grams per day) and the analysis is based on the figure at 6 months. Also, certain results showing greater weight loss on higher fat diets were omitted even when the results from alternative lower fat diets from the same study were included in the analysis (e.g. refs 73 and 83 in this paper). The conclusion presented in the paper is therefore ill founded.

Davey (2003): Gwyneth K Davey et al., *Public Health Nutrition,* 2003; 6: 259-268, EPIC-Oxford: lifestyle characteristics and nutrient intakes in a cohort of 33 883 meat-eaters and 31 546 non meat-eaters in the UK.

Friedman (2003): Jeffrey M Friedman, *Science,* 2003; 299: 856-858, A war on obesity not the obese.

Hill (2003): James O Hill et al., *Science,* 2003; 299: 853-855, Obesity and the Environment: Where do we go from here?

Key (1996): Timothy Key and Gwyneth Davey, *British Medical Journal,* 1996; 313: 816-817, Prevalence of obesity is low in people who do not eat meat.

Pirozzo (2003): S Pirozzo et al., *Obesity Reviews,* 2003; 4: 83-90, Should we recommend low fat diets for obesity?

Willett (1998): Walter C Willett, *American Journal of Clinical Nutrition,* 1998; 68: 1149-1150, Dietary fat and obesity: an unconvincing relationship.

Willett (2002): Walter C Willett, *Obesity Reviews,* 2002; 3: 59-68, Dietary fat plays a major role in obesity: no.

WHO (2003b): Diet, nutrition and the prevention of chronic disease, 2003, WHO Technical Report Series 916, Section 5.2.

Diabetes prevention studies

Diabetes Prevention Program Research Group (2002): Diabetes Prevention Program Research Group, *New England Journal of Medicine,* 2002; 346: 393-403, Reduction in incidence of type 2 diabetes with lifestyle intervention or metformin.

Tuomilehto (2001): Jaakko Tuomilehto et al., *New England Journal of Medicine,* 2001; 344: 1343-1350, Prevention of type 2 diabetes mellitus by changes in lifestyle among subjects with impaired glucose tolerance.

5. The health giving rainbow

Antioxidants and disease

De Waart (2001): F G de Waart et al., *International Journal of Epidemiology,* 2001; 30: 136-143, Serum carotenoids, α-tocopherol and mortality risk in a prospective study among Dutch elderly.

Giovannucci (1999): Edward Giovannucci, *Journal of the National Cancer Institute,* 1999; 91: 317-331, Tomatoes, tomato-based products, lycopene and cancer: review of the epidemiological literature.

Hennekens (1996): Charles H Hennekens et al., *New England Journal of Medicine,* 1996; 334: 1145-1149, Lack of effect of long-term supplementation with beta-carotene on the incidence of malignant neoplasms and cardiovascular disease.

Ito (2002): Yoshinori Ito et al., *International Journal of Vitamin and Nutrition Research,* 2002; 72: 237-250, Serum antioxidants and subsequent mortality rates of all causes or cancer among rural Japanese inhabitants.

Joshipura (2001): Kaumudi J Joshipura et al., *Annals of Internal Medicine,* 2001; 134: 1106-1114, The effect of fruit and vegetable intake on risk for coronary heart disease.

Khaw (2001): Kay-Tee Khaw et al., *The Lancet,* 2001, 357: 657-663, Relation between plasma ascorbic acid and mortality in men and women in EPIC-Norfolk prospective study: a prospective population study.

Kohlmeier (1997): Lenore Kohlmeier et al., *American Journal of Epidemiology,* 1997; 146: 618-626, Lycopene and myocardial infarction risk in the EURAMIC study.

Liu (2001): Simin Liu et al., *International Journal of Epidemiology,* 2001; 30: 130-135, Intake of vegetables rich in carotenoids and risk of coronary heart disease in men: The Physicians' Health Study.

Liu (2003): Meilin Liu et al., *American Journal of Clinical Nutrition,* 2003; 77: 700-706, Mixed tocopherols inhibit platelet aggregation in humans: potential mechanisms.

Omenn (1996): Gilbert S Omenn et al., *New England Journal of Medicine,* 1996; 334: 1150-1155, Effects of a combination of beta carotene and vitamin A on lung cancer and cardiovascular disease.

Rissanen (2003a): Tiina H Rissanen et al., *American Journal of Clinical Nutrition,* 2003; 77: 133-138, Serum lycopene concentrations and risk of carotid atherosclerosis: the Kuopio Ischaemic Heart Disease Risk Factor Study.

Rissanen (2003b): T H Rissanen et al., *Journal of Nutrition,* 2003; 133: 199-204, Low intake of fruits, berries and vegetables is associated with excess mortality in men: the Kuopio Ischaemic Heart Disease Risk Factor (KIHD) Study.

Schunemann (2002): Holger J Schunemann et al., *American Journal of Epidemiology,* 2002; 155: 463-471, Lung function in relation to intake of carotenoids and other antioxidant vitamins in a population-based study.

Antioxidants in plant foods

Halvorsen (2002): Bente L Halvorsen et al., *Journal of Nutrition,* 2002; 132: 461-471, A systematic screening of total antioxidants in dietary plants.

McBride (1996): Judy McBride, *Agricultural Research,* November 1996: 4-8, Plant pigments: paint a rainbow of antioxidants.

6. Homocysteine and Health

Homocysteine and all-cause mortality

Bostom (1999): Andrew G Bostom et al., *Archives of Internal Medicine*, 1999; 15: 1077-1080, Nonfasting plasma total homocysteine levels and all-cause and cardiovascular disease mortality in elderly Framingham men and women. (USA)

Hoogeveen (2000): Ellen K Hoogeveen et al., *Circulation*, 2000; 101: 1506-1511, Hyperhomocysteinemia increases risk of death, especially in Type 2 diabetes. (Netherlands)

Kark (1999): Jeremy D Kark et al., *Annals of Internal Medicine*, 1999; 131: 321-330, Nonfasting plasma total homocysteine level and mortality in middle-aged and elderly men and women in Jerusalem. (Israel)

Rea (2000): I M Rea et al., *Atherosclerosis*, 2000; 149: 207-214, Community-living nonagenarians in Northern Ireland have lower plasma homocysteine but similar methylene-tetrahydrofolate reductase thermolabile genotype prevalence compared to 70-89-year-old subjects.

Vollset (2001): Stein Emil Vollset et al., *American Journal of Clinical Nutrition*, 2001; 74: 130-136, Plasma total homocysteine and cardiovascular and noncardiovascular mortality: the Hordaland Homocysteine Study. (Norway)

Homocysteine and cardiovascular disease

Blacher (2002): Jacques Blacher et al., *The American Journal of Cardiology,* 2002; 90: 591-595, Relation of plasma total homocysteine to cardiovascular mortality in a French population.

Homocysteine studies collaboration (2002): *Journal of the American Medical Association,* 2002; 288: 2015-2022, Homocysteine and risk of ischemic heart disease and stroke: a meta-analysis.

Klerk (2002): Mariska Klerk et al., *Journal of the American Medical Association,* 2002; 288: 2023-2031, MTHFR 677C-T polymorphism and risk of coronary heat disease: a meta-analysis.

Rogers (2003): John D Rogers et al., *Archives of Neurology*, 2003; 60: 59-64, Elevated plasma homocysteine levels in patients treated with levodopa: association with vascular disease.

Wald (2002): David S Wald et al., *British Medical Journal,* 23 November, 2002; 325: 1202-1208, Homocysteine and cardiovascular disease: evidence on causality from a meta-analysis.

Homocysteine and birth defects

Afman (2001): L A Afman et al., *Quarterly Journal of Medicine*, 2001; 94: 159-166, Reduced vitamin B12 binding by transcobalamin II increases the risk of neural tube defects.

Kirke (1993): P N Kirke et al., *Quarterly Journal of Medicine*, 1993: 86: 703-708, Maternal plasma folate and vitamin B12 are independent risk factors for neural tube defects.

Refsum (2001): Helga Refsum, *British Journal of Nutrition,* 2001; 85(S2): S109-S113, Folate, vitamin B12 and homocysteine in relation to birth defects and outcome.

Ronnenberg (2002): Alayne G Ronnenberg et al., *American Journal of Clinical Nutrition,* 2002; 76: 1385-1391, Preconception homocysteine and B vitamin status and birth outcomes in Chinese women.

Vollset (2000): Stein Emil Vollset et al., *American Journal of Clinical Nutrition*, 2000; 71: 962-968, Plasma total homocysteine, pregnancy complications, and adverse pregnancy outcomes: the Hordaland Homocysteine Study.

Wilson (1999): Aaron Wilson et al., *Molecular Genetics and Metabolism,* 1999; 67: 317-323, A common variant in methionine synthase combined with low cobalamin (vitamin B12) increases risk for spina bifida.

Homocysteine and depression

Bottiglieri (2000): Teodoro Bottiglieri et al., *Journal of Neurology, Neurosurgery and Psychiatry*, 2000; 69: 228-232, Homocysteine, folate, methylation, and monoamine metabolism in depression.

Mischoulon (2002): David Mischoulon and Maurizio Fava, *American Journal of Clinical Nutrition,* 2002; 76: 1158S-1161S, Role of S-adenosyl-L-methionine in the treatment of depression: a review of the evidence.

Tiemeier (2002), Henning Tiemeier et al., *American Journal of Psychiatry,* 2002; 159: 2099-2101, Vitamin B12, folate and homocysteine in depression: the Rotterdam study.

Homocysteine, dementia and ageing

Hogervorst (2002): Eva Hogervorst et al., *Archives of Neurology,* 2002; 59: 787-793, Plasma homocysteine levels, cerebrovascular risk factors, and cerebral white matter changes (leukoaraiosis) in patients with Alzheimer disease.

Kado (2002): Deborah M Kado et al., *American Journal of Medicine,* 2002; 113: 537-542, Homocysteine levels and decline in physical function: MacArthur studies of successful aging.

McCaddon (2002): A McCaddon et al., *Neurology,* 2002; 58: 1395-1399, Functional vitamin B12 deficiency and Alzheimer disease.

Seshadri (2002): Sudha Seshadri et al., *New England Journal of Medicine,* 2002; 346: 476-483, Plasma homocysteine as a risk factor for dementia and Alzheimer's disease.

Intervention trials with B vitamins

Czeizel (1992): A E Czeizel and I Dudas, *New England Journal of Medicine,* 1992; 327: 1832-1835, Prevention of first occurrence of neural-tube defects by periconceptual vitamin supplementation.

Hackam (2000): Daniel G Hackam et al., *American Journal of Hypertension,* 2000; 13: 105-110, What levels of plasma homocyst(e)ine should be treated? Effects of vitamin therapy on progression of atherosclerosis in patients with homocyst(e)ine levels above and below 14 µmol/L.

MRC (1991): *The Lancet,* 1991; 338: 131-137, Prevention of neural tube defects: results of the Medical Research Council Vitamin Study.

Schnyder (2001): Guido Schnyder et al., *New England Journal of Medicine,* 2001; 345: 1593-1600, Decreased rate of coronary restenosis after lowering of plasma homocysteine levels.

Vermeulen (2000): E G J Vermeulen et al., *The Lancet,* 2000, 355: 517-522, Effect of homocysteine-lowering treatment with folic acid plus vitamin B6 on progression of subclinical atherosclerosis: a randomised, placebo-controlled trial.

B12, folate and homocysteine levels in vegetarians

Bissoli (2002) : T. Bissoli et al., *Annals of Nutrition and Metabolism,* 2002; 26: 73-79, Effect of vegetarian diet on homocysteine levels. (Italy 2002)

Chanarin (1985): I Chanarin et al., *The Lancet,* November 23, 1985; 1168-1172, Megaloblastic anaemia in a vegetarian community.

Crane (1994): Milton G Crane et al., *Journal of Nutritional Medicine,* 1994; 4: 419-430, Vitamin B12 studies in total vegetarians (vegans).

DeRose (2000): David J DeRose et al., *Preventive Medicine,* 2000; 30: 225-233, Vegan diet-based lifestyle program rapidly lowers homocysteine levels.

Donaldson (2000): Michael S Donaldson, *Annals of Nutrition and Metabolism,* 2000; 44: 229-234, Metabolic vitamin B12 status on a mostly raw vegan diet with follow-up using tablets, nutritional yeast, or probiotic supplements.

Haddad (1999): Ella H Haddad et al., *American Journal of Clinical Nutrition,* 1999; 70: 586S-593S, Dietary intake and biochemical, hematologic, and immune status of vegans compared with nonvegetarians. (USA 1999)

Herbert (1994): Victor Herbert, *American Journal of Clinical Nutrition,* 1994; 59: 1213S-1222S, Staging vitamin B-12 (cobalamin) status in vegetarians.

Herrmann (2001): Wolfgang Herrmann et al., *Clinical Chemistry,* 2001; 47: 1094-1101, Total homocysteine, Vitamin B12, and total antioxidant status in vegetarians. (Germany 2001)

Herrmann (2002): Wolfgang Herrmann and Jurgen Geisel, *Clinica Chemica Acta,* 2002; 326: 47-59, Vegetarian lifestyle and monitoring of vitamin B-12 status.

Herrmann (2003): Wolfgang Herrmann et al., *American Journal of Clinical Nutriion,* 2003; 78: 131-136, Vitamin B-12 status, particularly holotranscobalamin II and methylmalonic acid concentrations, and hyperhomocysteinemia.

Hokin (1999): Bevan D Hokin and Terry Butler, *American Journal of Clinical Nutrition,* 1999; 70: 576S-578S, Cyanocobalamin (vitamin B-12) status in Seventh-day Adventist ministers in Australia.

Hokin (2002): Bevan Hokin, Abstract 25, *Loma Linda Conference on Vegetarian Nutrition,* B12 Bioavailability and intervention studies.

Huang (2003): Yi-Chia Huang et al., *European Journal of Nutrition,* 2003; 42: 84-90, The status of plasma homocysteine in healthy young vegetarians and nonvegetarians. (Taiwan 2003)

Hung (2001): Chien-Jung Hung et al., *Journal of Nutrition,* 2001; 132: 152-158, Plasma homocysteine levels in Taiwanese vegetarians are higher than those of omnivores. (Taiwan 2001)

Koschizke (2002): Jochen Koschizke, Abstract 18, *Loma Linda Conference on Vegetarian Nutrition,* Cobalamin and homocysteine status of vegans – results of the German Vegan Study. (Germany 2002)

Krajcovicova-Kudlackova (2000): M. Krajcovicova-Kudlackova et al., *Annals of Nutrition and Metabolism,* 2000; 44: 135-138, Homocysteine levels in vegetarians versus omnivores. (Czechoslovakia 2000)

Mann (1999): N J Mann et al., *European Journal of Clinical Nutrition,* 1999; 53: 895-899, The effect of diet on plasma homocysteine concentrations in healthy male subjects. (Australia 1999)

Mezzano (1999): Diego Mezzano et al., *Thrombosis and Haemostasis,* 1999; 81: 913-7, Vegetarians and cardiovascular risk factors: hemostasis, inflammatory markers and plasma homocysteine. (Chile 1999)

Mezzano (2000): Diego Mezzano et al., *Thrombosis Research,* 2000; 100: 153-160, Cardiovascular risk factors in vegetarians: normalisation of hyperhomocysteinemia with vitamin B12 and reduction of platelet aggregation with n-3 fatty acids.

Obeid (2002): R Obeid et al., *European Journal of Haematology,* 2002; 69: 275-279, The impact of vegetarianism on some haematological parameters.

Rauma (1995): Anna-Liisa Rauma et al., *Journal of Nutrition,* 1995; 125: 2511-2515, Vitamin B-12 status of long-term adherents of a strict uncooked vegan diet ("living food diet") is compromised. (See also *Journal of Nutrition,* 1997; 127: 378-380)

Refsum (2001): Helga Refsum et al., *American Journal of Clinical Nutrition,* 2001; 74: 233-241, Hyperhomocysteinemia and elevated methylmalonic acid indicate a high prevalence of cobalamin deficiency in Asian Indians.

Lifestyle and diet determinants of homocysteine concentrations

Ganji (2003): Vijay Ganji and Mohammad R Kafai, *American Journal of Clinical Nutrition,* 2003; 77: 826-833, Demographic, health, lifestyle, and blood vitamin determinants of serum total homocysteine concentrations in the third National Health and Nutrition Examination Survey, 1988-1994.

Grubben (2000): Marina J Grubben et al., *American Journal of Clinical Nutrition,* 2000; 71: 480-484, Unfiltered coffee increases plasma homocysteine concentrations in healthy volunteers: a randomized trial.

Hodgson (2003): Jonathan M Hodgson et al., *American Journal of Clinical Nutrition,* 2003; 77: 907-911, Can black tea influence plasma total homocysteine concentrations?

Jacques (2001): Paul F Jacques et al., *American Journal of Clinical Nutrition,* 2001; 73: 613-621, Determinants of plasma total homocysteine concentration in the Framingham Offspring cohort.

Koehler (2001): Kathleen M Koehler et al., *American Journal of Clinical Nutrition,* 2001; 73: 628-637, Association of folate intake and serum homocysteine in elderly persons according to vitamin supplementation and alcohol use.

Stolzenberg-Solomon (1999): Rachael Z Stolzenberg-Solomon et al., *American Journal of Clinical Nutrition,* 1999; 69: 467-475, Association of dietary protein and coffee consumption with serum homocysteine concentrations in an older population.

How much B12 is needed to avoid increased risk of elevated homocysteine?

Herbert (1987): Victor Herbert, *American Journal of Clinical Nutrition,* 1987, 45: 671-678, Recommended dietary intakes (RDI) of vitamin B-12 in humans.

Selhub (1999): Jacob Selhub et al., *Annals of Internal Medicine,* 1999; 131: 331-339, Serum total homocysteine concentrations in the third National Health And Nutrition Examination Survey (1991-1994): Population reference ranges and contribution of vitamin status to high serum concentrations.

Tucker (2000): Katherine L Tucker et al., *American Journal of Clinical Nutrition,* 2000, 71: 514-522, Plasma vitamin B-12 concentrations relate to intake source in the Framingham Offspring Study.

Diagnosing B12 deficiency

Snow (1999): Christopher F Snow, *Archives of Internal Medicine,* 1999, 159: 1289-1298, Laboratory diagnosis of vitamin B12 and folate deficiency.

B12 needs of other primates

Personal communication with Monkey World primate rescue sanctuary www.monkeyworld.org

B12 and algae

Dagnelie (1991): Pieter C Dagnelie et al., *American Journal of Clinical Nutrition,* 1991; 53: 695-697, Vitamin B-12 from algae appears not to be bioavailable.

Kittaka-Katsura (2002): Hiromi Kittaka-Katsura et al., *Journal of Agricultural and Food Chemistry,* 2002; 50: 4994-4997, Purification and characterization of a corrinoid compound from chlorella tablets as an algal health food.

Miyamoto (2001): E Miyamoto et al., *Journal of Agricultural and Food Chemistry,* 2001; 49: 3486-3489, Characterization of a vitamin B12 compound from unicellular coccolithophorid alga (Pleurochrysis carterae).

Watanabe (1997): Fumio Watanabe et al., *Bioscience, Biotechnology and Biochemistry,* 1997; 61: 896-897, Occurrence of cobalamin coenzymes in the photosynthetic green alga, chlorella vulgaris.

Watanabe (1999): F Watanabe et al., *Journal of Agricultural and Food Chemistry,* 1999; 47: 4736-4741, Pseudovitamin B-12 is the predominant cobamide of an algal health food, spirulina tablets.

Watanabe (2002): Fumio Watanabe et al., *Journal of Nutritional Science and Vitaminology,* 2002; 48: 325-321, Characterization and bioavailability of vitamin B12-compounds from edible algae.

Yamada (1999): Keiko Yamada et al., *International Journal of Vitamin and Nutrition Research,* 1999; 69: 412-418, Bioavailability of dried asakusanori (Porphyra tenera) as a source of cobalamin (vitamin B12).

General information on B12 and homocysteine

Homocysteine in Health and Disease, ed. Ralph Carmel and Donald W Jacobsen, Cambridge University Press, 2001.

www.veganoutreach.org/health/b12rec.html
www.vegansociety.com/articles/homocysteine1
www.vegansociety.com/html/info/b12sheet.htm

7. Balancing calcium

Calcium balance versus calcium intake

National Institutes of Health Consensus conference (1994): NIH consensus development panel on optimal calcium intake, *Journal of the American Medical Association,* 1994; 272: 1942-1948, Optimal calcium intake.

Nordin (2000): B E Christopher Nordin, *American Journal of Clinical Nutrition,* 2000; 71: 1381-1383, Calcium requirement is a sliding scale.

Calcium balance, blood pressure and stroke

Appel (1997): Lawrence J Appel et al., *New England Journal of Medicine,* 1997; 336: 1117-1124, A clinical trial of the effects of dietary patterns on blood pressure.

Ascherio (1998): A Ascherio et al., *Circulation,* 1998; 98: 1198-1204, Intake of potassium, magnesium, calcium, and fiber and risk of stroke among US men.

Browner (1993): Warren S Browner et al., *Stroke,* 1993; 24: 940-946, Association between low bone density and stroke in women.

Cappucio (1997): Francesco P Cappucio et al., *The Lancet,* 1997; 350: 850-854, Double-blind randomised trial of modest salt restriction in older people.

Cappucio (1999a): Francesco P Cappucio, *American Journal of Hypertension,* 1999; 12: 93-95, The "calcium antihypertension theory".

Cappucio (1999b): Francesco P Cappucio, *The Lancet,* 1999; 354: 971-975, High blood pressure and bone-mineral loss in elderly white women: a prospective study.

Elliott (1996): Paul Elliott et al., *British Medical Journal,* 1996; 312: 1249-1253, Intersalt revisited: further analyses of 24 hour salt excretion and blood pressure within and across populations.

Green (2002): D M Green et al., *Neurology,* 2002; 59: 314-320, Serum potassium level and dietary potassium intake as risk factors for stroke.

Griffith (1999): Lauren E Griffith et al., *American Journal of Hypertension,* 1999; 12: 84-92, The influence of dietary and nondietary calcium supplementation on blood pressure: an updated metaanalysis of randomized controlled trials.

Gruchow (1988): Harvey W Gruchow et al., *American Journal of Clinical Nutrition,* 1988; 48: 1463-1470, Calcium intake and the relationship of dietary sodium and potassium to blood pressure.

He (2001): Feng J He and Graham MacGregor, *British Medical Journal,* 2001; 323: 497-501, Beneficial effects of potassium.

Heaney (2002): Robert P Heaney, *Nutrition Research,* 2002; 22: 153-178, Ethnicity, bone status and the calcium requirement.

Iso (1999): Hiroyasu Iso et al., *Stroke,* 1999; 30: 1772-1779, Prospective study of calcium, potassium, and magnesium intake and risk of stroke in women.

Karanja (1998): N Karanja et al., *Journal of the American Society of Nephrology,* 1998; 9: 151A, Mineral metabolism, blood pressure and dietary patterns: findings from the DASH trial.

Khaw (1987): Kay-Tee Khaw et al., *New England Journal of Medicine,* 1987; 316: 235-240, Dietary potassium and stroke-associated mortality: a 12-year prospective study.

Kwok (2003): T C Y Kwok et al., *European Journal of Clinical Nutrition,* 2003; 57: 299-304, Relationship of urinary sodium/potassium excretion and calcium intake to blood pressure and prevalence of hypertension among older Chinese vegetarians.

McCarron (1999): David A McCarron, *Journal of the American College of Nutrition,* 1999; 18: 398S-405S, Finding consensus in the dietary calcium-blood pressure debate.

Robertson (2003): J Ian S Robertson, *Journal of Evaluation in Clinical Practice,* 2003; 9: 1-22, Dietary salt and hypertension: a scientific issue or a matter of faith?

Sacks (2001): Frank M Sacks et al., *New England Journal of Medicine,* 2001; 344: 3-10, Effects on blood pressure of reduced dietary sodium and the Dietary Approaches to Stop Hypertension (DASH) diet.   (plus correspondence in *New England Journal of Medicine*, 2001; 344: 1716-1719)

Vegetarian diet and blood pressure

Appleby (2002): Paul N Appleby et al., *Public Health Nutrition,* 2002; 645-654, Hypertension and blood pressure among meat eaters, fish eaters, vegetarians and vegans in EPIC-Oxford.

Beilin (1995): L J Beilin and V Burke, *Clinical and Experimental Pharmacology and Physiology,* 1995; 22: 195-198, Vegetarian diet components, protein and blood pressure: which nutrients are important.

Margetts (1986): Barrie M Margetts et al., *British Medical Journal,* 1986; 293: 1468-1471, Vegetarian diet in mild hypertension: a randomised controlled trial.

Rouse (1983): Ian L Rouse et al., *The Lancet,* January 1/8, 1983: 5-9, Blood-pressure-lowering effect of a vegetarian diet: controlled trial in normotensive subjects.

Sacks (1988): Frank M Sacks and Edward H Cass, *American Journal of Clinical Nutrition,* 1988; 48: 795-800, Low blood pressure in vegetarians: effects of specific foods and nutrients.

Calcium balance and obesity

Barr (2003): Susan I Barr, *Journal of Nutrition,* 2003; 133: 245S-248S, Increased dairy product or calcium intake: is body weight or composition affected in humans?

This review found an apparently beneficial effect in only one randomised trial on calcium supplementation, and adverse effects in another calcium supplementation trial and in two dairy supplementation trials. Many other trials showed no significant effect. This suggests that if there is a beneficial effect of higher calcium intakes, as suggested by within-population correlations in the USA, then it either occurs when moving from calcium intakes below 500 milligrams per day to higher intakes or occurs over an extended period of time.

Melanson (2003): E L Melanson et al., *International Journal of Obesity,* 2003; 27: 196-203, Relation between calcium intake and fat oxidation in adult humans.

Parikh (2003): Shamik J Parikh and Jack A Yanovski, *American Journal of Clinical Nutrition,* 2003; 77: 281-287, Calcium intake and adiposity.

Pereira (2002): Mark A Pereira et al., *Journal of the American Medical Association,* 2002; 287: 2081-2089, Dairy consumption, obesity, and the insulin resistance syndrome in young adults: The CARDIA Study

The headline finding in this paper is that increased dairy consumption was linked to lower risk of a combination of obesity, high blood pressure, low HDL cholesterol, high triglycerides and elevated blood glucose in overweight individuals. This may relate to improved calcium balance, reduced glycaemic load or simply less junk food consumption in the high dairy consumers. High fibre intake appeared to be at least as protective as high dairy intake.

Teegarden (2003): Dorothy Teegarden, *Journal of Nutrition,* 2003; 133: 249S-251S, Calcium intake and reduction in weight or fat mass.

Zemel (2002): Michael B Zemel, *Journal of the American College of Nutrition,* 2002; 21: 146S-151S, Regulation of adiposity and obesity risk by dietary calcium: mechanisms and implications.

Calcium balance and bone health

Cohen (2000): A J Cohen and F J C Roe, *Food and Chemical Toxicology,* 2000; 38: 237-253, Review of risk factors for osteoporosis with particular reference to a possible aetiological role of dietary salt.

Cumming (1997): Robert G Cumming et al., *American Journal of Epidemiology,* 1997; 145: 926-934, Calcium intake and fracture risk: results from the Study of Osteoporotic Fractures.

Devine (1995); Amanda Devine et al., *American Journal of Clinical Nutrition*, 1995; 62: 740-745, A longitudinal study of the effect of sodium and calcium intakes on regional bone density in postmenopausal women.

Feskanich (1997): Diane Feskanich et al., *American Journal of Public Health*, 1997; 87: 992-997, Milk, dietary calcium and bone fractures in women: a 12-year prospective study.

Feskanich (2003): Diane Feskanich et al., *American Journal of Clinical Nutrition,* 2003; 77: 504-511, Calcium, vitamin D, milk consumption, and hip fractures: a prospective study among postmenopausal women.

Fujiwara (1997): Saeko Fujiwara et al., *Journal of Bone and Mineral Research*, 1997; 12: 998-1004, Risk factors for hip fracture in a Japanese cohort.

Giannini (1998): S Giannini et al., *Clinical Nephrology*, 1998; 50: 94-100, Bone density and skeletal metabolism are altered in idiopathic hypercalciuria.

Heaney (2000): Robert P Heaney, *Journal of the American College of Nutrition*, 2000; 19: 83S-99S, Calcium, dairy products and osteoporosis.

Hirota (1992): Takako Hirota et al., *American Journal of Clinical Nutrition*, 1992; 55: 1168-1173, Effect of diet and lifestyle on bone mass in Asian young women.

Holbrook (1988): Troy L Holbrook et al., *The Lancet*, 1988; ii: 1046-1049, Dietary calcium and risk of hip fracture: 14-year prospective population study.

Honkanen (2001): Risto Honkanen et al., Effect of calcium on bone loss and fractures according to estrogen repletion status, in *Nutritional Aspects of Osteoporosis*, ed. Peter Burckhardt et al., 2001, ISBN 0-12-141703-4

Hu (1993): Ji-Fan Hu et al., *American Journal of Clinical Nutrition*, 1993; 58: 219-227, Dietary calcium and bone density among middle-aged and elderly women in China.

Lau (2001): E M C Lau et al., *Journal of Bone and Mineral Research*, 2001; 16: 572-580, Risk factors for hip fracture in Asian men and women: the Asian Osteoporosis Study.

Martini (2000): L A Martini, *Clinical Nephrology*, 2000; 54: 85-93, High sodium chloride is associated with low bone density in calcium stone-forming patients.

Matkovic (1995): Velimir Matkovic et al., *American Journal of Clinical Nutrition*, 1995; 62: 417-425, Urinary calcium, sodium, and bone mass of young females.

Tucker (1999): Katherine L Tucker et al., *American Journal of Clinical Nutrition*, 1999; 69: 727-736, Potassium, magnesium, and fruit and vegetable intakes are associated with greater bone mineral density in elderly men and women.

Tucker (2002): Katherine L Tucker et al., *American Journal of Clinical Nutrition*, 2002; 76: 245-252, Bone mineral density and dietary patterns in older adults: the Framingham osteoporosis study.

Effects of protein on calcium balance, bone and kidneys

Barzel (1998): Uriel S Barzel and Linda K Massey, *Journal of Nutrition*, 1998; 128: 1051-1053, Excess dietary protein can adversely affect bone.

Breslau (1988): Neil A Breslau et al., *Journal of Clinical Endocrinology and Metabolism*, 1988; 66: 140-146, Relationship of animal protein-rich diet to kidney stone formation and calcium metabolism.

Bushinsky (2000): David A Bushinsky and Kevin K Frick, *Current Opinion in Nephrology and Hypertension*, 2000; 9: 369-379, The effects of acid on bone.

Dawson-Hughes (2002): Bess Dawson-Hughes and Susan S Harris, *American Journal of Clinical Nutrition*, 2002; 75: 773-779, Calcium intake influences the association of protein intake with rates of bone loss in elderly men and women.

This paper has been used to support the idea that high protein intakes are beneficial to bone when accompanied by high calcium intakes. However, the study found a benefit from protein only in relation to bone gain during the remodelling transient in the year or so following supplementation with calcium and vitamin D. No evidence was found of improved calcium balance 18 months after supplementation started: indeed, the study results suggest that calcium balance at 18 months decreased with increasing protein intake in both supplemented and unsupplemented groups.

Dawson-Hughes (2003): Bess Dawson-Hughes, *Journal of Nutrition*, 2003; 133: 852S-854S, Interaction of dietary calcium and protein in bone health in humans.

Feskanich (1996): Diane Feskanich et al., *American Journal of Epidemiology*, 1996; 143: 472-479, Protein consumption and bone fractures in women.

Frassetto (1996): Lynda A Frassetto et al., *American Journal of Physiology*, 1996; 271: F1114-F1122, Effect of age on blood acid-base composition in adult humans: role of age-related renal functional decline.

Frassetto (2000): Lynda A. Frassetto et al., *Journal of Gerontology: Medical Sciences*, 2000; 55A: M585-M592, Worldwide incidence of hip fracture in elderly women: relation to the consumption of animal and vegetable foods.

Giannini (1999): Sandro Giannini et al., *American Journal of Clinical Nutrition*, 1999; 69: 267-271, Acute effects of moderate dietary protein restriction in patients with idiopathic hypercalciuria and calcium nephrolithiasis.

Hannan (2000): Marian T Hannan et al., *Journal of Bone and Mineral Research*, 2000; 15: 2504-2512, Effect of dietary protein on bone loss in elderly men and women: the Framingham osteoporosis study.

Hannan (2001): Marian T. Hannan, Dietary protein and effects upon bone health in elderly men and women, in *Nutritional Aspects of Osteoporosis*, ed. Peter Burckhardt et al., 2001, ISBN 0-12-141703-4

Heaney (1998): Robert P Heaney, *Journal of Nutrition*, 1998; 128: 1054-1057, Excess dietary protein may not adversely affect bone.

Heaney (2000): Robert P Heaney, *American Journal of Clinical Nutrition*, 2000; 72: 758-61, Dietary protein and phosphorus do not affect calcium absorption.

Kerstetter (1997): Jane E Kerstetter et al., *American Journal of Clinical Nutrition*, 1997; 66: 1188-1196, Increased circulating concentrations of parathyroid hormone in healthy, young women consuming a protein-restricted diet.

Kerstetter (1998): Jane E Kerstetter et al., *American Journal of Clinical Nutrition*, 1998; 68: 859-865, Dietary protein affects intestinal calcium absorption.

Kerstetter (1999): Jane E Kerstetter et al., *Journal of Clinical Endocrinology and Metabolism,* 1999; 84: 1052-1055, Changes in bone turnover in women consuming different levels of protein.

Kerstetter (1997, 1998, 1999) confirms the adverse effect of high protein intake on calcium balance: calcium balance was about 34 mg worse on the high protein diet compared with the low protein diet and bone resorption was increased. A less predictable observation was a dramatic increase in parathyroid hormone (PTH) and calcitriol on the low protein diet, even though protein intake was still 0.7 grams per kilogram of body weight. Bone resorption is known to reduce as blood pH rises with reduced protein intake or increased alkali intake. These studies suggest that intestinal calcium absorption also decreases with decreased protein intake at given levels of PTH and calcitriol, but that the overall effect of high protein intake on calcium balance remains negative. In contrast to the increase in absorption that partly compensated for increased losses in the young women in Kerstetter's papers, Heaney (2000) found no relationship between long term protein intake and calcium absorption in older women, suggesting a stronger adverse effect of protein in older women than in young women.

Kerstetter (2000): J E Kerstetter et al., *Calcified Tissue International*, 2000; 63: 313, Low dietary protein and low bone density.

Knight (2003): Eric L Knight et al., *Annals of Internal Medicine*, 2003; 138: 460-467, The impact of protein intake on renal function decline in women with normal renal function or mild renal function insufficiency.

This paper found an association between protein intake and decline in kidney function with age in women who had mildly impaired kidney function at the start of the study. Associations differed for non-dairy animal protein, dairy protein and plant protein, but these differences may be artefacts of the different associations between these individual protein sources and total protein intake rather than reflecting a distinct biological effect of each source.

Massey (2003): Linda K Massey, *Journal of Nutrition,* 2003; 133: 862S-865S, Dietary animal and plant protein and human bone health: a whole foods approach.

Munger (1999): Ronald G Munger et al., *American Journal of Clinical Nutrition,* 1999; 69: 147-152, Prospective study of dietary protein intake and risk of hip fracture in postmenopausal women.

New (2000): Susan A New et al., *American Journal of Clinical Nutrition,* 2000; 71: 142-151, Dietary influences on bone mass and bone metabolism: further evidence of a positive link between fruit and vegetable consumption and bone health?

Promislow (2002): Joanne H E Promislow, *American Journal of Epidemiolgy,* 2002; 155: 636-644, Protein consumption and bone mineral density in the elderly: the Rancho Bernardo study.

Remer (1994): Thomas Remer and Friedrich Manz, *American Journal of Clinical Nutrition,* 1994; 59: 1356-61, Estimation of the renal net acid excretion by adults consuming variable amounts of protein.

Remer (1995): Thomas Remer and Friedrich Manz, *Journal of the American Dietetic Association,* 1995; 95: 791-797, Potential renal acid load of foods and its influence on urine pH.

Schurch (1998): Marc-Andre Schurch, *Annals of Internal Medicine,* 1998; 128: 801-809, Protein supplements increase serum insulin-like growth factor-I levels and attenuate proximal femur bone loss in patients with recent hip fracture: a randomized, double-blind, placebo-controlled trial.

Sellmeyer (2001): Deborah E Sellmeyer et al., *American Journal of Clinical Nutrition,* 2001; 73: 118-122, A high ratio of dietary animal to vegetable protein increases the rate of bone loss and the risk of fracture in postmenopausal women.

Stawasz (2001): L Stawasz et al., *Bone,* 2001; 28: S187, Bone mineral density and content in premenopausal women consuming a vegan or omnivore diet.

Wood (2003): Marcia Wood, *Agricultural Research,* March 2003; 8-9, Boning up on osteoporosis.

The latter two papers directly examine Western vegans' bone mineral density and bone turnover and find modest evidence of an advantage for the vegans over the omnivores.

Effect of potassium and alkali on calcium balance

Alpern (1997): Robert J Alpern and Khashayar Sakhaee, *American Journal of Kidney Diseases,* 1997; 29: 291-302, The clinical spectrum of chronic metabolic acidosis: homeostatic mechanisms produce significant morbidity.

Frassetto (1998): Lynda A Frassetto et al., *American Journal of Clinical Nutrition,* 1998; 68: 576-583, Estimation of net endogenous noncarbonic acid production from diet potassium and protein contents.

Hu (1993): Ji-Fan Hu et al., *American Journal of Clinical Nutrition,* 1993; 58: 398-406, Dietary intakes and urinary excretion of calcium and acids: a cross-sectional study of women in China.

Lemann (1993): Jacob Lemann Jr et al., *Journal of Nutrition,* 1993; 123: 1623-1626, Potassium causes calcium retention in healthy adults.

Lemann (1998): Jacob Lemann Jr, *Nephron,* 1998; 81 (supp 1): 18-25, Relationship between urinary calcium and net acid excretion as determined by dietary protein and potassium: a review.

This review argues that the effect of both protein and potassium rich foods is determined by their effect on urinary acid excretion. This conclusion is based on a regression dominated by non-physiological doses of ammonium chloride. If the data are restricted to physiological changes induced by variations in protein or potassium bicarbonate intakes, it is clear that the effect of protein on calcium excretion is much greater than the effect of potassium bicarbonate for a given change in urinary acid excretion.

Lutz (1984): Josephine Lutz, *American Journal of Clinical Nutrition,* 1984; 39: 281-288, Calcium balance and acid-base status of women as affected by increased protein intake and by sodium bicarbonate ingestion.

This paper provides direct confirmation that the effect of protein on urinary calcium loss is much greater than would be expected based on its effect on alkali balance.

Sebastian (1994): Anthony Sebastian et al., *The New England Journal of Medicine,* 1994; 330: 1776-1781, Improved mineral balance and skeletal metabolism in postmenopausal women treated with potassium bicarbonate.

Sellmeyer (2002): Deborah E Sellmeyer et al., *Journal of Clinical Endocrinology and Metabolism,* 2002; 87: 2008-2012, Potassium citrate prevents increased urine calcium excretion and bone resorption induced by a high sodium chloride diet.

Sodium and calcium balance

Ho (2001): S C Ho et al., *Osteoporosis International*, 2001; 12: 723-731, Sodium is the leading dietary factor associated with urinary calcium excretion in Hong Kong Chinese adults.

Itoh (1996): Roichi Itoh and Yasuo Suyama, *American Journal of Clinical Nutrition,* 1996; 63: 735-740, Sodium excretion in relation to calcium and hydroxyproline excretion in a healthy Japanese population.

Lemann (1995): Jacob Lemann Jr et al., *Kidney International,* 1995; 47: 899-906, Dietary NaCl-restriction prevents the calciuria of KCl-deprivation and blunts the calciuria of KHCo3-deprivation in healthy adults.

Massey (1996): Linda K Massey and Susan J Whiting, *Journal of Bone and Mineral Research*, 1996; 11: 731-736, Dietary salt, urinary calcium and bone loss.

Sodium intake and mortality

Alderman (1995): Michael H Alderman et al., *Hypertension,* 1995; 25: 1144-1152, Low urinary sodium is associated with greater risk of myocardial infarction among treated hypertensive men.

He (1999): Jiang He et al., *Journal of the American Medical Association,* 1999; 282: 2027-2034, Dietary sodium intake and subsequent risk of cardiovascular disease in overweight adults.

Tuomilehto (2001): Jaakko Tuomilehto et al., *The Lancet,* 2001; 357: 848-851, Urinary sodium excretion and cardiovascular mortality in Finland: a prospective study.

Calcium absorption

Agnusdei (1998): D Agnusdei et al., *Calcified Tissue International*, 1998; 63: 197-201, Age-related decline of bone mass and intestinal calcium absorption in normal males.

Barger-Lux (1995a): M Janet Barger-Lux et al., *Journal of Clinical Endocrinology and Metabolism,* 1995; 80: 406-411, An investigation of sources of variation in calcium absorption efficiency.

Barger-Lux (1995b): M J Barger-Lux and R P Heaney, *Osteoporosis International*, 1995; 5: 97-102, Caffeine and the calcium economy revisited.

Benway (1993): Denise A Benway and Connie M Weaver, *Journal of Food Science,* 1993; 58: 605-608, Assessing chemical form of calcium in wheat, spinach and kale.

Ensrud (2000): Kristine E Ensrud et al., *Annals of Internal Medicine*, 2000; 132: 345-353, Low fractional calcium absorption increases the risk for hip fracture in women with low calcium intake.

Gonnelli (2001): Stefano Gonnelli et al., Intestinal calcium absorption in normal men and women, in *Nutritional Aspects of Osteoporosis*, ed. Peter Burckhardt et al., 2001, ISBN 0-12-141703-4

Heaney (1986): Robert P Heaney and Robert R Recker, *American Journal of Clinical Nutrition,* 1986; 43: 299-305, Distribution of calcium absorption in middle-aged women.

Heaney (1994): Robert P Heaney and Robert R Recker, *Journal of Bone and Mineral Research*, 1994; 9: 1621-1627, Determinants of endogenous fecal calcium in healthy women.

Heaney (1999): Robert P Heaney et al., *Osteoporosis International,* 1999; 9: 13-18, Urinary calcium in perimenopausal women: normative values.

Recker (1977): Robert R Recker et al., *Annals of Internal Medicine*, 1977; 87: 649-655, Effect of estrogens and calcium carbonate on bone loss in postmenopausal women.

Recker (1985): Robert R Recker and Robert P Heaney, *American Journal of Clinical Nutrition*, 1985; 41: 254-263, The effect of milk supplements on calcium metabolism, bone metabolism and calcium balance.

Weaver (1993): C M Weaver et al., *Journal of Food Science*, 1993; 58: 1401-1403, Absorbability of calcium from common beans.

Weaver (1997): C M Weaver et al., *Journal of Food Science,* 1997; 62: 524-525, Calcium bioavailability from high oxalate vegetables: Chinese vegetables, sweet potatoes and rhubarb.

Weaver (1999): Connie M Weaver et al., *American Journal of Clinical Nutrition*, 1999; 70: 543S-548S, Choices for achieving adequate dietary calcium with a vegetarian diet.

Weaver (2002): C M Weaver et al., *Journal of Food Science,* 2002; 67: 3144-3147, Bioavailability of calcium from tofu as compared with milk in premenopausal women

Retinol and bone health

Binkley (2000): Neil Binkley and Diane Krueger, *Nutrition Reviews*, 2000; 58: 138-144, Hypervitaminosis A and bone.

Feskanich (2002): Diane Feskanich et al., *Journal of the American Medical Association*, 2002; 287: 47-54, Vitamin A intake and hip fractures among postmenopausal women.

Johansson (2001): S Johansson and H Melhus, *Journal of Bone and Mineral Research*, 2001; 16: 1899-1905, Vitamin A antagonises calcium response to vitamin D in man.

Melhus (1998): Hakan Melhus et al., *Annals of Internal Medicine*, 1998; 129: 770-778, Excessive dietary intake of vitamin A is associated with reduced bone mineral density and increased risk for hip fracture.

Michaelsson (2003): Karl Michaelsson et al., *New England Journal of Medicine,* 2003; 348: 287-294, Serum retinol levels and risk of fracture.

Vitamin K and bone health

Booth (2000): Sarah L Booth et al., *American Journal of Clinical Nutrition*, 2000; 71: 1201-1208, Dietary vitamin K intakes are associated with hip fracture but not with bone mineral density in elderly men and women.

Booth (2003): Sarah L Booth et al., *American Journal of Clinical Nutrition*, 2003; 77: 512-516, Vitamin K intake and bone mineral density in women and men.

Feskanich (1999): Diane Feskanich et al., *American Journal of Clinical Nutrition*, 1999; 69: 74-79, Vitamin K intake and hip fractures in women: a prospective study.

Kaneki (2001): Masao Kaneki et al., *Nutrition,* 2001; 17: 315-321, Japanese fermented soybean food as the major determinant of the large geographical difference in circulating levels of vitamin K2: possible implications for hip fracture risk.

Knapen (1989): Marjo H J Knapen et al., *Annals of Internal Medicine*, 1989; 111: 1001-1005, The effect of vitamin K supplementation on circulating osteocalcin (bone Gla protein) and urinary calcium excretion.

Shearer (1996): Martin J Shearer et al., *Journal of Nutrition*, 1996; 126: 1181S-1186S, Chemistry, nutritional sources, tissue distribution and metabolism of vitamin K with special reference to bone health.

Weber (2001): Peter Weber, *Nutrition*, 2001; 17: 880-887, Vitamin K and bone health.

Vitamin D and bone health

Chapuy (1992): Marie C Chapuy et al., *New England Journal of Medicine*, 1992; 327: 1637-1642, Vitamin D3 and calcium to prevent hip fractures in elderly women.

Chapuy (1994): Marie C Chapuy et al., *British Medical Journal*, 1994; 308: 1081-1082, Effect of calcium and cholecalciferol treatment for three years on hip fractures in elderly women.

Dawson-Hughes (1997), Bess Dawson-Hughes et al., *The New England Journal of Medicine*, 1997; 337: 670-676, Effect of calcium and vitamin D supplementation in men and women 65 years of age or older.

Feskanich (1998): Diane Feskanich et al., *Epidemiology*, 1998; 9: 535-539, Vitamin D receptor genotype and the risk of bone fractures in women.

Lamberg-Allardt (2001): Christel J E Lamberg-Allardt *Journal of Bone and Mineral Research,* 2001; 16: 2066-2073, Vitamin D deficiency and bone health in healthy adults in Finland: could this be of concern in other parts of Europe.

Lips (1996): Paul Lips et al., *Annals of Internal Medicine*, 1996; 124: 400-406, Vitamin D supplementation and fracture incidence in elderly persons: a randomized, placebo-controlled clinical trial.

Outila (2000a): Terhi Aulikki Outila et al., *Journal of the American Dietetic Association,* 2000; 100: 434-441, Dietary intake of vitamin D in premenopausal, healthy vegans was insufficient to maintain concentrations of serum 25-hydroxyvitamin D and intact parathyroid hormone within normal ranges during the winter in Finland.

Outila (2000b): Terhi Aulikki Outila et al., *Journal of the American Dietetic Association,* 2000; 100: 629, Ergocalciferol supplementation may positively affect lumbar spine bone mineral density of vegans.

Peacock (2000): Munro Peacock et al., *Journal of Clinical Endocrinology and Metabolism*, 2000; 85: 3011-3019, Effect of calcium and 25OH vitamin D3 dietary supplementation on bone loss at the hip in men and women over the age of 60.

Trivedi (2003): Dapksa P Trivedi et al., *British Medical Journal,* 2003, 326: 469-474, Effect of four monthly oral vitamin D3 (cholecalciferol) supplementation on fractures and mortlaity in men and women living in the community: randomised double blind controlled trial.

Oestrogen and bone health

Riggs (1998): B Lawrence Riggs et al., *Journal of Bone and Mineral Research*, 1998; 13: 763-773, A unitary model for involutional osteoporosis: estrogen deficiency causes both type I and type II osteoporosis in postmenopausal women and contributes to bone loss in aging men.

Omega-3s and bone health

Kruger (1998): M C Kruger et al., *Aging Clinical and Experimental Research*, 1998; 10: 385-394, Calcium, gamma-linolenic acid and eicosapentaenoic acid supplementation in senile osteoporosis.

Requirand (2000): P Requirand et al., *Clinical Nutrition*, 2000; 19: 271-276, Serum fatty acid imbalance in bone loss: example with periodontal disease.

Watkins (2001): Bruce A Watkins et al., *Experimental Biology and Medicine*, 2001; 226: 485-497, Omega-3 polyunsaturated fatty acids and skeletal health.

Homocysteine and bone health

Abrahamsen (2003): Bo Abrahamsen et al., *Journal of Bone and Mineral Research,* 2003; 18: 723-729, A common methylenetetrahydrofolate reductase (C677T) polymorphism is associated with low bone mineral density and increased fracture incidence after menopause: longitudinal data from the Danish Osteoporosis Prevention Study.

Dhonukshe-Rutten (2003): Rosalie A M Dhonukshe-Rutten et al., *Journal of Nutrition,* 2003; 133: 801-807, Vitamin B-12 status is associated with bone mineral content and bone mineral density in frail elderly women but not in men.

Magnesium and bone health

Sojka (1995): J E Sojka and C M Weaver, *Nutrition Reviews*, 1995; 53: 71-80, Magnesium supplementation and osteoporosis.

Exercise and bone health

Anderson (2000): John J B Anderson, *American Journal of Clinical Nutrition,* 2000; 71: 1384-1386, The important role of physical activity in skeletal development: how exercise may counter low calcium intake.

Uusi-Rasi (1998): Kirsti Uusi-Rasi et al., *Journal of Bone and Mineral Research*, 1998; 13: 133-142, Associations of physical activity and calcium intake with bone mass and size in healthy women at different ages.

Wang (2003); May-Choo Wang et al., *American Journal of Clinical Nutrition,* 2003; 77: 495-503, Diet in midpuberty and sedentary activity in prepuberty predict peak bone mass.

Wolff (1999): I Wolff et al., *Osteoporosis International*, 1999; 9: 1-12, The effect of exercise training programs on bone mass: a meta-analysis of published controlled trials in pre- and postmenopausal women.

Evolutionary perspectives on calcium balance

Eaton (1991): S Boyd Eaton and Dorothy A Nelson, *American Journal of Clinical Nutrition*, 1991, 54; 281S-287S, Calcium in evolutionary perspective.

Milton (1999): Katharine Milton, *Nutrition*, 1999; 15: 488-498, Nutritional characteristics of wild primate foods: do the diets of our closest living relatives have lessons for us?

Calcium supplementation trials

Heaney (2001): Robert P Heaney, *Nutrition Reviews*, 2001; 59: 327-334, The bone remodelling transient: interpreting interventions involving bone-related nutrients.

Recker (1996): Robert R Recker et al., *Journal of Bone and Mineral Research*, 1996; 11: 1961-1966, Correcting calcium nutritional deficiency prevents spine fractures in elderly women.

Reid (1995): Ian R Reid et al., *The American Journal of Medicine*, 1995; 98: 331-335, Long-term effects of calcium supplementation on bone loss and fractures in postmenopausal women: a randomized controlled trial.

Riggs(1998): B Lawrence Riggs et al., *Journal of Bone and Mineral Research*, 1998; 13: 168-174, Long-term effects of calcium supplementation on serum parathyroid hormone level, bone turnover, and bone loss in elderly women.

Adverse effects of high calcium diets

Whiting (1997): Susan J Whiting and Richard J Wood, *Nutrition Reviews*, 1997; 55: 1-9, Adverse effects of high-calcium diets in humans.

8.　Fats for health　9.　Fat wars

Dietary fats and mortality

Kris-Etherton (2001): Penny M Kris-Etherton et al., *Nutrition Reviews,* 2001; 59: 103-111, The effect of nuts on coronary heart disease risk.

Kromhout (1995): Daan Kromhout et al., *Preventive Medicine,* 1995, 24: 308-315, Dietary saturated and trans fatty acids and cholesterol and 25-year mortality from coronary heart disease: The Seven Countries Study.

Menotti (1999): Alessandro Menotti et al., *European Journal of Epidemiology,* 1999; 15: 507-515, Food intake patterns and 25-year mortality from coronary heart disease: cross-cultural correlations in the Seven Countries Study.

WHO (2003b): Diet, nutrition and the prevention of chronic disease, 2003, WHO Technical Report Series 916, Chapter 5.

Fats in evolutionary diets

Chamberlain (1993): J Chamberlain et al., *Experientia,* 1993; 49: 820-824, Fatty acid profiles of major food sources of howler monkeys (Alouatta palliate) in the neotropics.

Cordain (2000): Loren Cordain et al., *American Journal of Clinical Nutrition,* 2000; 71: 682-692, Plant-animal subsistence ratios and macronutrient energy estimations in worldwide hunter-gatherer diets.

Eaton (1985): S Boyd Eaton and Melvin Konner, *New England Journal of Medicine,* 1985; 312: 283-289, Paleolithic Nutrition: a consideration of its nature and current implications.

Eaton (1997): S B Eaton et al., *European Journal of Clinical Nutrition,* 1997; 51: 207-216, Paleolithic nutrition revisited: a twelve-year retrospective on its nature and implications.

Eaton (1998): S Boyd Eaton et al., *World Review of Nutrition and Dietetics,* 1998; 83: 12-23, Dietary intake of long-chain polyunsaturated fatty acids during the Paleolithic.

Guil-Guerrero (1999): Jose L Guil-Guerrero and Ignacio Rodriguez-Garcia, *European Food Research and Technology,* 1999; 209: 313-316, Lipid classes, fatty acids and carotenes of the leaves of six edible wild plants.

Milton (2000): Katharine Milton, *American Journal of Clinical Nutrition,* 2000; 71: 665-667, Hunter-gatherer diets – a different perspective.

Trials using plant oils rich in ALNA to reduce heart disease deaths

De Lorgeril (1994): Michel de Lorgeril et al., *The Lancet,* 1994; 343: 1454-1459, Mediterranean alpha-linolenic acid-rich diet in secondary prevention of coronary heart disease.

De Lorgeril (1998): Michel de Lorgeril et al., *Archives of Internal Medicine,* 1998; 158: 1181-1187, Mediterranean dietary pattern in a randomised trial: prolonged survival and possible reduced cancer rate.

De Lorgeril (1999): Michel de Lorgeril et al., *Circulation,* 1999; 99: 779-785, Mediterranean diet, traditional risk factors, and the risk of cardiovascular complications after myocardial infarction.

Natvig (1968): Haakon Natvig et al., *Scandinavian Journal of Clinical and Laboratory Investigation Supplementum,* 1968; 105: 1-20, A controlled trial of the effect of linolenic acid on incidence of coronary heart disease: The Norwegian vegetable oil experiment of 1965-66.

Renaud (1995): Serge Renaud et al., *American Journal of Clinical Nutrition,* 1995; 61: 1360S-1367S, Cretan Mediterranean diet for prevention of coronary heart disease.

Singh (1997): Ram B Singh et al., *Cardiovascular Drugs and Therapy,* 1997; 11: 485-491, Randomized, double-blind, placebo-controlled trial of fish oil and mustard oil in patients with suspected acute myocardial infarction: The Indian experiment of infarct survival – 4.

Trials on fish oils

Bucher (2002): Heiner C Bucher et al., *American Journal of Medicine,* 2002; 112: 298-304, N-3 polyunsaturated fatty acids in coronary heart disease: a meta-analysis of randomized controlled trials.

Burr (1989): M L Burr et al., *The Lancet* ii, 1989, 757-761, Effects of changes in fat, fish and fibre intakes on death and myocardial reinfarction: Diet And Reinfarction Trial (DART).

Burr (2001): M L Burr, *European Heart Journal Supplements,* 2001; 3 (Supp D), D75-D78, Reflections on the diet and reinfarction trial (DART).

GISSI (1999): GISSI-Prevenzione Investigators, *The Lancet,* 1999; 354: 447-455, Dietary supplementation with n-3 polyunsaturated fatty acids and vitamin E after myocardial infarction: results of the GISSI-Prevenzione trial.

Marchioli (2001): Roberto Marchioli et al., *Lipids,* 2001; 36: S119-S126, Efficacy of n-3 polyunsaturated fatty acids after myocardial infarction, results of the GISSI-Prevenzione trial.

Other studies on omega-3 fatty acids

Albert (2002): Christine M Albert et al., *New England Journal of Medicine,* 2002; 346: 1113-1118, Blood levels of long-chain n-3 fatty acids and the risk of sudden death.

Ascherio (1996): Alberto Ascherio et al., *British Medical Journal,* 1996; 313: 84-90, Dietary fat and risk of coronary heart disease in men: cohort follow up study in the United States.

This is a fascinating study. Each 5% increase in saturated fat was associated with a 61% increase in fatal coronary heart disease. Adjustment for standard risk factors had little effect, but additional adjustment for fibre intake reduced the increase in risk to about 30%. Every 2% increase in trans fats was associated with a 71% increase in fatal coronary heart disease, but this was eliminated entirely by adjustment for fibre intake. Neither linoleic acid nor alpha-linolenic acid showed a significant effect until after adjustment for total fat intake – after which both showed a protective effect (a 30% reduction in risk for an additional 5% of calories as linoleic acid and a 40% reduction in risk for an additional 1% of calories as alpha-linolenic acid). While these results show the difficulty of unravelling the contribution of interrelated factors, they are very much consistent with the recommendations in this book of 4% to 6% of calories as linoleic acid, 1% to 2% as alpha-linolenic acid, less than 7% saturated fat, less than 1% trans fats and plenty of fibre from unrefined plant foods.

Djousse (2001): Luc Djousse et al., *American Journal of Clinical Nutrition*, 2001; 74: 612-619, Relation between dietary linolenic acid and coronary artery disease in the National Heart, Lung, and Blood Institute Family Heart Study.

Djousse (2003): Luc Djousse et al., *American Journal of Clinical Nutrition*, 2003; 77: 819-825, Dietary linolenic acid and carotid atherosclerosis: the National Heart, Lung, and Blood Institute Family Heart Study.

Dolecek (1992): Therese A Dolecek, *Proceedings of the Society for Experimental Biology and Medicine*, 1992; 200: 177-182, Epidemiological evidence of relationships between dietary polyunsaturated fatty acids and mortality in the Multiple Risk Factor Intervention Trial.

Freese (2001): Riita Freese, *European Journal of Lipid Science and Technology,* 2001; 103: 483-489, Low-erucic acid rapeseed oil and platelet function.

Hu (1999): Frank B Hu et al., *American Journal of Clinical Nutrition*, 1999; 69: 890-897, Dietary intake of alpha-linolenic acid and risk of fatal ischemic heart disease among women

Hu (2002): Frank B Hu et al., *Journal of the American Medical Association*, 2002; 287: 1815-1821, Fish and omega-3 fatty acid intake and risk of coronary heart disease in women.

Lemaitre (2003): Rozenn N Lemaitre et al., *American Journal of Clinical Nutrition,* 2003; 77: 319-325, n-3 polyunsaturated fatty acids, fatal ischemic heart disease, and nonfatal myocardial infarction in older adults: the Cardiovascular Health Study.

Marckmann (1999): P Marckmann and M Gronbaek, *European Journal of Clinical Nutrition*, 1999; 53: 585-590, Fish consumption and coronary heart disease mortality. A systematic review of prospective cohort studies.

Oomen (2001): Claudia M Oomen et al., *American Journal of Clinical Nutrition*, 2001; 74: 457-463, Alpha-linolenic acid intake is not beneficially associated with 10-y risk of coronary artery disease incidence: the Zutphen Elderly Study.

Pietinen (1997): Pirjo Pietinen et al., *American Journal of Epidemiology*, 1997; 145: 876-887, Intake of fatty acids and risk of coronary heart disease in a cohort of Finnish men.

Renaud (1986): Serge Renaud et al., *American Journal of Clinical Nutrition*, 1986; 43: 136-150, Influence of long-term diet modification on platelet function and composition in Moselle farmers.

Zhang (1999): Jianjun Zhang et al., *Preventive Medicine,* 1999; 28: 520-529, Fish consumption and mortality from all causes, ischemic heart disease, and stroke: an ecological study.

This study claims a clear protective association between fish consumption and overall mortality in comparisons between countries, but the apparent association is greatly exaggerated by the inclusion of five Eastern European countries with low fish consumption and high mortality. This is inappropriate as Eastern European countries differ from established market economies in many other factors which contribute to mortality. If these countries are removed from the analysis, a much weaker association is found and even this weaker association is due largely to one country: Japan. While omega-3 consumption from fish may be beneficial if mercury contamination is low, this study clearly overstates any such benefit from fish.

Environmental issues related to fish

Guallar (2002): Eliseo Guallar et al., *New England Journal of Medicine,* 2002; 347: 1747-1754, Mercury, fish oils and the risk of myocardial infarction.

Pauly (2002): Daniel Pauly et al., *Nature,* 2002; 418: 689-695, Towards sustainability in world fisheries.

Rissanen (2000): Tiina Rissanen et al., *Circulation*, 2000; 102: 2677-2679, Fish oil-derived fatty acids, docosahexaenoic acid and docosapentaenoic acid, and the risk of acute coronary events.

Salonen (1995): Jukka Salonen et al., *Circulation*, 1995; 91: 645-655, Intake of mercury from fish, lipid peroxidation, and the risk of myocardial infarction and coronary, cardiovascular, and any death in Eastern Finnish men.

Schober (2003): Susan E Schober et al., *Journal of the American Medical Association,* 2003; 289: 1667-1674, Blood mercury levels in US children and women of childbearing age, 1999-2000.

Sorensen (1999): N Sorensen et al., *Epidemiology*, 1999; 10: 370-375, Prenatal methylmercury exposure as a cardiovascular risk factor at seven years of age.

Yoshizawa (2002): Kazuko Yoshizawa et al., *New England Journal of Medicine,* 2002; 347: 1755-1760, Mercury and the risk of coronary heart disease in men.

Note: both Guallar (2002) and Yoshizawa (2002) found an increase in heart disease risk with methyl mercury (the form found in fish). In the former European study, the relative risk for a first heart attack for the highest quintile of mercury was 1.47, increasing to 1.86 when adjusted for DHA intake. There was no significant benefit for high DHA level until after adjustment for mercury level, indicating that the effect of mercury was countering the effect of omega-3 fatty acids. In the latter US study, the relative risk for high mercury levels in non-dentists was 1.27, rising to 1.70 after adjustment for EPA and DHA, but was not statistically significant due to small numbers. The results of the two studies are nevertheless highly consistent.

Dairy fat, calcium and heart disease

Al-Delaimy (2003): Wael K Al-Delaimy et al., *American Journal of Clinical Nutrition,* 2003; 77: 814-818, A prospective study of calcium intake from diet and supplements and risk of ischemic heart disease among men.

Bostick (1999): Roberd M Bostick et al., *American Journal of Epidemiology,* 1999; 149: 151-161, Relation of calcium, vitamin D, and dairy foods to ischemic heart disease mortality among postmenopausal women.

Hu (1999): Frank B Hu et al., *American Journal of Clinical Nutrition,* 1999; 70: 1001-1008, Dietary saturated fats and their food sources in relation to the risk of coronary heart disease in women.

Fat, alpha-linolenic acid, animal products and cancer

Bingham (2003): Sheila A Bingham et al., *The Lancet,* 2003; 361: 1496-1501, Dietary fibre in food and protection against colorectal cancer in the European Prospective Investigation into Cancer and Nutrition (EPIC): an observational study.

Chan (2001): June M Chan et al., *American Journal of Clinical Nutrition,* 2001; 74: 549-554, Dairy products, calcium, and prostate cancer risk in the Physicians' Health Study.

Colditz (2000): Graham A Colditz, *Cancer Causes and Controls,* 2000; 11: 677-678, Changing dietary patterns and cancer prevention: alpha-linolenic acid health risks and benefits.

De Stefani (2000): Eduardo de Stefani et al., *Cancer Epidemiology, Biomarkers and Prevention,* 2000; 9: 335-338, α-linolenic acid and risk of prostate cancer: a case-control study in Uruguay.

Gann (1994): Peter H Gann et al., *Journal of the National Cancer Institute,* 1994; 86: 281-286, Prospective study of plasma fatty acids and risk of prostate cancer.

Giovannucci (1993): Edward Giovannucci, *Journal of the National Cancer Institute,* 1993; 85: 1571-1579, A prospective study of dietary fat and risk of prostate cancer.

Giovannucci (1998): Edward Giovannucci et al., *Cancer Research,* 1998; 58: 442-447, Calcium and fructose intake in relation to risk of prostate cancer.

Holmes (1999): Michelle D Holmes et al., *Journal of the American Medical Association,* 1999; 281: 914-920, Association of dietary intake of fatty acids with risk of breast cancer.

Hsing (2000): Ann W Hsing et al., *International Journal of Cancer,* 2000; 85: 60-67, International trends and patterns of prostate cancer incidence and mortality.

Hunter (1996): David J Hunter et al., *New England Journal of Medicine,* 1996; 334: 356-361, Cohort studies of fat intake and the risk of breast cancer – a pooled analysis.

Key (2002): Timothy J Key et al., *The Lancet,* 2002; 360: 861-868, The effect of diet on risk of cancer.

Kushi (2002): Lawrence Kushi and Edward Giovannucci, *American Journal of Medicine,* 2002; 113(9B): 63S-70, Dietary fat and cancer.

Michaud (2001): Dominique S Michaud et al., *Cancer Causes and Control,* 2001; 12: 557-567, A prospective study of animal products and risk of prostate cancer.

Missmer (2002): Stacey A Missmer et al., *International Journal of Epidemiology,* 2003; 31: 78-85, Meat and dairy food consumption and breast cancer: a pooled analysis of cohort studies.

Sandhu (2001): Manjinder S Sandhu et al., *Cancer Epidemiology, Biomarkers and Prevention,* 2001; 10: 439-446, Systematic review of the prospective cohort studies on meat consumption and colorectal cancer risk: a meta-analytical approach.

Schuurman (1999a): Agnes G Schuurman et al., *Cancer,* 1999; 86: 1019-

1027, Association of energy and fat intake with prostate carcinoma risk: Results from the Netherlands Cohort Study.

Schuurman (1999b): A G Schuurman et al., *British Journal of Cancer,* 1999; 80: 1107-1113, Animal products, calcium and protein and prostate cancer risk in the Netherlands Cohort Study.

Terry (2003): Paul D Terry et al., *American Journal of Clinical Nutrition,* 2003; 77: 532-543, Intakes of fish and marine fatty acids and the risks of cancers of the breast and prostate and of other hormone-related cancers: a review of the epidemiological evidence.

Willett (1998): Walter Willett, *Nutritional Epidemiology,* 2nd edition, Chapter 16, Dietary fat and breast cancer. ISBN 0-19-512297-6.

Conversion of alpha-linolenic acid to longer chain omega-3s, and vegetarian omega-3 levels

Agren (1995): Jyrki J Agren et al., *Lipids,* 1995; 30: 365-369, Fatty acid composition of erythrocyte, platelet and serum lipids in strict vegans.

Bemelmans (2000): W J E Bemelmans, *European Journal of Clinical Nutrition,* 2000; 54: 865-871, Associations of α-linolenic acid and linoleic acid with risk factors for coronary heart disease.

Bemelmans (2002): Wanda J E Bemelmans, *American Journal of Clinical Nutrition,* 2002; 75: 221-227, Effect of increased α-linolenic acid and group nutritional education on cardiovascular risk factors: The Mediterranean Alpha-linolenic Enriched Grongingen Dietary Intervention (MARGARIN) study.

Burdge (2002a): Graham C Burdge et al., *British Journal of Nutrition,* 2002; 88: 355-363, Eicosapentaenoic and docosapentaenoic acids are the principal products of α-linolenic acid metabolism in young men.

Burdge (2002b): Graham C Burdge and Stephen A Wootton, *British Journal of Nutrition,* 2002; 88: 411-420, Conversion of α-linolenic acid to eicosapentaenoic, docosapentaenoic and docosahexaenoic acids in young women.

Cleland (1992): Leslie G Cleland et al., *American Journal of Clinical Nutrition,* 1992; 55: 395-399, Linoleate inhibits EPA incorporation from dietary fish-oil supplements in human subjects.

Cunnane (1993): Stephen C Cunnane et al., *British Journal of Nutrition,* 1993; 69, 443-453, High α-linolenic acid flaxseed (Linum usitatisssimum): some nutritional properties in humans.

Emken (1994): Edward A Emken et al., *Biochimica et Biophysica Acta,* 1994; 1213: 277-288, Dietary linoleic acid influences desaturation and acylation of deuterium-labeled linoleic and linolenic acids in young adult males.

Ezaki (1999): Osamu Ezaki et al., *Journal of Nutritional Science and Vitaminology,* 1999; 45: 759-772, Long-term effects of dietary α-linolenic acid from perilla oil on serum fatty acids composition and on the risk factors of coronary heart disease in Japanese elderly subjects.

Finnegan (2003): Yvonne E Finnegan et al., *American Journal of Clinical Nutrition,* 2003; 77: 783-795, Plant- and marine-derived n-3 polyunsaturated fatty acids have different effects on fasting and postprandial blood lipid concentrations and on the susceptibility of LDL to oxidative modification in moderately hyperlipidemic subjects.

Fokkema (2000a): M R Fokkema et al., *Prostaglandins, leukotrienes and essential fatty acids,* 2000; 63: 279-285, Polyunsaturated fatty acid status of Dutch vegans and omnivores.

Fokkema (2000b): M R Fokkema et al., *Prostaglandins, leukotrienes and essential fatty acids,* 2000; 63: 287-292, Short-term supplementation of low-dose γ-linolenic acid (GLA) and α-linolenic acid (ALA), or GLA plus ALA does not augment LCPω3 status of Dutch vegans to an appreciable extent.

Francois (2003): Cindy A Francois et al., *American Journal of Clinical Nutrition,* 2003; 77: 226-233, Supplementing lactating women with flaxseed oil does not increase docosahexaenoic acid in their milk.

Gerster (1998): Helga Gerster, *International Journal of Vitamin and Nutrition Research,* 1998; 68: 159-173, Can adults adequately convert α-linolenic acid (18: 3n-3) to eicosapentaenoic acid (20: 5n-3) and docosahexaenoic acid (22: 6n-3)?

Ghafoorunissa (1992): Indu M, Ghafoorunissa, *Nutrition Research,* 1992; 12: 569-582, n-3 fatty acids in Indian diets – comparison of the effects of precursor (alpha-linolenic acid) vs product (long chain n-3 polyunsaturated fatty acids).

Katan (1997): Martijn B Katan et al., *Journal of Lipid Research,* 1997; 38: 2012-2022, Kinetics of the incorporation of dietary fatty acids into serum cholesteryl esters, erythrocyte membranes and adipose tissue: an 18-month controlled study.

Krajcovicova-Kudlackova (1997): M. Krajcovicova-Kudlackova et al., *Annals of Nutrition and Metabolism,* 1997; 41: 365-370, Plasma fatty acid profile and alternative nutrition.

Li (1999a): Duo Li et al., *Clinical Science*, 1999; 97: 175-181, Lipoprotein(a), essential fatty acid status and lipoprotein lipids in female Australian vegetarians.

Li (1999b): Duo Li et al., *American Journal of Clinical Nutrition*, 1999; 69: 872-882, Effect of dietary α-linolenic acid on thrombotic risk factors in vegetarian men.

Mantzioris (1994): Evangeline Mantzioris et al., *American Journal of Clinical Nutrition*, 1994; 59: 1304-1309, Dietary substitution with α-linolenic acid-rich vegetable oil increases eicosapentaenoic acid concentrations in tissues.

Mantzioris (1995): Evangeline Mantzioris et al., *American Journal of Clinical Nutrition*, 1995; 61: 320-324, Differences exist in the relationships between dietary linoleic and α-linolenic acids and their respective long-chain metabolites.

Melchert (1987): H-U Melchert et al., *Atherosclerosis*, 1987; 65: 159-166, Fatty acid patterns in triglycerides, diglycerides, free fatty acids, cholesteryl esters and phosphatidylcholine in serum from vegetarians and non-vegetarians.

Pawlosky (2001): Robert J Pawlosky et al., *Journal of Lipid Research*, 2001; 1257-1265, Physiological compartmental analysis of α-linolenic metabolism in adult humans.

This paper is widely cited as showing very limited conversion of alpha-linolenic acid to EPA. This conclusion is an artefact of an error in the model used which assumes that when alpha-linolenic acid disappears from plasma (a rapid transition) it is irrevocably lost. In fact, alpha-linolenic acid is stored in the liver and steadily released over a period of a few weeks in cholesteryl esters.

Phinney (1990): Stephen D Phinney et al., *American Journal of Clinical Nutrition*, 1990; 51: 385-392, Reduced arachidonate in serum phospholipids and cholesteryl esters associated with vegetarian diets in humans.

Renaud and Nordoy (1983): S Renaud and A Nordoy, *The Lancet*, May 21, 1983; 1169, "Small is beautiful": α-linolenic acid and eicosapentaenoic acid in man.

Sanders (1978): T A B Sanders et al., *American Journal of Clinical Nutrition*, 1978, 31: 805-813, Studies of vegans: the fatty acid composition of plasma choline phosphoglycerides, erythrocytes, adipose tissue, and breast milk, and some indicators of susceptibility to ischemic heart disease in vegans and omnivore controls.

Sanders (1981): T A B Sanders and Katherine M Younger, *British Journal of Nutrition,* 1981; 45: 613-616, The effect of dietary supplements of ω3 polyunsaturated fatty acids on the fatty acid composition of platelets and plasma choline phosphoglycerides.

Sanders (1983): T A B Sanders and Farah Roshanai, *Clinical Science,* 1983; 64: 91-99, The influence of different types of ω3 polyunsaturated fatty acids on blood lipids and platelet function in healthy volunteers.

Sanders (1992): T A B Sanders and Sheela Reddy, *Journal of Pediatrics,* 1992; 120: S71-S77, The influence of a vegetarian diet on the fatty acid composition of human milk and the essential fatty acid status of the infant.

Optimal intake of linoleic acid

A research committee (1968): *The Lancet,* 28 September 1968; 693-699, Controlled trial of soya-bean oil in myocardial infarction.

Dayton (1969): Seymour Dayton et al., *American Heart Association Monograph Number 25,* 1969, A controlled clinical trial of a diet high in unsaturated fat. (*Circulation,* 1969; 40 (Supp II): 1-69)

Frantz (1989): Ivan D Frantz, *Arteriosclerosis,* 1989; 9: 129-135, Test of effect of lipid lowering by diet on cardiovascular risk: The Minnesota Coronary Survey.

Hjermann (1981), I Hjermann et al., *The Lancet,* 12 December 1981; 1303-1310, Effect of diet and smoking intervention on the incidence of coronary heart disease.

Hjermann (1986): I Hjermann et al., *American Journal of Medicine,* 1986; 80 (S2A): 7S-11S, Oslo diet and antismoking trial.

Leren (1970): Paul Leren, *Circulation,* 1970; XLII: 935-942, The Oslo Diet-Heart Study: Eleven-year report.

Simopoulos (2000): A P Simopoulos et al., *Prostaglandins, Leukotrienes and Essential Fatty Acids,* 2000; 63: 119-121, Workshop statement on the essentiality of and recommended dietary intakes for omega-6 and omega-3 fatty acids.

Singh (1992): *British Medical Journal,* 1992; 304: 1015-1019, Randomised controlled trial of cardioprotective diet in patients with recent acute myocardial infarction: results of one year follow up.

WHO (2003b): Diet, nutrition and the prevention of chronic disease, 2003, WHO Technical Report Series 916

Glycaemic load

Augustin (2002): L S Augustin et al., *European Journal of Clinical Nutrition,* 2002; 56: 1049-1071, Glycemic index in chronic disease: a review.

Liu (2000): Simin Liu et al., *American Journal of Clinical Nutrition,* 2000; 71: 1455-1461, A prospective study of dietary glycemic load, carbohydrate intake and risk of coronary heart disease in US women.

Liu (2001): Simin Liu et al., *American Journal of Clinical Nutrition,* 2001; 73: 560-566, Dietary glycemic load assessed by food-frequency questionnaire in relation to plasma high-density-lipoprotein cholesterol and fasting plasma triacylglycerols in postmenopausal women.

Trials of low fat diets

Barnard (2000): Neal D Barnard et al., *American Journal of Cardiology,* 2000; 85: 969-972, Effectiveness of a low-fat vegetarian diet in altering serum lipids in healthy premenopausal women.

McDougall (1995): John McDougall et al., *Journal of the American College of Nutrition,* 1995; 14: 491-496, Rapid reduction of serum cholesterol and blood pressure by a twelve-day, very low fat, strictly vegetarian diet.

Ornish (1990): Dean Ornish et al., *The Lancet,* 1990; 336: 129-133, Can lifestyle changes reverse coronary heart disease?

Ornish (1998): Dean Ornish et al., *Journal of the American Medical Association,* 1998; 280: 2001-2007, Intensive lifestyle changes for reversal of coronary heart disease.

Effect of diet on cholesterol levels and cardiovascular disease

Ascherio and Willett (1997): Alberto Ascherio and Walter C Willett, *American Journal of Clinical Nutrition,* 1997; 66S: 1006S-1010S, Health effects of trans fatty acids.

Baum (2000): Charles L Baum and Melissa Brown, *Nutrition Reviews,* 2000; 58: 148-151, Low-fat, high-carbohydrate diets and atherogenic risk.

Connor (1999): William E Connor, *American Journal of Clinical Nutrition,* 1999; 70: 951-952, Harbingers of coronary heart disease: dietary saturated fatty acids and cholesterol. Is chocolate benign because of its stearic acid content?

Dreon (1999): Darlene M Dreon et al., *American Journal of Clinical Nutrition,* 1999; 69: 411-418, A very-low-fat diet is not associated with improved lipoprotein profiles in men with a predominance of large, low-density lipoproteins.

Dreon (2000): Darlene M Dreon et al., *American Journal of Clinical Nutrition,* 2000; 71: 1611-1616, Reduced LDL particle size in children consuming a very-low-fat diet is related to parental LDL subclass patterns.

Gillman (1997): Matthew W Gillman et al., *Journal of the American Medical Association,* 1997: 278: 2145-2150, Inverse association of dietary fat with development of ischemic stroke in men.

Katan (1997): Martijn B Katan, *American Journal of Clinical Nutrition,* 1997; 66S: 974S-979S, High-oil compared with low-fat, high-carbohydrate diets in the prevention of ischemic heart disease.

Katan (1998): Martijn B Katan, *American Journal of Clinical Nutrition,* 1998; 67S: 573S-576S, Effect of low-fat diets on high-density lipoprotein concentrations.

Katan (2000): Martijn B Katan, *Nutrition Reviews,* 2000; 58: 188-191, Trans fatty acids and plasma lipoproteins.

Kris-Etherton and Yu (1997): Penny M Kris-Etherton and Shaomei Yu, *American Journal of Clinical Nutrition,* 1997; 65S: 1628S-1644S, Individual fatty acid effects on plasma lipids and lipoproteins: human studies.

Morgan (1997): Sally A Morgan et al., *Journal of the American Dietetic Association,* 1997: 97: 151-156, A low fat diet supplemented with monounsaturated fat results in less HDL-C lowering than a very-low fat diet.

Cholesterol levels and mortality

Golomb (1998): Beatrice A Golomb, *Annals of Internal Medicine,* 1998; 128: 478-487, Cholesterol and violence: is there a connection?

Iribarren (1995a): Carlos Iribarren et al., *Journal of the American Medical Association,* 1995; 273: 1926-1932, Serum total cholesterol and mortality.

Iribarren (1995b): Carlos Iribarren et al., *Circulation,* 1995; 92: 2396-2403, Low serum cholesterol and mortality: Which is the cause and which is the effect?

Jacobs (1992): David Jacobs et al., *Circulation,* 1992; 86: 1046-1060, Report of the conference on low blood cholesterol: mortality associations.

Jacobs (2000): David R Jacobs and Carlos Iribarren, *American Journal of Epidemiology,* 2000; 151: 748-751, Invited commentary: Low cholesterol and nonatherosclerotic disease risk: a persistently perplexing question.

Kinosian (1994): Bruce Kinosian et al., *Annals of Internal Medicine,* 1994; 121: 641-647, Cholesterol and coronary heart disease: predicting risks by levels and ratios.

Law (1994): M R Law et al., *British Medical Journal,* 1994; 308: 367-373, By how much and how quickly does reduction in serum cholesterol concentration lower risk of ischemic heart disease.

National Heart, Lung and Blood Institute (2001): Excel-based risk calculator (http://hin.nhlbi.nih.gov/atpiii/riskcalc.htm) prepared by Ralph B. D'Agostino, Sr., Ph.D. and Lisa M. Sullivan, Ph.D., Boston University and The Framingham Heart Study and Daniel Levy, M.D., Framingham Heart Study, National Heart, Lung and Blood Institute.

Pekkanen (1992): Juha Pekkanen et al., *American Journal of Epidemiology,* 1992: 135: 1251-8, Short and long-term associations of serum cholesterol with mortality: The 25-year follow-up of the Finnish Cohorts of the Seven Countries study.

Stamler (1999): Jeremiah Stamler et al., *Journal of the American Medical Association,* 1999; 282: 2012-2018, Low risk-factor profile and long-term cardiovascular and noncardiovascular mortality and life expectancy: Findings for 5 large cohorts of young adult and middle-aged men and women.

Effect of diet on C-reactive protein and other inflammation markers

Caughey (1996): Gillian E Caughey et al., *American Journal of Clinical Nutrition,* 1996; 63: 116-122, The effect on human tumour necrosis factor α and interleukin 1β production of diets enriched in n-3 fatty acids from vegetable oil or fish oil.

Liu (2002): Simin Liu et al., *American Journal of Clinical Nutrition,* 2002; 75: 492-498, Relation between a diet with a high glycemic load and plasma concentrations of high-sensitivity C-reactive protein in middle-aged women.

Madsen (2003): Trine Madsen et al., *British Journal of Nutrition,* 2003; 89: 517-522, The effect of dietary n-3 fatty acids on serum concentrations of C-reactive protein: a dose-response study.

Mezzano (2000): Diego Mezzano et al., *Thrombosis Research,* 2000; 100: 153-160, Cardiovascular risk factors in vegetarians: normalisation of hyperhomocysteinemia with vitamin B12 and reduction of platelet aggregation with n-3 fatty acids.

Rallidis (2003): Loukianos S Rallidis et al., *Atherosclerosis,* 2003; 167: 237-242, Dietary alpha-linolenic acid decreases C-reactive protein, serum amyloid A and interleukin-6 in dyslipidaemic patients.

Sierksma (2002): A Sierksma et al., *European Journal of Clinical Nutrition,* 2002; 56: 1130-1136, Moderate alcohol consumption reduces plasma C-reactive protein and fibrinogen levels; a randomized, diet-controlled intervention study.

Vikram (2003): Naval K Vikram et al., *Atherosclerosis,* 2003; 168: 305-313, Correlations of C-reactive protein with anthropometric profile, percentage of body fat and lipids in healthy adolescents and young adults in urban North India.

C-reactive protein, other inflammation markers and mortality

Danesh (2000): John Danesh et al., *British Medical Journal,* 2000; 321: 199-204, Low grade inflammation and coronary heart disease: prospective study and updated meta-analyses (supplementary tables on www.bmj.com).

Ridker (2002): Paul M Ridker et al., *New England Journal of Medicine,* 2002; 347: 1557-1565, Comparison of C-reactive protein and low-density lipoprotein cholesterol in the prediction of first cardiovascular events.

10. Natural imperfections

Vitamin D and type 1 diabetes

Hypponen (2001): Elina E Hypponen, *The Lancet,* 2001; 358: 1500-1503, Intake of vitamin D and risk of type 1 diabetes: a birth-cohort study.

Mayer (2002): Jean Mayer, *Nutrition Reviews,* 2002; 60: 118-121, Can vitamin D supplementation in infancy prevent type 1 diabetes.

Skrabic (2003): Veselin Skrabic et al., *Diabetes Research and Clinical Practice,* 2003; 59: 31-35, Vitamin D receptor polymorphism and susceptibility to type 1 diabetes in the Dalmatian population.

Stene (2000): L C Stene et al., *Diabetologia,* 2000; 43: 1093-1098, Use of cod liver oil during pregnancy associated with lower risk of Type I diabetes in the offspring.

Vitamin D and cancer

Ahonen (2000): Merja H Ahonen et al., *Cancer Causes and Control,* 2000; 11: 847-852, Prostate cancer risk and prediagnostic serum 25-hydroxyvitamin D levels (Finland).

Ainsleigh (1993): H Gordon Ainsleigh, *Preventive Medicine,* 1993; 22: 132-140, Beneficial effects of sun exposure on cancer mortality.

John (1999): Esther M John et al., *Cancer, Epidemiology, Biomarkers and Prevention,* 1999; 8: 399-406, Vitamin D and Breast cancer risk: The NHANES I epidemiologic follow-up study, 1971-1975 to 1992.

Myung-Hee Shin (2002): Myung-Hee Shin et al., *Journal of the National Cancer Institute,* 2002; 94: 1301-1311, Intake of dairy products, calcium, and vitamin D and risk of breast cancer.

Vitamin D and other conditions

Thys-Jacobs (1999): Susan Thys-Jacobs et al., *Steroids,* 1999; 64: 430-435, Vitamin D and calcium dysregulation in the polycystic ovarian syndrome.

Thys-Jacobs (2000): Susan Thys-Jacobs, *Journal of the American College of Nutrition,* 2000; 19: 220-227, Micronutrients and the premenstrual syndrome: the case for calcium.

Required amounts of vitamin D

Department of Health (1991): *Dietary Reference Values for food energy and nutrients for the United Kingdom,* 1991, The Stationery Office.

Vieth (1999): Reinhold Vieth, *American Journal of Clinical Nutrition,* 1999; 69: 842-856, Vitamin D supplementation, 25-hydroxyvitamin D concentrations and safety.

Vieth (2001): Reinhold Vieth et al., *American Journal of Clinical Nutrition,* 2001; 73: 288-294, Efficacy and safety of vitamin D3 intake exceeding the lowest observed adverse effect level.

Optimal iodine intakes

Dunn (2001): John T Dunn and Francois Delange, *Journal of Clinical Endocrinology and Metabolism,* 2001; 86: 2360-2363, Damaged reproduction: the most important consequence of iodine deficiency.

Lee (1999): Kelly Lee et al., *Nutrition Reviews,* 1999; 57: 177-181, Too much versus too little: the implications of current iodine intake in the United States.

Iodine intakes in vegans and omnivores

Appleby et al., (1999): Paul N Appleby et al., *American Journal of Clinical Nutrition,* 1999; 70: 523S-531S, The Oxford Vegetarian Study: an overview.

Lee (1994): Susan M Lee et al., *British Journal of Nutrition,* 1994; 72: 435-446, Iodine in British foods and diets.

Lightowler (2002): H J Lightowler and G J Davies, *European Journal of Clinical Nutrition,* 2002; 56: 765-770, Assessment of iodine intake in vegans by dietary record vs duplicate portion technique.

Rasmussen (2002): Lone B Rasmussen et al., *American Journal of Clinical Nutrition,* 2002; 76: 1069-1076, Relations between various measures of iodine intake and thyroid volume, thyroid nodularity, and serum thyroglobulin.

Shaikh (2003): M G Shaikh et al., *Journal of Pediatric Endocrinology and Metabolism,* 2003; 16: 111-113, Transient neonatal hypothyroidism due to a maternal vegan diet.

www.people.virginia.edu/~jtd/iccidd   International council for the control of iodine deficiency disorders – summarises iodine status by country.

Hypothyroidism and elevated homocysteine

Lien (2000): E A Lien et al., *Journal of Clinical Endocrinology and Metabolism,* 2000; 85: 1049-1053, Plasma total homocysteine levels during short-term iatrogenic hypothyroidism.

Morris (2001): Martha Savaria Morris, *Atherosclerosis,* 2001; 155: 195-200, Hyperhomocysteinemia and hypercholesterolemia associated with hypothyroidism in the third US National Health And Nutrition Examination Survey.

Selenium requirements

Rayman (2000): Margaret P Rayman, *The Lancet,* 2000; 356: 233-241, The importance of selenium to human health.

Selenium and cancer

Clark (1998): L C Clark et al., *British Journal of Urology,* 1998; 81: 730-734, Decreased incidence of prostate cancer with selenium supplementation: results of a double-blind cancer prevention trial.

Nomura (2000): Abraham M Y Nomura et al., *Cancer, Epidemiology, Biomarkers and Prevention,* 2000; 9: 883-887, Serum selenium and subsequent risk of prostate cancer.

Yoshizawa (1998): Kazuko Yoshizawa et al., *Journal of the National Cancer Institute,* 1998; 90: 1219-1224, Study of prediagnostic selenium level in toenails and the risk of advanced prostate cancer.

Selenium intakes in vegetarians

Clarke (2003): Don B Clarke et al., *Food Chemistry,* 2003; 81: 287-300, Levels of phytoestrogens, inorganic trace-elements, natural toxicants and nitrate in vegetarian duplicate diets.

Judd (1997): Patricia A Judd et al., *British Medical Journal*, 1997; 314: 1834, Vegetarians and vegans may be most at risk from low selenium intakes.

11. Unnecessary fears

Protein, calorie and amino acid requirements

Department of Health (1991): *Dietary Reference Values for food energy and nutrients for the United Kingdom*, 1991, The Stationery Office.

Kurpad (2002a): Anura V Kurpad et al., *American Journal of Clinical Nutrition*, 2002; 76: 404-412, Lysine requirements of healthy adult Indian subjects receiving long-term feeding, measured with a 24-h indicator amino acid oxidation and balance technique.

Kurpad (2002b): Anura V Kurpad et al., *American Journal of Clinical Nutrition*, 2002; 76: 789-797, Threonine requirements of healthy Indian men, measured by a 24-h indicator amino acid oxidation and balance technique.

Kurpad (2003): Anura V Kurpad et al., *American Journal of Clinical Nutrition*, 2003; 77: 101-10, Lysine requirements of chronically undernourished Indian men, measured by a 24-h indicator amino acid oxidation and balance technique.

National Research Council (1989): *Recommended dietary allowances (10th edition)*, 1989, National Academy Press. (USA)

Rand (2003): William M Rand et al., *American Journal of Clinical Nutrition*, 2003; 77: 109-127, Meta-analysis of nitrogen balance studies for estimating protein requirements in healthy adults.

Iron requirements and absorption

Hallberg (2000): Leif Hallberg and Lena Hulthen, *American Journal of Clinical Nutrition*, 2000; 71: 1147-1160, Prediction of dietary iron absorption: an algorithm for calculating absorption and bioavailability of dietary iron.

Hallberg (2001): Leif Hallberg, *Annual Reviews of Nutrition*, 2001; 21: 1-21, Perspectives on nutritional iron deficiency.

Hunt (2000): Janet R Hunt and Zamzam K Roughead, *American Journal of Clinical Nutrition*, 2000; 71: 94-102, Adaptation of iron absorption in men consuming diets with high or low iron bioavailability.

Institute of Medicine (2001): *Dietary reference intakes for vitamin A, vitamin K, arsenic, boron, chromium, copper, iodine, iron, manganese, molybdenum, nickel, silicon, vanadium, and zinc*, 2001, National Academy Press.

Adverse effects of excess iron

Ascherio (2001): Alberto Ascherio et al., *Circulation,* 2001; 103: 52-57, Blood donations and risk of coronary heart disease in men.

Corti (1997): Maria-Chiara Corti et al., *American Journal of Cardiology,* 1997: 120-127, Serum iron level, coronary artery disease, and all-cause mortality in older men and women.

Danesh (1999): John Danesh and Paul Appleby, *Circulation,* 1999; 99: 852-854, Coronary heart disease and iron status: meta-analyses of prospective studies.

Fernandez-Real (2002): Jose Manuel Fernandez-Real et al., *Diabetes,* 2002; 51: 2348-2354, Cross-talk between iron metabolism and diabetes.

Hua (2001): Nancy W Hua et al., *British Journal of Nutrition,* 2001; 86: 515-519, Low iron status and enhanced insulin sensitivity in lacto-ovo vegetarians.

Klipstein-Grobusch (1999): Kerstin Klipstein-Grobusch et al., *American Journal of Clinical Nutrition,* 1999; 69: 1231-1236, Serum ferritin and the risk of myocardial infarction in the elderly: the Rotterdam study.

Sullivan (1999): Jerome L Sullivan, *Circulation,* 1999; 100: 1260-1263, Iron and the genetics of cardiovascular disease.

Tuomainen (1998): Tomi-Pekka Tuomainen et al., *Circulation,* 1998; 97: 1461-1466, Association between body iron stores and risk of acute myocardial infarction in men.

Van Jaarsveld (2002): Henretha van Jaarsveld and Gertruida F Pool, *Atherosclerosis,* 2002; 161: 395-402, Beneficial effects of blood donation on high density lipoprotein concentration and the oxidative potential of low density lipoprotein.

Iron status in vegetarians and non-vegetarians

Ball (1999): Madeline J Ball and Melinda A Bartlett, *American Journal of Clinical Nutrition,* 1999; 70: 353-358, Dietary intake and iron status of Australian vegetarian women.

12.5% of omnivores and 18% of vegetarians had serum ferritin levels below 12 micrograms per litre (not statistically significant).

Cowin (2001); I Cowin et al., *European Journal of Clinical Nutrition,* 2001; 55: 278-286, Association between composition of the diet and haemoglobin and ferritin levels in 18-month-old children.

Low haemoglobin levels were found in 29% of children eating no meat compared with 19% overall; haemoglobin was higher in children who ate any fruit or any vegetables; and ferritin was lower in children consuming unfortified cow's milk.

Fleming (2002): Diana J Fleming et al., *American Journal of Clinical Nutrition,* 2002; 76: 1375-1384, Dietary factors associated with the risk of high iron stores in the elderly Framingham Heart Study cohort.

Supplemental iron, red meat and fruit each increased risk of high iron stores while higher whole grain intake reduced risk.

Larsson (2002): Christel L Larsson and Gunnar K Johansson, *American Journal of Clinical Nutrition,* 2002; 76: 100-106, Dietary intake and nutritional status of young vegans and omnivores in Sweden.

20% of omnivores and 23% of vegans showed low iron status.

Nathan (1996): Indira Nathan et al., *British Journal of Nutrition,* 1996; 75: 533-544, The dietary intake of a group of vegetarian children aged 7-11 years compared with matched omnivores.

The abstract to this paper misleadingly highlights that 47.5% of vegetarian children showed low haemoglobin. The text notes that 33% of non-vegetarians also showed low levels by the same standard and that the difference was not statistically significant.

Nelson (1993): Michael Nelson et al., *British Journal of Nutrition,* 1993; 70: 147-155, Haemoglobin, ferritin and iron intakes in British children aged 12-14 years: a preliminary investigation.

25% (4 out of 16) vegetarians were anaemic compared with 9% of non-vegetarians. Statistical significance was not claimed, and a follow-up study (Nelson, 1994) found no difference. Higher vitamin C intakes reduced risk of anaemia and risk of ferritin concentrations less than 20 micrograms per litre.

Nelson (1994): M Nelson et al., *British Journal of Nutrition,* 1994; 72: 427-433, Iron-deficiency anaemia and physical performance in adolescent girls from different ethnic backgrounds.

20% of vegetarians and 20% of non-vegetarians had haemoglobin less than 120 grams per litre.

Thane (2000): C W Thane and C J Bates, *Journal of Human Nutrition and Dietetics,* 2000; 13: 149-162, Dietary intakes and nutrient status of vegetarian preschool children from a British national survey.

Vegetarians had lower ferritin concentrations than omnivores, but similar haemoglobin.

Zinc status in vegetarians and non-vegetarians

Ball (2000): M J Ball and M L Ackland, *British Journal of Nutrition,* 2000; 83: 27-33, Zinc intake and status in Australian vegetarians.

Vegetarians had higher serum zinc (14.5 micromoles per litre) than omnivorous men (12.4) and vegan men (13.1). Serum zinc was correlated with zinc intake in vegetarian women and was similar on average to omnivore women.

Donovan (1995): Ursula M Donovan and Rosalind S Gibson, *Journal of the American College of Nutrition,* 1995; 14: 463-472, Iron and zinc status of young women consuming vegetarian and omnivorous diets.

2.5% of vegetarians compared with 3.5% of omnivores were anaemic and 29% of vegetarians compared with 17% of omnivores had serum ferritin concentrations less than 12 micrograms per litre. Serum zinc was 11.6 micromoles per litre in the vegetarians compared with 12.0 in the omnivores. Serum zinc was inversely associated with the dietary phytate to zinc ratio.

Hunt (1998): Janet R Hunt et al., *American Journal of Clinical Nutrition,* 1998; 67: 421-430, Zinc absorption, mineral balance, and blood lipids in women consuming controlled lactoovovegetarian and omnivorous diets for 8 wk.

Absorbed zinc was 35% lower on the vegetarian diet due to reduced zinc content and reduced absorption, but plasma zinc was reduced by just 5% and zinc balance was maintained.

Hunt (2002): Janet R Hunt, *Nutrition Reviews,* 2002; 60: 127-134, Moving toward a plant-based diet: are iron and zinc at risk?

Hunt notes that most vegetarian women do not have serum ferritin concentrations below 15 micrograms per litre and suggests that lowering serum ferritin without increasing anaemia might confer a health advantage. She also suggests that phytate to zinc ratios above 15 to 1 should be avoided.

Phytates and mineral absorption

Lopez (2002): H Walter Lopez et al., *International Journal of Food Science and Technology,* 2002; 37: 727-737, Minerals and phytic acid interactions: is it a real problem for human nutrition?

Protein, zinc and IGF-1

Allen (2000): N E Allen et al., *British Journal of Cancer,* 2000; 83: 95-97, Hormones and diet: low insulin-like growth factor-I but normal bioavailable androgens in vegan men.

Allen (2002): Naomi E Allen et al., *Cancer Epidemiology, Biomarkers and Prevention,* 2002; 11: 1441-1448, The associations of diet with serum insulin-like growth factor I and its main binding proteins in 292 women meat-eaters, vegetarians and vegans.

Cadogan (1997): Joanna Cadogan et al., *British Medical Journal,* 1997; 315: 1255-1260, Milk intake and bone mineral acquisition in adolescent girls: randomised, controlled intervention trial.

Cappola (2003): Anne R Cappola et al., Journal of Clinical Endocrinology and Metabolism, 2003; 88: 2019-2025, Insulin-like growth factor I and interleukin-6 contribute synergistically to disability and mortality in older women.

Chan (1998): June M Chan et al., *Science,* 1998; 279: 563-566, Plasma insulin-like growth factor-I and prostate cancer risk: a prospective study.

Devine (1998): Amanda Devine et al., *American Journal of Clinical Nutrition,* 1998; 68: 200-206, Effects of zinc and other nutritional factors on insulin-like growth factor I and insulin-like growth factor binding proteins in postmenopausal women.

Giovannucci (2001): Edward Giovannucci, *Journal of Nutrition,* 2001; 131: 3109S-3120S, Insulin, insulin-like growth factors and colon cancer: a review of the evidence.

Giovannucci (2003): Edward Giovannucci et al., *Cancer Epidemiology, Biomarkers and Prevention,* 2003; 12: 84-89, Nutritional predictors of insulin-like growth factor I and their relationships to cancer in men.

Hankinson (1998): Susan E Hankinson et al., *The Lancet,* 1998; 351: 1393-1396, Circulating concentrations of insulin-like growth factor-I and risk of breast cancer.

Heaney (1999): Robert P Heaney et al., *Journal of the American Dietetic Association,* 1999; 99: 1228-1233, Dietary changes favourably affect bone remodelling in older adults.

Holmes (2002): Michelle D Holmes et al., *Cancer Epidemiology, Biomarkers and Prevention,* 2002; 11: 852-861, Dietary correlates of plasma insulin-like growth factor I and insulin-like growth factor binding protein 3 concentrations.

Key (2001): T J Key and N E Allen, *The Breast,* 2001; 10 (Supp 3): 9-13, Nutrition and breast cancer.

Li (2001): Benjamin D L Li et al., *International Journal of Cancer,* 2001; 91: 736-739, Free insulin-like growth factor-I and breast cancer risk.

Ma (2001): Jing Ma et al., *Journal of the National Cancer Institute,* 2001; 93: 1330-1336, Milk intake, circulating levels of insulin-like growth factor-I, and risk of colorectal cancer in men.

Yu (2000): Herbert Yu and Thomas Rohan, *Journal of the National Cancer Institute,* 2000; 92: 1472-1489, Role of the insulin-like growth factor family in cancer development and progression.

12. From birth to old age

Pregnancy and growth in vegans

Carter (1987): James P Carter et al., *Southern Medical Journal,* 1987; 80: 692-697, Preeclampsia and reproductive performance in a community of vegans.

O'Connell (1989): Joan M O'Connell et al., *Pediatrics,* 1989; 84: 475-481, Growth of vegetarian children: The Farm study.

Sanders (1988): Thomas A B Sanders, *American Journal of Clinical Nutrition,* 1988; 48: 822-825, Growth and development of British vegan children.

Omega-3 fatty acids and infant development

Gibson (2000): Robert A Gibson and Maria Makrides, *American Journal of Clinical Nutrition,* 2000; 71: 251S-255S, n-3 Polyunsaturated fatty acid requirements of term infants.

Helland (2003): Ingrid B Helland et al., *Pediatrics,* 2003; 111: e39-e44, Maternal supplementation with very-long-chain n-3 fatty acids during pregnancy and lactation augments children's IQ at 4 years of age.

Hornstra (2000): Gerard Hornstra, *American Journal of Clinical Nutrition,* 2000; 71: 1262S-1269S, Essential fatty acids in mothers and their neonates.

Reddy (1994): S Reddy et al., *European Journal of Clinical Nutrition,* 1994; 48: 353-368, The influence of maternal vegetarian diet on essential fatty acid status of the newborn.

Sanders (1992): T A B Sanders and Sheela Reddy, *Journal of Pediatrics,* 1992; 120: S71-S77, The influence of a vegetarian diet on the fatty acid composition of human milk and the essential fatty acid status of the infant.

Sanders (1999): Thomas A B Sanders, *American Journal of Clinical Nutrition,* 1999; 70, 555S-559S, Essential fatty acid requirements of vegetarians in pregnancy, lactation and infancy.

Soya infant formula

Mendez (2002): Michelle A Mendez et al., *Journal of Nutrition*, 2002; 132: 2127-2130, Soy-based formulae and infant growth and development: a review.

Strom (2001): Brian L Strom et al., *Journal of the American Medical Association*, 2001; 286: 807-814, Exposure to soy-based formula in infancy and endocrinological and reproductive outcomes in young adulthood.

Adolescent vegetarian diets

Larsson (2002): Christel L Larsson and Gunnar K Johansson, *American Journal of Clinical Nutrition*, 2002; 76: 100-106, Dietary intake and nutritional status of young vegans and omnivores in Sweden.

Perry (2002): Cheryl L Perry et al., *Archives of Pediatric and Adolescent Medicine*, 2002; 156: 431-437, Adolescent vegetarians: how well do their dietary patterns meet the Healthy People 2010 objectives.?

Omega-3 fatty acids and depression

Adams (1996): Peter B Adams et al., *Lipids*, 1996; 31: S157-S161, Arachidonic acid to eicosapentaenoic acid ratio in blood correlates positively with clinical symptoms of depression.

Edwards (1998): Rhian Edwards et al., *Journal of Affective Disorders*, 1998; 48: 149-155, Omega-3 polyunsaturated fatty acid levels in the diet and in red blood cell membranes of depressed patients.

Hibbeln (1995): Joseph R Hibbeln and Norman Salem Jr, *American Journal of Clinical Nutrition*, 1995; 62: 1-9, Dietary polyunsaturated fatty acids and depression: when cholesterol does not satisfy.

Maes (1996): Michael Maes et al., *Journal of Affective Disorders*, 1996; 38: 35-46, Fatty acid composition in major depression: decreased ω3 in cholesteryl esters and increased C20:4ω6/C20:5ω3 ratio in cholesteryl esters and phospholipids.

Maes (1999): Michael Maes et al., *Psychiatry Research*, 1999; 85: 275-291, Lowered ω3 polyunsaturated fatty acids in serum phospholipids and cholesteryl esters of depressed patients.

Alzheimer's disease, cognitive decline and diet.

Engelhart (2002): Marianne J Engelhart et al., *Journal of the American Medical Association*, 2002; 287: 3223-3229, Dietary intake of antioxidants and risk of Alzheimer disease.

Heude (2003): Barbara Heude et al., *American Journal of Clinical Nutrition,* 2003; 77: 803-808, Cognitive decline and fatty acid composition of erythrocyte membranes – The EVA study.

Michikawa (2003): Makoto Michikawa, *Journal of Neuroscience Research,* 2003; 72: 141-146, Cholesterol paradox: Is high total or low HDL cholesterol a risk for Alzheimer's disease.

Morris (2002): Martha Clare Morris et al., *Journal of the American Medical Association,* 2002; 287: 3230-3237, Dietary intake of antioxidant nutrients and the risk of incident Alzheimer disease in a biracial community study.

Homocysteine, depression and dementia
See references for chapter 6.

Variation in effect of meat-free diets with age

Key (1999): Timothy J Key et al., *Proceedings of the Nutrition Society,* 1999; 58: 271-275, Health benefits of a vegetarian diet.

Snowdon (1984): David A Snowdon et al., *Preventive Medicine,* 1984; 13: 490-500, Meat consumption and fatal ischemic heart disease.

Cancer, B12 and folate

Kim (2000): Young-In Kim, *Nutrition Reviews,* 2000; 58: 205-209, Methylenetetrahydrofolate reductase polymorphisms, folate and cancer risk: a paradigm of gene-nutrient interactions in carcinogenesis.

Potter (1999): John D Potter, *Journal of the National Cancer Institute,* 1999; 91: 916-932, Colorectal cancer: molecules and populations.

13. Variations on a theme

Crete, Japan and the Seven Countries Study

Kromhout (1989): Daan Kromhout et al., *American Journal of Clinical Nutrition,* 1989; 49: 889-894, Food consumption patterns in the 1960s in seven countries.

Kromhout (2000): Daan Kromhout et al., *International Journal of Epidemiology,* 2000; 29: 260-265, Saturated fat, vitamin C and smoking predict long-term population all-cause mortality rates in the Seven Countries Study.

Kromhout (2001): Daan Kromhout et al., *International Journal of Obesity,* 2001; 25: 301-306, Physical activity and dietary fibre determines population body fat levels: the Seven Countries Study.

Menotti (2001): A Menotti et al., *European Journal of Epidemiology,* 2001; 17: 337-346, Cardiovascular risk factors as determinants of 25-year all-cause mortality in the Seven Countries Study.

Sandker (1993): G W Sandker et al., *European Journal of Clinical Nutrition,* 1993; 47: 201-208, Serum cholesteryl esters and their relation with serum lipids in elderly men in Crete and The Netherlands.

Sugano (1996): Michihiro Sugano, *Lipids,* 1996; 31: S283-S286, Characteristics of fats in Japanese diets and current recommendations.

Sugano (2000): Michihiro Sugano and Fumiko Hirahara, *American Journal of Clinical Nutrition,* 2000; 71: 189S-196S, Polyunsaturated fatty acids in the food chain in Japan.

WHO (1997): World Health Organisation, *Atlas of mortality in Europe,* WHO regional publications: European series No. 75.

Alcohol and mortality

Doll (1994): Richard Doll et al., *British Medical Journal,* 1994; 309: 911-918, Mortality in relation to consumption of alcohol: 13 years' observations on male British doctors.

Hart (1999): Carole L Hart et al., *British Medical Journal,* 1999; 318: 1725-1729, Alcohol consumption and mortality from all causes, coronary heart disease, and stroke: results from a prospective cohort study of Scottish men with 21 years of follow up.

Liao (2000): Youlian Liao et al., *American Journal of Epidemiology,* 2000; 151: 651-659, Alcohol intake and mortality: Findings from the national health interview surveys (1988 and 1990).

Tsugane (1999): Shoichiro Tsugane et al., *American Journal of Epidemiology,* 1999; 150: 1201-1207, Alcohol consumption and all-cause and cancer mortality among middle-aged Japanese men: Seven-year follow-up of the JHPC study cohort I.

WHO (2003a): The World Health Report 2002, World Health Organisation, www.who.int/whr/2002/en

Biological effects of soya

Alekel (2000): D Lee Alekel et al., *American Journal of Clinical Nutrition,* 2000; 72: 844-852, Isoflavone-rich soy protein attenuates bone loss in the lumbar spine of perimenopausal women.

Anderson (1995): James W Anderson et al., *New England Journal of Medicine,* 1995; 333: 276-282, Meta-analysis of the effects of soy protein on serum lipids.

Cassidy (1994): Aedin Cassidy et al., *American Journal of Clinical Nutrition,* 1994; 60: 333-340, Biological effects of a diet of soy protein rich in isoflavones on the menstrual cycle of premenopausal women.

Ganry (2002): O Ganry, *European Journal of Cancer Prevention,* 2002; 11: 519-522, Phytoestrogen and breast cancer prevention.

Jacobsen (1998): Bjarne K Jacobsen et al., *Cancer Causes and Control,* 1998; 9: 553-557, Does high soy milk intake reduce prostate cancer incidence? The Adventist Health Study (United States).

Verksalo (2001): Pia K Verksalo et al., *British Journal of Nutrition,* 2001; 86: 415-421, Soya intake and plasma concentrations of diadzein and genistein: validity of dietary assessment among eighty British women (Oxford arm of the European Prospective Investigation into Cancer and Nutrition).

White (2000): Lon R White et al., *Journal of the American College of Nutrition,* 2000; 19: 242-255, Brain aging and midlife soya consumption.

Peptides and autism

Reichelt (1997): Wenche H Reichelt et al., *Development and Brain Dysfunction,* 1997; 10: 44-55, Urinary peptide levels and patterns in autistic children from seven countries and the effect of dietary intervention after 4 years.

Byproducts of cooking

Mucci (2003): L A Mucci et al., *British Journal of Cancer,* 2003; 88: 84-89, Dietary acrylamide and cancer of the large bowel, kidney, and bladder: absence of an association in a population-based study in Sweden.

Vlassara (2002): Helen Vlassara et al., *Proceedings of the National Academy of Sciences,* 2002; 99: 15596-15601, Inflammatory mediators are induced by dietary glycotoxins, a major risk factor for diabetic angiopathy.

Adverse effects of excessive beta-carotene

Kemmann (1983): Ekkehard Kemmann et al., *Journal of the American Medical Association,* 1983; 249: 926-929, Amenorrhea associated with carotenemia.

Raw food diets and health

Donaldson (2001): Michael S Donaldson, *Nutrition and Food Science, 2001;* 31: 293-303, Food and nutrient intake of Hallelujah dieters.

Koebnick (1999): C Koebnick et al., *Annals of Nutrition and Metabolism,* 1999; 43: 69-79, Consequences of a long-term raw food diet on body weight and menstruation: results of a questionnaire survey.

Meyer (1971a): B J Meyer et al., *South African Medical Journal,* 1971; 45: 191-195, Some physiological effects of a mainly fruit diet in man.

Meyer (1971b): B J Meyer et al., *South African Medical Journal,* 1971; 45: 253-261, Some biochemical effects of a mostly fruit diet in man.

Strassmann (1996): Beverly I Strassmann, *The Quarterly Review of Biology,* 1996; 71: 181-220, The evolution of endometrial cycles and menstruation.

General references

Harvard Medical School recommendations

Eat, drink, and be healthy: The Harvard Medical School guide to healthy eating, 2001, Walter C Willett. ISBN 0-684-86337-5

Nutrients in foods

Food Standards Agency (2002): *McCance and Widdowson's The composition of foods* (Sixth summary edition).

USDA (2002), U.S. Department of Agriculture, Agricultural Research Service, 2002, USDA nutrient database for standard reference, Release 15, Nutrient data laboratory home page, http://www.nal.usda.gov/fnic/foodcomp

Index

THE

Vegan

SOCIETY

7 Battle Road,
St Leonards-on-Sea,
East Sussex TN37 7AA, UK.
Tel. (local rate) 0845 458 8244
or (+44) 1424 448820
Fax 01424 717064
Email: **info@vegansociety.com**

The Vegan Society is an educational charity founded in 1944. The Society promotes a way of life free from animal products, for the benefit of people, animals and the environment. In keeping with this objective, it provides information on all aspects of veganism, especially sound plant-based nutrition.

The most common motive for becoming vegan is the wish to avoid animal suffering, but many people also cite environmental, health or spiritual reasons and concern for the developing world.

For an information pack, including a catalogue with details of a wide range of vegan cookery books and other merchandise, send your name and address and two 1st class stamps. Or visit our website **www.vegansociety.com** which offers a wealth of information as well as an on-line shop.

If you are already a vegan or sympathise with vegan ideals, please support the Society and help to expand its work by joining as a member or supporter or by making a donation. Members receive a quarterly full colour magazine packed with news and features of interest to those wishing to follow a plant-based diet for health, animal welfare or environmental reasons.

The Vegan Society supports all vegans and others wishing to replace animal products in their diet and seeks to further their interests in the media and in discussions with national and international organisations.

I wish to become a member and support the work of The Vegan Society

name

address

postcode

email

tel

Date of Birth

(for security purposes)

occupation

◯ Please tick this box if you are a dietary vegan. This entitles you to voting rights in the Society's elections if aged 18+

◯ Please treat my membership subscription as Gift Aid. I have paid UK income or capital gains tax equal to the amount the Society reclaims.

giftaid it

A copy of the Society's rules (Memo & Articles of Association) can be viewed on our website or at our office. Alternatively you may buy a copy for £5

how to pay

membership: £21   donation: £

total: £

☐ I enclose a cheque/PO payable to The Vegan Society

☐ Please debit my Visa/Mastercard/Electron/eurocard/Switch/Visa Delta/Connect card

issue no. start / expiry /

signature

The Vegan Society, 7 Battle Road, St. Leonards-on-Sea, East Sussex TN37 7AA
www.vegansociety.com   membership@vegansociety.com
Tel: 0845 458 8244 Fax: 01424 717064

The International Vegetarian Union (IVU)

The IVU is a non-profit umbrella organisation for the vegan/vegetarian movement and has been holding congresses around the world since 1908 when the first congress was held in Dresden, Germany. More recent venues include Thailand (1999), Canada (2000), Scotland (2002) and Brazil (2004). For the full list and details of the next congress, see **www.ivu.org** World congresses are open to all, and catering is entirely animal free (vegan). National and regional congresses and festivals are also organised by member groups.

Membership of IVU is open to any non-profit organisation whose primary purpose is to promote vegetarianism and which is governed exclusively by vegetarians. A Supporter of IVU may be any individual, family or organisation, whether vegetarian or not, who supports the objectives of IVU.

The IVU promotes the establishment and growth of vegetarian organisations throughout the world and co-operation between them. It encourages non-animal research into all aspects of vegetarianism and the collection and publication of relevant material. It also seeks to represent the vegetarian cause to international bodies such as the World Health Organisation and to speak on behalf of the global cause when appropriate. Cooperation among scientists is encouraged through the IVU Science email discussion group.

The ivu website is the ultimate multilingual, multicultural vegetarian resource encompassing:

> Thousands of entirely plant-based recipes searchable by country and by ingredient;
>
> Archives on the history and philosophy of vegetarianism;
>
> Quotations from famous vegetarians;
>
> Details of vegan and vegetarian groups, restaurants and products around the world;
>
> And much, much more.

Visit www.ivu.org and find out more!

IVU Membership/Supporter Form

Send to: IVU, c/o Parkdale, Dunham Road, Altrincham, Cheshire
WA14 4QG, UK. Fax: +44 (0)161 926 9182

Annual subscription rates:

£12 sterling for societies up to 150 members, £30 up to 650 members and £20 per additional 500 members or part thereof up to a maximum of £150.   The low initial figure is to help small societies and may even be waived if a society can show that it is unable to make the full payment.

Supporters:
Individuals and non-profit agencies: £12 per annum.
Business supporters: £25 per annum.

Patrons: Become an individual supporter for life for a donation of £125 or more.

Payment in any currency other than sterling should be increased by the equivalent of £3 towards bank charges on conversion. You can also join on-line through the secure server at **www.ivu.org**

Name of organisation or individual:

Number of members: Address for correspondence:

Phone/fax/email/website:

Subscription enclosed   ....
Donation to help promote vegetarianism worldwide   ....
Total amount   ....

I/we enclose cheque/international money order/bank draft payable to **International Vegetarian Union**
or
Please debit Visa / MasterCard / Amex / Switch / Delta card no.:

Holder name and address:

Expiry date: Signature:

VEGAN PASSPORT

純素食者護照

ΔIABAΘHΡΙΟΝ BHFKAN

و یگن پاسپورت

完全菜食主義者のパスポート

ПАСПОРТ ВЕГАНА דרכון טבעוני

This economically priced, lightweight and handy little book explains what vegans do and don't eat in 38 languages, covering 95 per cent of the world's population. Invaluable for the adventurous diner both at home and abroad. If you want to avoid inadvertently eating minced dog or skylark's eggs when off the beaten track, this is the book for you. The Vegan Society also stocks guides to vegetarian travel in the United Kingdom, France, Spain and Europe as a whole.

www.Vegansociety.com/SHOP

Have you ever wondered what vegans are like and how they live? Are you a vegan yourself and interested in the experiences of fellow vegans from around the world? This collection of true life stories comes from vegans from age 2 to 92, from a variety of social, cultural and religious backgrounds and with an amazing variety of tales to tell, and all in their own words. If you ever thought vegans were all alike, this collection will persuade you otherwise.

This regularly updated pocket-sized guide details thousands of proucts in UK shops and supermarkets which are acceptable to vegans and others who wish to avoid meat, fish and dairy products. It also provides information on additives and other substances to be avoided and on goods available on-line and by mail order.

Get your copy now.